THE
LINGUISTIC SHAPING
OF ACCOUNTING

THE LINGUISTIC SHAPING OF ACCOUNTING

AHMED RIAHI-BELKAOUI

QUORUM BOOKS
Westport, Connecticut • London

Library of Congress Cataloging-in-Publication Data

Riahi-Belkaoui, Ahmed.
    The linguistic shaping of accounting / Ahmed Riahi-Belkaoui.
       p.   cm.
    Includes bibliographical references and index.
    ISBN 0–89930–992–5 (alk. paper)
    1. Communication in accounting. 2. Accounting—Language.
  I. Title.
  HF5657.R496 1995
657'.014—dc20   95–19470

British Library Cataloguing in Publication Data is available.

Library of Congress Catalog Card Number: 95–19470
ISBN: 0–89930–992–5

First published in 1995

Quorum Books, 88 Post Road West, Westport, CT 06881
An imprint of Greenwood Publishing Group, Inc.

Printed in the United States of America

The paper used in this book complies with the
Permanent Paper Standard issued by the National
Information Standards Organization (Z39.48–1984).

10 9 8 7 6 5 4 3 2

To my family

CONTENTS

PREFACE

Accounting is first a communication tool. Communication is accomplished by a specific language with its own logical and grammatical characteristics. As with any language, accounting faces specific situations that explain its relevance and its impact. First, accounting needs to reach adequate levels of readability and understandability to guarantee the effectiveness of accounting communications. Second, accounting as a language predisposes users to a given method of perception and behavior, a thesis derived from the linguistic relativity school emphasizing the role of accounting language as a mediator and shaper of the environment. Third, the existence of various accounting repertoires used by different accounting professional groups, the schism in accounting between academic and the world of practice, and the observed different performance of novices and experts point to the existence of a sociolinguistic thesis in accounting. Fourth, the global economy requirement to be proficient in more than one language to facilitate intercultural communication and interaction is also present in the accounting world, pointing to the potential impact of the bilingual thesis in accounting. This book examines each of the four specific situations in the following order:

1. Chapter 1 introduces accounting as a language and examines its readability and understandability.
2. Chapter 2 attempts to systematize the "Sapir-Whorf hypothesis" in accounting, that is, the hypothesis that the clerical and grammatical characteristics of accounting shape users' perception.
3. Chapter 3 introduces the sociolinguistic thesis in accounting.
4. Chapter 4 introduces the bilingual thesis in accounting.

The book should be of value to all those interested in international accounting issues, including professional accountants, business executives, teachers and researchers, and students.

Many people helped in the development of this book. I received considerable assistance from University of Illinois at Chicago research assistant Claire Howard. I also thank Mr. Eric Valentine and Ms. Bridget M. Austiguy at Greenwood Publishing for their continuous and intelligent support. Finally, to Janice and Hedi, thanks for making everything possible and enjoyable.

THE
LINGUISTIC SHAPING
OF ACCOUNTING

1

ACCOUNTING AS A LANGUAGE

One of the most important purposes of accounting is to communicate relevant information between and among producers and users of such information. The communication is accomplished by the use of specific words and techniques that are very much characteristic of a specific language. That is exactly the objective of this first chapter: to show that accounting can be referred to and viewed as a language. The success of the messages conveyed by the accounting language rests on the level of readability of these messages and their correct perception by users. That is the second objective of this chapter: to evaluate the readability and the perception of the meaning of accounting messages as examined in the accounting research literature.

ACCOUNTING AS A LANGUAGE

References to Accounting as a Language

Accounting has often been called the language of business.[1] Laudie refers to it as a process of bidirectional and interpersonal communication.[2] As a result,

[w]hen we study systematically the users of this language we need to ask what kinds of meaning are being communicated in it, and what coordinative functions the use of this language permits. Language is not just talk, it is our way of seeing the real world. It is a process of mutual adjustment and communication in which the knowledge socially generated by the participants in this process is greater than that possessed by any of them individually. This has, I think, pro-

foundly radical implications for the way we should conduct research in accounting theory and for the way we understand the role of accounting practices in the economic process.[3]

This perception of accounting as a language is emphasized in most accounting textbooks. Horngren observes that "[a]ccounting is a language with a special vocabulary aimed at conveying the financial story of organizations. To understand corporate annual reports, a reader must learn the fundamentals of the language."[4] Similarly, Anthony and Reece state:

As in the case with language, accounting has many dialects. There are differences in terminology and practices among industries and among companies within industries. . . . Accounting also resembles a language in that some of its rules are definite, whereas others are not, and there are differences of opinions among accountants as to how a given event should be recorded just as there are differences of opinions among grammarians as to many matters of sentence structure, punctuation, and choice of words.[5]

Finally, Ijiri contends:

As the language of business, accounting has many things in common with other languages. The various business activities of a firm are reported in accounting statements using accounting language, just as news events are reported in newspapers in the English language. To express an event in accounting or in English, we must follow certain rules. Without following certain rules diligently, not only does one run the risk of being misunderstood, but also risks a penalty for misrepresentation, lying, or perjury. Comparability of statements is essential to the effective functioning of a language whether it is in English or in accounting. At the same time, language has to be flexible enough to adapt to a changing environment.[6]

A recognition of accounting language is provided by Mills,[7] who notes the dependence of accounting on a specialized vocabulary and terminology and posits that close attention to the key words of accounting is an important part of the practice of accounting history. The concern follows from Brandel's call for greater attention to the key words of the vocabulary of history.[8] As stated by Brandel: "The key words of the vocabulary of history should only be used after asking a number of questions. Where do they come from? How do they come down to us? Are they likely to mislead us?"[9] Mills's analysis focused on the French terms of *ratio* and *compte*.[10] It led to the following suggestion:

This illustration yields a number of tentative but provocative insights concerning the development of accounting. Similarly, it suggests that in the medieval world the account was considered essentially a memorial with juridical functions; and that over the course of the early modern period, this legacy was eroded by new, more strictly quantitative conceptions which were important to the development of modern ideas of accountability. In addition, the illustration uncovers several technical usages, the explication of which may make understanding accounting records and literature of the period an easier task.[11]

The importance of accounting as a language is also very much evident in the proliferation of dictionaries of accounting.[12, 13, 14, 15, 16, 17, 18, 19, 20]

A review of some of these dictionaries has been provided by Forrester and Grant.[21] They conclude:

These vocabularies are intended largely to provide glossaries for accounts and texts put together in a more orderly manner. They offer definitions of varying length, and might be expected not merely to enunciate received use, but rather to trace origins, to find redundant and confusing synonyms, incompatibilities and inconsistencies of logic. If hierarchic and relational definitions have been attempted, international uniformities of the past would surely have been found relevant. This might have found a welcome if it were seen as a further effort by English-speaking accountants to determine and control business concepts in the interests of financial capital.[22]

The reference to accounting as a language highlights the need for quality in accounting communication. With regard to the communication issue, the Financial Accounting Standards Board's *Statement of Financial Accounting Concepts No. 1: Objectives of Financial Reporting by Business Enterprises* declared that "[t]he information [presented in financial statements] should be comprehensible to those who have a reasonable understanding of business and economic activities and are willing to study the information with reasonable diligence."[23]

Notion of Accounting as a Language

What makes accounting a language? To answer this question, Belkaoui examined the possible parallels existing between accounting and a language.[24] Hawes defines a language as follows:

Man's symbols are not randomly arranged signs which lead to the conceptualization of isolated and discrete referents. Rather, man's symbols are arranged in a systematic or patterned fashion with certain rules governing their usage. This arrangement of symbols is called a language and the rules which influence the patterning and usage of the symbols constitute the grammar of the language.[25]

It appears from the above definition and others that there are two components to a language—namely, symbols and grammatical rules. Thus, the recognition of accounting as a language rests on the identification of these two components as the two levels of accounting.

The *symbols* or logical characteristics of a language are the "meaningful" units or words identifiable in any language. These symbols are linguistic objects used to identify particular concepts. Concerning this effect, Zaltman et al. state: "Concepts are located in the world of thought rather than in the world of actual things referred here as objects, including linguistic objects commonly referred to as terms."[26] Symbolic representations do exist in accounting. For example, McDonald[27] identified numerals and words, and debits and credits, as the only symbols, respectively, accepted and unique to the accounting discipline.

The *grammatical rules* of a language refer to the syntactical arrangements existing in any given language. Such rules exist in accounting. They refer to the general set of procedures used for the creation of all financial data. Jain established the following parallel between grammatical rules and accounting rules:

The CPA (the expert in accounting) certifies the correctness of the application of the accounting rules as does an accomplished speaker of a language for the grammatical correctness of the sentence. Accounting rules formalize the structure of accounting in the same way as grammar formalizes the inherent structure of a natural language.[28]

Given the existence of the components identified—symbols and grammatical rules—accounting may be defined a priori as a language. As a result, accounting and language have a number of similarities. As stated by Jain:

A language represents phenomena in the real world while accounting represents phenomena in the business world. Accounting practices are the basic objects of study for formulating accounting theories and policies. They are like our daily conversation in linguistics. Based on these similarities we may draw the conclusion that inferences drawn from the field of linguistics will be equally applicable in the field of accounting.[29]

READABILITY IN ACCOUNTING

The Importance of Readability

Accounting is aimed at facilitating decision making. One paramount characteristic of accounting language use is its ability to facilitate the communication process. This notion is best expressed by the American Accounting Association's Committee to Prepare a Statement of Basic Accounting Theory:

The development of accounting information is only part of the accounting function. A necessary companion aspect of the function is the development of the communication process so that information can be transmitted and so that those to whom information is provided understand it. . . . Communication is a vital link in accounting activity. It is of no less importance than that of developing the information itself.[30]

There is, however, a definite problem with the understandability of the authoritative pronouncements of standard-setting bodies. Most, for example, state that certain Financial Accounting Standards Board (FASB) "statements . . . were long, verbose, and often obscure."[31] The same accusation was made about Securities and Exchange Commission (SEC) pronouncements. For example, Kelly-Newton states that "a second aspect of the communication factor is the clarity with which the requirements are stated. The SEC often neglects this aspect. A frequent criticism of ARS(s) (is) the use of ambiguous terms . . . resulting in uncertainty regarding the implementation and fostering incomparable disclosures among firms."[32] The problem resides in the language of accounting used, which affects mostly the readability of the statements.

Readability is one of the qualities of information sought by users. For example, Swanson[33] and Zmud[34] suggested that user perception of information had four basic dimensions:

1. Significance, usefulness, or helpfulness of information;
2. Accuracy, factualness, and timeliness of information;
3. Quality of format and readability of information; and
4. Meaningfulness or reasonableness of information.[35]

Similar findings were presented by Larcker and Vessig.[36]

One way of evaluating the comprehensibility of accounting messages is to assess the readability of these messages. Readability is adequately defined by Smith and Smith as:

an objective and quantitative measure of the ease of comprehension of written matter. The principal purpose of readability is to enable an objective evaluation of "what is." By knowing the state of affairs that exists, steps can be taken to modify printed matter whose comprehension ease is unsuitable for the appropriate audience. Thus, readability provides the type of immediate feedback to the writer.[37]

Measurement of Readability

Readability formulas provide a simple, quick, and inexpensive yardstick for assessing communication effectiveness. The formula is applied to prose passage to assess its readability to a target audience. It measures elements in writing of importance in the creation of readable message, such as content, style, format, and organization. It allows a matching of the levels of reader and text to render the meaning comprehensive and communication effective. As Smith and Smith state about effective communication:

[T]he meanings intended by the information source are assigned to the financial statement messages by the destination. Proper meaning assignment necessitates that the information source encode and transmit the selected messages such that the destination is capable of assigning the intended meanings.[38]

The readability formula determines the appropriate age needed to understand a written communication, providing therefore a matching between the level of difficulty in readability and the age or level of education. Various readability formulas have been proposed in the literature. The "mainstream" readability formulas are presented next.

1. *The Dale-Chall* formula assesses vocabulary difficulty on the basis of a list of 3,000 words deemed known by eight-year-olds in the United States. The formula is:

U.S. grade = (0.1579 × PERCENT UFMWDS) + (0.0496 + WDS/SEN)

UFMWDS = Unfamiliar words

WDS/SEN = Average number of words per sentence

UK Grade = 5 + U.S. grade.[39]

2. *The Flesch formula* assesses adult reading materials, relating to a notional comprehension score out of 100 rather than a grade level.[40] Scores more than 30 denote very difficult reading. The formula is:

Reading ease = 206.835 − (0.846 × SYLLS/100W) − (1.015 × WDS/SEN)

SYLLS/100W = Syllables per 100 words

WDS/SEN = Average number of words per sentence.[41]

3. *The Flesch-Kincaid formula* is a more recent index needed to reflect the higher education level and better reading ability of the U.S. population since the Flesch Reading Ease Scale was published in 1948.[42] The formula is:

Grade level = (0.39 × SL) + (11.8 × SYL) − 15.59

SL = Average sentence length in words

SYL = Average number of syllables per word.

4. *The Fog formula* is comparable to the Flesch formula, with a focus, however, on the percentage of polysyllabic words (i.e., words of three or more syllables) in a passage.[43] The formula is:

U.S. grade = 0.4 (WDS/SEN + %PSW)

WDS/SEN = Average number of words per sentence

%PSW = Percentage of polysyllabic words

UK grade = U.S. grade + 5.[44]

5. *The Kwolek formula* is a modification of the Fog formula through a change in the weight given to the words per sentence and hard words variables.[45] The formula is:

Readability index = 0.593 (W/2 + H)

W = Words per sentence

H = Percentage of hard words.[46]

6. *The Lix formula* assesses readability across language and focuses on word and sentence factors.[47] The formula is:

Lix = Word length + sentence length

Word length = Percentage of words of more than six letters

Sentence length = Average number of words per sentence.[48]

7. *The Gunning test* relies on the average length of sentences and the percentage of polysyllabic words.[49] A range of at least 100 words is selected. Computations include: (a) the average length of sentence as the number of words in the passage divided by number of sentences and (b) the percentage of polysyllabic words as the number of words of three syllables or more divided by the number of words in the passage. The sum of the average sentence length and the percentage of polysyllabic words is multiplied by 0.4, which gives an estimate of readability approximating years of education.

8. Lewis et al. recanted the Dale-Chall, Flesch, Fog, Kwolek, and Lix formulas in the following useful manner:

DALE-CHALL = $15.79(U)/(W) + 0.0496(W)/(S)$

FLESCH = $-84.6(L)/(W) - 1.015(W)/(S) + 206.835$

FOG = $40(P)/(W) + 0.4(W)/(S)$

KWOLEK = $59.3(H)/(W) + 0.2965(W)/(S)$

LIX = $100(B)/(W) + 1.0(W)/(S)$

where:

W = Number of words

S = Number of sentences

U = Number of "unfamiliar" words

L = Number of syllables

P = Number of polysyllabic words

H = Number of "hard" words

B = Number of "big" (> 6 letters) words.[50]

9. Frazier et al. introduced a methodology for the analysis of narrative accounting disclosures.[51] The methodology is a content analysis system, called WORDS, which is based on a word-frequency congruity logic: "[T]hat is, certain words in a narrative that occur, and co-occur, frequently are assumed to represent the content of the narrative."[52] WORDS is a process emphasizing words and their statistical interrelationships. As defined by Isler:

Our unit of information is the word itself. Dividing an interview into segments of time, i.e., one minute segments, we count the frequency . . . with which each word appears in each time segment. Using these data, intercorrelations among words are obtained; operationally, these correlations represent the degree of . . . association between words as they are observed across successive segments of interview time. Our assumption is that words which correlate highly with each other have much in common in defining topic or content reference while those with low correlations have little in common. We therefore factor-analyze this matrix of word intercorrelations to determine in a systematic fashion, if there are common factors which can account for the obtained correlations in an efficient and meaningful way.[53]

The process was applied to the Management Analyses of the Results of Operations from the 1978 annual reports of 74 firms, showing its potential application for systematic clarification and quantification of accounting disclosures and data.

10. Lewis et al. investigated the application of readability formulas to the "Managing Director" and "Operations Review" extracts of a sample of corporate financial reports to employees.[54] The formulas used included the Flesch, Fog, Kwolek, and Dale-Chall readability indexes as well as the Lix formula and the Fry graph. The results show that the financial reports to employees, which ought to be written in a language understandable to employees without financial training, were pitched a "difficult to read" level over the period studied. There was a certain degree of consistency in the results provided by the different formulas. The Lix formula emerged as a particularly useful tool for the following cited reasons:

1. Relative ease of calculation.
2. Applicability across languages.
3. Total score results that appear to be similar to those produced by formula already known to accounting researchers.
4. A means of diagnosing relative importance of, and changes in, factors contributing to the readability score.
5. A predictor of likely ex post Cloze readability assessments.[55]

Studies on the Readability of the Content of Accounting Statements

The first readability study by Pashalian and Crissy[56] investigated the readability of 26 annual reports of corporations listed in the Billion-Dollar Club of *Business Week*, June 11, 1949, by means of the Flesch readability formulas.[57, 58] The results were bleak, showing the general level of reading to be difficult, the human interest to be dull, and the presence of language beyond the language experience and fluent comprehension of approximately 75 percent of the U.S. adult population.[59] A replication of the study by Soper and Dolphin[60] using corporate annual reports for the year 1961 showed that the reading ease has not improved from 1948 to 1961, where reading ease is a vital factor in aiding comprehension of the reports by reader.

A second replication of the study by Holley and Early,[61] using corporate annual reports for 1976, showed that the 1976 reports were very difficult and dull because of the inclusion of more technical materials in annual reports. As a result, the following practical suggestion is made:

Despite the frequent assertion that annual reports are often only a form of promotional a public relations media, the content continues to require a relatively high level of technical ability and self-motivation on the part of the reader. If an objective of annual reports is to communicate with individual investors and other parties whose main source of information is that provided by the business enterprise through the Annual Report, perhaps a simplified, less comprehensive, more readable style should be considered as a secondary, supplementary reporting format. The traditionally prepared annual report could continue to serve its present function in conjunction with the alternative of a less rigorous report available to user.[62]

A third replication by Wagley and Dolphin[63] using 19 corporate annual reports for 1974 showed that there has been no improvement in the reading ease of these reports during the 1948 to 1974 period, with an average reading score in 1974 of 16.05 (very difficult), representing a decrease of 15.37 points since 1948 (31.42). The range was 44–1.

Smith and Smith examined the readability of footnotes in U.S. corporate annual reports using both the Flesch Reading Ease formula and the Dale-Chall formula.[64] The results showed that the readability level of the financial statement notes were restrictive and that there were no relationships between the identity of external auditors and the comprehension ease level of notes to financial statements.

Parker suggested that the annual report is inaccessible to a large majority because of its failure to meet their information needs and its inaccessibility to unsophisticated audiences.[65] *Social accessibility* referred to situations where certain message decoding skills are not available to all members of the participating society. To find evidence on the social accessibility of Australian reports, he applied the Fog index test both to the chairman's or director's "review of operations" and to the "footnotes" of ten randomly selected 1980 Australian corporate reports. The average Fog index score was 19.1 for the review of operations and 20.1 for the notes. The range was 14–25.7 for the review of operations and 16.1–24.4 for the notes. The scores indicates that both documents may be inaccessible to a large proportion of private lay shareholders. Such an audience lacks the necessary decoding skills to have access to the annual reports. One major consequence follows:

Audiences themselves can restrict the accessibility of reports by rejecting them for moral reasons, by perceiving the reports to be inappropriate to their needs or for political or social reasons only indirectly connected with the reports. A politically left-wing audience for instance may consistently misinterpret or disbelieve profits, asset valuations or director's reports because it suspects a politically conservative bias in presentation. Some shareholders may completely reject explanations of current activities and future prospects because they regard the activities of a company as socially irresponsible. Indeed, there may be little that accountants can do to overcome this source of social inaccessibility to their reports.[66]

Hoskins investigated the readability of the general overview section and the chairman's letter from the 1980 annual reports of 25 corporations in the *Fortune 500* Directory, using the Flesch index.[67] The average Flesch Reading Ease score was 43.25 for the chairman's letter and 34.20 for the overview section. The ranges were 12–44 for the overview section and 26–61 for the chairman's letter. The results indicate that annual reports were at least difficult for the general public to read.

Heath and Phelps investigated the readability of the 1981 annual reports of 20 randomly selected *Fortune 500* companies using the Gunning's list.[68] While the readability scores varied with different sections of the report, the financial disclosure sections still proved to be the most difficult. As a result, they gave the following assessment:

Public relations professionals should have more control over the level of vocabulary than they do over any other aspect of the writing of annual reports. Perhaps management will not allow them to supply types of information stockholders seek. And because of legal requirements and corporate policy, writers of annual reports often must include accounting and managerial jargon which usually is not understood by the average shareholder. But they should be free to make the reports as readable as possible by shortening sentence length and by reducing the complexity of diction. Increased readability should be possible while maintaining credibility with investors and complying with SEC and Financial Accounting Standards Board regulations.

At a time when several billion dollars are spent annually on corporate image and issue campaigns, the least that can be done is to create a readable report.[69]

Courtis examined readability levels of 1982 and 1983 Canadian annual report components, specifically the chairman's address and footnotes to the financial statements, using both Flesch and Fog readability formulas.[70] The average Flesch Reading Ease score for the chairman's address was 31.34 in 1982 and 28.96 in 1983. For the footnotes, the score was 28.06 for 1982 and 25.96 in 1983. The average Fog index score for the chairman's address was 18.95 in 1982 and 19.48 in 1983. For the footnotes, the score was 20.07 in 1982 and 20.32 in 1983. For both years, the readability level was found to be either very difficult or difficult, requiring at least a university undergraduate to comprehend fully the messages contained in the report. The poor-quality readability led to the following good suggestion:

The claim remains that on the basis of formula scores the reading ease of annual reports is predicted to be presently too difficult on average for most recipients. Since annual reports are the primary formal means of communication between a corporation and groups external to the organization, it would seem incumbent on those who are responsible for annual report preparation to become more aware of how their own corporation's report scores on readability measures. Scores which predict difficult comprehension levels are indicative of the need for remedial writing. By itself, shorter sentence lengths and selection of words with less than three syllables should improve formula scores, but such alterations may "trick" the formulas. Although these two variables are associated with reading difficulty, they will not necessarily improve the true understandability of the message being communicated. Instead, therefore, annual report preparers should (1) try to write sentences that are as simple as possible and (2) test the readability of their sentences for ease of comprehension with a small sample of their own employees or other non-technical people. Annual report messages may then become more comprehensible to the population in general, as well as to the remaining 56.1% of shareholders without any university education. To stimulate such a reaction, perhaps annual awards of excellence for annual reports should be extended to the "golden bill" award for the worst and most horrid example of corporate gobbledegook each year.[71]

Jones investigated the readability of the chairman's narrative of a UK company's reports from 1952 to 1985 using the Flesch score.[72] The study's two objectives were "(1) [w]hether the readability of the chairman's narrative has changed over time, and (2) whether any of five factors—financial performance, turnover, different chairmen, change in legal form, change in title of the chairman's narrative—have been key influences on readability."[73] The results supported earlier research that corporate reports had remained difficult to read over time. In addition, there were clear negative correlations between readability and turnover and time. As time passed and turnover increased, readability declined and even deteriorated. Jones gives the following warning:

If a serious communication breakdown between the providers and users of accounting information is therefore not to occur, standardization must be accompanied by more understandable, readable accounts. If this does not happen, and corporate reports remain largely unreadable, they will remain largely unread.[74]

Schroeder and Gibson examined the readability of Management's Discussion and Analysis (MD&A).[75] MD&A is required for firms by the SEC. With the footnotes, MD&A constitutes the third form of narrative information provided by annual reports. The firms used were selected from the 1986 *Fortune 500* and the 1986 *Fortune Service 500*. Variables used to estimate readability included use of the passive voice, word length, sentence length, and the Flesch index. The results showed that (1) management makes much less use of the passive voice in the MD&As and president's letter than in the footnotes, (2) average word length in the MD&As is significantly longer than that found in the president's letters, (3) the sentence length was initially the same for all three narratives, and (4) the president's letters were significantly more readable than the MD&As. The following relevant advice is given:

Writers concerned with readability need to choose their words and write their sentences with the reader in mind. Readability can be improved by limiting vocabulary to common words whenever technical terminology is not required. Writing sentences in the active voice will help hold the reader's interest. Readability can also be improved by using the shorter word when synonyms exist. Finally, holding down average sentence length will improve the reader's understanding of the narrative. . . . The results of this study show that many firms are missing an opportunity to improve financial reporting communications. The MD&A can be made more readable and comprehensible to users. Managers responsible for communicating financial information in narrative form must remember that the narrative should "express" rather than "impress."[76]

Schroeder et al. compared the readability of annual report footnotes on the New York Stock Exchange with a matched group of U.S.-based

firms traded on the same exchange.[77] The comparison involved the vocabulary, grammar, sentence structure, and readability of financial information directed at the U.S. investment community. The addition to
objective measures of vocabulary and sentence structure, the readability
levels, was assessed by the Flesch Reading Ease formula and the Flesch-
Kincaid index. The Flesch-Kincaid formula is computed as follows:

Grade level $= (0.39 \times SL) + (11.8 \times SYL) - 15.59$

SL $=$ Average sentence length in words

SYL $=$ Average number of syllables per word.

The results showed no difference in vocabulary levels but significant
differences in grammar, sentence structure, and readability. Three implications of these results follow:

The differences noted in this study imply that individuals reading translated
Japanese financial reports may face higher information costs because these reports are more difficult to read than reports of comparable U.S. companies. These
findings may have two other implications. First, translation difficulties may contribute to segmentation of capital markets. Second, Japanese companies may be
able to increase their access to U.S. markets and lower their cost of capital by
improving the quality of the translation used in preparing English language annual reports.[78]

Gibson and Schroeder examined the readability of narrative disclosure
in UK and U.S. financial reports directed at the U.S. capital market.[79]
Three variables were used for assessing readability: average word length,
use of the passive voice, and average sentence length. In addition, readability levels were estimated using the Flesch-Kincaid index. The results
indicate that (1) overall readability of management discussions in UK
reports were comparable to those in U.S. reports, (2) there are differences
in average word length and average sentence length of both reports, and
(3) there are differences in the readability of management letter to shareholder and MD&A. The following interesting research questions were
also raised:

[F]urther research on narrative disclosure [should] be conducted. Are the semantic and syntactic differences between U.K. and U.S. financial disclosure
unique or are these differences present in other professional narratives originat-
ing in the United Kingdom and the United States? Are these differences due to
competitive environment, culture, level of education, philosophy of education,
or a combination of these and other factors? These and other questions need to
be addressed in order to develop a theory explaining why differences in semantics and syntax would occur in U.K. and U.S. financial disclosure.
Research should also examine English-language financial reporting narratives

from other countries and cultures. Are semantic and syntactic differences found when these narratives are compared with U.S. financial disclosure? Does the level and/or direction of such (if any) depend on identifiable factors such as culture, language group, or level of disclosure regulation in the "home" securities market? Further research on the effectiveness of narrative financial communication would provide useful information for both financial analysts and those involved in regulation of financial disclosure.[80]

Schroeder and Gibson investigated the linguistic characteristics and estimated readability of financial statement footnotes in English-language reports of major international banks in nine countries.[81] The rationale for the study is stated as follows:

Increased linguistic complexity and/or poor readability of narrative disclosure could have an adverse effect on financial statement user efforts to analyze and interpret the measurement information explained by the narrative. Thus, linguistic characteristics of narrative disclosure are as likely as measurement information to affect deposition, investor, and borrower uncertainty. Uncertainty has the potential to affect borrowing and lending decisions on the cost of capital of international banks.[82]

The variables used to assess readability were average word length, average sentence length, use of the passive voice, and the Flesch-Kincaid index.[83] The results showed differences in vocabulary level and readability-related linguistic characteristics in the English-language annual report footnotes of international banks, implying that international banks depositors, investors, and borrowers in some countries may be facing higher information costs. The following research agenda is proposed:

Future academic research needs to develop a theory explaining why to expect differences in readability of English language financial reports from different countries and where to expect these differences to occur. For example, is there a relationship between readability estimates and complexity of reporting standards? Does readability of financial reports correlate to readability of the financial reporting standards with which the financial reports conform (e.g., FASB versus IASC)? Does readability of financial reports correlate to readability of the financial reporting examples published by official and/or semiofficial sources (e.g., the annual *Accounting Trends and Techniques* published by the American Institute of CPAs)? Follow-up research may include using academic readability research findings to explain differences in banking growth cost of capital, or volume of borrower activity in banks of different countries.[84]

Healy investigated the readability of footnotes in 50 New Zealand public corporations.[85] The difficulty of readability of this report was evident in the overall average score of 30.19, with a range of 7.35–53.04.

Still investigated the readability of chairmen's letters in 50 randomly selected UK annual reports.[86] The overall average Flesch Reading Ease score of 42.51, with a range of 18–71.9, indicates that the reports were beyond the fluent comprehension of most users of information in the United Kingdom.

Pound investigated the readability of corporate employee reports for 30 Australian public companies.[87] The readability of these reports was better than those of annual reports and very much accessible to the general Australian workforce.

Pound also investigated the readability of the audit report of a random sample of 120 audit reports.[88] The Flesch score obtained indicated that the level of education required to understand the messages contained in the audit reports was at least a university undergraduate level.

Readability and Performance

The general difficulty level of readability in annual reports and the variations observed among firms over time raised the question of whether readability is related to the financial performance of a firm. Various studies examined this question with different results:

1. Adelberg investigated the relationship between productivity and changes and earning per share.[89] His findings were that management is introducing an interpretative bias in nonstandard footnotes and qualified auditor's reports but not in the standardized footnotes or management analyses. The implication suggested is that management may be obfuscating failures and underscoring successes.

2. Courtis found a nonsignificant relationship between readability and the variables of current ratio, leverage, earnings variability, and return on total assets.[90]

3. Jones found a significant relationship between readability and the variables of return on capital employed, turnover, private/public status, and chairman's title and a nonsignificant relationship with net profit to sales.[91]

4. Baker and Klare found a significant relationship between readability and total assets and return on equity and a nonsignificant relationship with common shares and net profit to sales.[92]

5. Smith and Taffler found poor readability to be associated with poor performance and ease of readability with financial success.[93] The relationship was especially significant with profit, liquidity, and risk and nonsignificant with gearing.

6. Subramarian et al. found a significant relationship between readability and absolute net profit/loss.[94] They suggest the following research agenda:

   For example, future studies should examine the impact of external corporate communication on market performance of firms. The ethical issues involved in companies pursuing distinct strategies for communicating good and bad performance news provides another research direction worth exploring. Finally, other aspects of the style of annual reports, such as the tone used to deliver the message and the techniques of analysis and de-emphasis used, need to be studied to complement the existing understanding of current practices in external corporate communication methods.[95]

Assessments of Readability in Accounting

An exhaustive review of readability studies is shown in Exhibit 1.1. All the research studies covered in the previous section indicate a serious problem in the readability of annual reports. The contents of annual reports appear to be dull and difficult for the average reader. Whether or not their style of communication is deliberate, it presents a challenge to the relevance and acceptability of accounting messages, given that readability is a crucial factor in aiding comprehension of the reports by users of accounting information. The problem is aggravated by the findings that (1) investors—current as well as potential—use both text and financial statements from annual reports to make important decisions[96] and (2) the letter to the stockholders section of a corporation's annual report is often used by investors to make their investment decisions[97] and is the most widely read part of the annual report.[98, 99] Various solutions are possible.

1. Because some of the accounting information requires a high level of technical knowledge, firms may elect to disclose two annual reports, one conventional report and another written in a simplified and more readable style.

2. Corporate jargon should be reduced or eliminated in favor of more readable reports that include shorter sentence length and reduction in the complexity of diction. In addition, the readability of annual reports should be tested before their release for ease of comprehension by a small sample of users.

3. Firms may also have to resort to a report of facial expressions as a potentially useful way of communicating financial information.[100] This technique is supported as follows:

At the very least, the technique may have value in the scanning of large numbers of observations in order to detect extreme values. It might ease the task of bank loan officers in assessing credit-worthiness by clearly distinguishing those cases which are acceptable/unacceptable and those which require more detailed examination. Similarly, the provision of facial expressions allows the detection of multivariate trends over time in a manner which is apparently difficult using numerical or conventional graphical expositions.

Researchers have devoted very little attention to the question of data presentation in a financial environment. To date more emphasis has been placed on the

Exhibit 1.1
Analysis of Empirically Based Readability Studies

Researchers Publication Date & Country	Purpose	Recording Unit	Coding Method	Measurement Model	Findings
Pashalian & Crissy [1952] USA	To assess readability using Flesch index.	words, syllables, and sentences from every other page in 1948 corporate reports	manual 100-word samples	descriptive statistics means	Reading ease mean score 34.37. Reports therefore difficult to read.
Soper & Dolphin [1964] USA	To assess readability using Flesch index, verified by judges.	words, syllables, and sentences from every other page in 1961 corporate reports	manual 100-word samples	descriptive statistics means	Reading ease mean score declined from 34.2 to 28.76. Reports therefore very difficult to read.
Smith & Smith [1971] USA	To assess readability using Flesch, Dale-Chall indexes.	words, syllables, and sentences from footnotes in 1969 corporate reports	manual four 100-word samples per 2000 words	descriptive statistics means	Mean score (Flesch) 23.49 very difficult to understand. No relationship between external auditors and comprehension level.
Still [1972] UK	To assess readability using Flesch index.	words, syllables, and sentences from Chairman's statement in 1971 corporate reports	manual 100-word samples	descriptive statistics means	Mean score 42.5. Difficult to read.
Dolphin & Wagley [1977] USA	To assess readability using Flesch index.	words, syllables, and sentences from every other page in 1974 corporate reports	manual 100-word samples	descriptive statistics means	Mean score had declined from 31.42 (difficult) to 16.05 (very difficult).
Healy [1977] NZ	To assess readability using Flesch index.	words, syllables, and sentences from notes to accounts in 1976 corporate reports	manual random 100-word samples	descriptive statistics means	Mean score 30.19 difficult to read.

Exhibit 1.1 (continued)

Researchers Publication Date & Country	Purpose	Recording Unit	Coding Method	Measurement Model	Findings
Worthington [1977; 1978] USA	To assess readability using Dale-Chall index.	words, syllables, and sentences from footnotes in 1974 corporate reports	manual all footnotes	descriptive statistics means	Financial footnotes are understood only by an audience considerably more sophisticated in reading ability than average investors. Mean grade score 9.5 equivalent to 1-3 years of college.
Barnett & Leoffler [1979] USA	To assess readability using Flesch index.	words, syllables, and sentences from footnotes and auditors' reports in 1975 corporate reports	manual	descriptive statistics means Mann-Whitney test	Mean footnote readability declined from 23.5 in 1969 to 12.88 in 1975, both very difficult to understand. No relationship established between auditors' identity and difficulty of footnotes. Auditors' report mean score, calculated by Jones and Shoemaker from authors' figures - 18.1, very difficult. Only one auditors' report scored positively.
Worthington [1979] USA	To assess readability using Dale-Chall index.	words, syllables, and sentences from footnotes on replacement cost data in 1976 corporate reports	manual	descriptive statistics means	Average grade level 10.7, very difficult to read at college level.
Holley & Early [1980] USA	To assess readability using Flesch index.	words, syllables, and sentences from every other page in 1976 corporate reports	manual 100-word samples	descriptive statistics means	Mean score 23.05 (very difficult). Declined from 34.1 (difficult) in 1961 and 28.6 (very difficult) in 1961.
Pound [1980] AUST	To assess readability using Flesch index.	words, syllables, and sentences from narrative presentations, e.g.. Chairman's statements in 1977/78 corporate reports and employee reports	manual probably 100-word samples	descriptive statistics	Twenty-eight of thirty shareholder reports very difficult or difficult to read. Twenty-seven of thirty employee reports difficult or fairly difficult to read. No means given.

Exhibit 1.1 (continued)

Researchers Publication Date & Country	Purpose	Recording Unit	Coding Method	Measurement Model	Findings
Means [1981] USA	To assess readability using Dale-Chall index.	words, syllables, and sentences from every page containing text in 1977/78 corporate reports	manual 100-word samples	descriptive statistics means coefficient of correlation	Fifty percent annual reports (very difficult). 43% (difficult and 7% (fairly difficult). No correlation was found between stockholder reactions to the annual report and readability, regardless of educational attainment. Reactions established from 549 questionnaires.
Pound [1981] AUST	To assess readability using Flesch index.	words, syllables, and sentences from auditors' reports in 1978 corporate reports	manual	descriptive statistics means student t test	Sixty-five found very difficult, 41 difficult, 8 fairly difficult, 6 standard difficulty. No means given. Technical literature, socially inaccessible to a significant proportion of population.
Parker [1982] AUST	To assess readability using Fog index.	words, syllables, and sentences from Chairman's or Directors' Review and footnotes in 1980 corporate reports	manual	descriptive statistics means Student t and Wilcoxon test	Fog index 19.1 for 'review of operations'; 20.1 for footnotes. Chairman's or Directors' Review and notes to accounts, no significant difference. Inaccessible to a large proportion of population.
Razek et al. [1982] USA	To assess readability using Flesch index.	words, syllables, and sentences from passages from 12 intermediate and advanced accounting textbooks	manual 100 words every chapter	descriptive statistics means	Textbooks overall very difficult to read. Flesch mean score 29.7 for intermediate and 22.2 for advanced textbooks.
Heath and Phelps [1984] USA	To assess readability using Fog index	words, syllables, and sentences from President's Letter, general text, and footnotes in 1981 corporate reports	manual about 200-word samples	descriptive statistics means ANOVA	President's Letter 14.2. General Selection 14.18, footnotes 15.92. Even most readable section difficult for 50% of readers. Annual reports not as readable as business publications.

19

Exhibit 1.1 (continued)

Researchers Publication Date & Country	Purpose	Recording Unit	Coding Method	Measurement Model	Findings
Avard & White [1986] USA	To assess readability using Flesch, Fog, and Smog indexes.	words, syllables, and sentences from passages from 10 financial management textbooks	manual twelve passages from each textbook	descriptive statistics means	Different readability measures failed to agree on ranking the texts. Writing style potential problem.
Courtis [1986] CAN	To assess readability using Flesch and Fog indexes.	words, syllables, and sentences from Chairman's address and footnotes in 1982 and 1983 corporate reports	manual random 100-word samples	descriptive statistics means student t, and Mann-Whitney U test	Flesch 31.34 [1982] and 28.96 [1982] for Chairman's address; 28.06 [1982] and 25.96 [1983] for footnotes. Fog 18.99 [1982] and 19.48 [1983] for Chairman's address; 20.07 [1982] and 20.32 [1983] for footnotes. Reports therefore very difficult or difficult; socially inaccessible. Difficulty levels not associated with corporate risk or profitability.
Lewis et al. [1986] AUST	To assess readability using Flesch, Fog, Kwolek, Dale-Chall, Lix, and Fry indexes.	words, syllables, and sentences from Managing Director's Report and Review of Operations in 1977-80 employee reports	manual 100-word samples	descriptive statistics means Kendall coefficient of concordance, and Spearman rank correlation coefficient	Financial reports to employees generally fairly difficult to very difficult to read. General conclusion readability did not improve noticeably over time, but Flesch showed slight increase in difficulty on Managing Director's extracts.
Courtis [1987] CAN	To assess readability using Fry, Smog, Lix, and Rix indexes.	words, syllables, and sentences from President's Letter in 1984 corporate reports	manual 100-word samples	descriptive statistics means	Fry mean 176 syllables and 4.6 sentences per 100 words; Smog score 15.2; Rix score 7.64; and Lix score 56.4. All difficult or very difficult requiring a college level education.

20

Exhibit 1.1 (continued)

Researchers Publication Date & Country	Purpose	Recording Unit	Coding Method	Measurement Model	Findings
Karlinsky & Koch [1987] USA	To evaluate the ability of accounting professionals to understand written tax law using Flesch, Fog, and Reading Complexity Elicitation indexes.	words, syllables, and sentences in passages of tax law	manual	MANOVA tests of differences and non-parametric correlation coefficient	Presentation style affected ability to correctly understand written tax law. The author generated Reading Complexity Elicitation was a more reliable measure of reading complexity than traditional indexes.
Jones [1988] UK	To assess readability using Flesch index.	words, syllables, and sentences from Chairman's narrative in one company's corporate reports 1952-1985	manual 100-word samples	descriptive statistics means student t tests, and regression analysis	Annual report readability declined over time from fairly difficult to difficult. Overall mean 47.2. Correlations between readability and sales as well as time. Readability declined when company became public.
Schroeder & Gibson [1990] USA	To assess readability using Flesch index.	words, syllables, and sentences from Management Discussion and Analysis, President's Letter, and footnotes in 1986 corporate reports	manual complete text	descriptive statistics Spearman rank Correlation	Relative judgments only made. MD&A and footnotes estimated 17.66 and 17.88 grade readability. President's Letter easier at 16.03.
Dorrell & Darsey [1991] USA	To assess readability using Flesch-Kincaid index.	words, syllables, and sentences from President's Letter in 1987 corporate reports	all (?) using GRAMMATIK II computer package	descriptive statistics means, median, and mode	Range from grade 8 - college senior, mode 12. median 12.8. Conclusion "appropriate for the target audience" (p. 81).

Exhibit 1.1 (continued)

Researchers Publication Date & Country	Purpose	Recording Unit	Coding Method	Measurement Model	Findings
Hussey & Everitt [1991] UK	To assess readability using Flesch index.	words, syllables, and sentences from Chairman's Narrative and Chief Executive's message in 1990 employee reports	manual	descriptive statistics means	More than half difficult or very difficult to read.
Baker & Kare [1992] USA	To assess readability using Flesch and Readability indexes.	words, syllables, and sentences from President's Letter in corporate reports Circa 1990(?)	all (?) used Rightwriter Computer Program	descriptive statistics means correlation co-efficient	Mean Flesch score 39 (difficult), readability index grade 13 requiring college-level education for comprehension. Large firms more readable than small firms. Flesch positively correlated at 95% level to return on equity. no significant correlation with net profit.
Flory et al. [1992] USA	To assess differences in readability using Flesch and Fog indexes.	words, syllables, and sentences from passages from 7 intermediate accounting textbooks	manual 30 pages	Kruskal-Wallis ANOVA and Mann-Whitney U test	Insignificant differences between textbooks using Flesch and Kruskal-Wallis. Kruskal-Wallis and Fog indexes showed at least one textbook to be significantly different.
Martindale et al. [1992] USA	To assess the complexity of income tax law using Flesch, Flesch-Kincaid and Reading Complexity Evaluation indexes.	words, syllables, and sentences from sections 179 and 318 of the Internal Revenue Code	manual	MANOVA tests of differences and non-parametric correlation coefficients	The Reading Complexity Evaluation Index, devised by authors, proved a better measure for evaluating technical writing than standard reading tests.

22

Exhibit 1.1 (continued)

Researchers Publication Date & Country	Purpose	Recording Unit	Coding Method	Measurement Model	Findings
Schroeder & Gibson [1992] USA	To assess readability using Flesch-Kincaid index.	words, syllables, and sentences from every other page in 1986 corporate reports and 1987 simplified annual reports (SAR)	manual 100-word samples, every other page containing over 100 words	descriptive statistics means Wilcoxon Signed Ranks test	Corporate annual report grade level 14.7, simplified reports grade level 14.0.
Smith & Taffler [1992a, b] UK	To assess readability and understandability using cloze, Lix, and Flesch indexes.	words, syllables, and sentences from Chairman's narratives in 1978-85 corporate reports	whole statement using Oxford Concordance computer program	descriptive statistics means student t test, and product moment coefficient of correlation	Lix score mean (56.5) and Flesch score (34.2). 97% and 96% respective scores show Chairman's narratives at least difficult. Lix and Flesch well correlated, Flesch did not correlate with cloze. Authors suggest a mismatch between readability and understandability. Lix scores significantly higher and Flesch scores significantly lower for failed companies.
Subramanian et al. [1993] USA	To assess readability using Flesch-Kincaid index.	words, syllables, and sentences from President's Letter in 1987 and 1988 corporate reports	computer paragraphs totaling 200 words using Rightwriter	descriptive statistics means student t	Compared mean readability levels of good performance companies (10.1 grade level), with poor performing companies (14.1 grade level). Readability levels significantly different. The annual reports of good performers were easier to read than those of poor performers.
Urbancic [1993] USA	To assess tax instruction readability for individuals using Flesch and Fog indexes.	words, syllables, and sentences from three passages from 44 resident instruction booklets	manual	descriptive statistics means	Tax instruction readability found to be in general, difficult or very difficult to read.

Source: M. J. Jones and P. A. Shoemaker, "Accounting Narratives: A Review of Empirical Studies of Content and Readability," *Journal of Accounting Literature* 13 (1994): 153–159. Reprinted with permission from the *Journal of Accounting Literature*.

accuracy and content of accounting statements. Despite the unconventional nature of the form of visual representation discussed here, it highlights the possible relationships that may exist between the predictive ability of a data set and its method of presentation. A novel and humorous approach to data representation can certainly be defended if more accurate and effective decisions result.[101]

4. Students who may have to contribute to the writing of accounting communications need to have their communication skills improved. One way would be to introduce writing in the accounting curriculum. Surveys of academics, practitioners, and students about writing skills showed several consistent conclusions (see Exhibit 1.2):

1. Practitioners and academics believe that communication skills are important.
2. Practitioners and academics believe communication skills are more important than students do.
3. Practitioners, academics and students believe that students are not well-prepared in communication skills.
4. Academic programs to improve communication skills are expanding and students are becoming more prepared.
5. There are many ways to improve communication skills.[102]

The call for improving communication skills has also been made forcefully by various official organizations as follows:

Communication skills learned in general education should be reinforced in the business and accounting segments.[103]

Practitioners must be able to present and defend their views through formal and informal, written and oral, presentation.[104]

Ability to present, discuss, and defend views effectively through formal and informal, written and spoken language.[105]

MEANING IN ACCOUNTING

The previous section investigated the readability of accounting messages over time with the overall conclusion that the level of readability remained difficult. This section shows a more serious situation, as several studies investigating the understandability of the meaning of accounting messages by various groups of users show either a lack of understandability or a differential understandability among groups of users. These studies are summarized below:

Haried examined in a first paper the semantic problems of external accounting communication.[106] He makes two points. First, to the extent semantic problems exist, accountants have the primary responsibility for reducing these problems in external accounting communication; and sec-

Exhibit 1.2
Surveys of Writing in Accounting Curriculum

Survey Reference	Research Topic	Participants	Selected Findings
Estes [1979]	Report on importance of wide range of skill and knowledge areas to accountants' work.	111 senior corporate accountants; 63 junior corporate accountants; 89 senior government accountants; 72 junior government accountants; 68 senior public accountants; 88 junior public accountants; 86 educators	1. Written communications ranks in the top four most important skills/knowledge areas (out of 57). 2. Senior corporate accountants ranked written communications higher than junior corporate accountants.
Andrews and Koester [1979]	Opinion of communications skills of recent accounting graduates.	122 public accountants; 43 corporate accountants; 30 government accountants; 149 recent accounting graduates; 77 accounting educators; 69 accounting students	1. New accountants are less effective in written communications than oral communications. 2. New accountants perceive fewer written communication problems than their employers do. 3. Employers perceive new accountants spend more time on narrative communications (as opposed to numerical) than new accountants do. 4. The most additional training in communication skills is needed in nonnumerical report writing.
Ingram and Frazier [1980]	Report of communication skills needed by and found in new accountants and of training in communication skills.	64 CPAs, 70 corporate accountants, 114 academicians	1. Communication skills are needed, but deficient; academicians view communication skills as more necessary than practitioners. 2. Communication skills affect hiring decisions. 3. Emphasis on communication skills in accounting programs is increasing.
Addams [1981]	Report of importance of writing on measures of success of new accountants. Opinion on preferred writing training and communication task difficulty.	164 Big 8 accountants with 1 year experience from 45 states	1. Writing ability is important in appraisal, promotion and raises, and maintaining relationships with others. 2. Training in the writing of financial statements, audit programs, letters, and analytical reports is most desired. 3. In-house writing training is most desired form of training. 4. The most difficult communication tasks are oral presentations, writing to clients, and writing within the firm.

Exhibit 1.2 (continued)

Survey Reference	Research Topic	Participants	Selected Findings
Andrews & Sigband [1984]	Opinion of communication skills and education of new accountants.	90 accounting department chairs in AACSB accredited universities; 38 managing partners of large accounting firms	1. 70% of CPA firm partners rate new accountants' writing skills "inadequate." (Chairs' responses not reported.) 2. Memos, reports, and letters are considered the most important writing skills. 3. Current education is considered inadequate, and curriculum/instructional time changes are suggested.
Rebele [1985]	Opinion of relative importance of communication skills for success in public accounting.	118 junior and senior accounting students at Indiana University	1. Students perceive oral communication skills as moderately influential in success in public accounting. 2. Students perceive written communication skills as least influential in success in public accounting.
Gingras [1987]	Opinion on importance of writing, satisfaction with writing education and preferred training in writing. Report of writing activities and training.	654 Idaho CPAs	1. Less-experienced accountants and corporate and government accountants do more nontechnical writing than public accountants. 2. Newer CPAs and CPAs with advanced degrees are more satisfied with their education in writing than more experienced CPAs and CPAs with B.A.s. 3. Most CPAs suggest additional writing instruction both in college and post-college.
Henry and Razzouk [1988]	Opinion of adequacy of accounting training and hiring criteria.	82 managing partners in 4 counties in Southern California	1. CPAs rate "Effective Communication Skills" the most important hiring criterion. 2. CPAs are least satisfied with ability of accounting graduates in writing skills.
May and May [1989]	Report of communication programs offered.	263 accounting programs department heads	Description of communication instruction program and communication skills taught, current and planned.
Novin and Pearson [1989]	Opinion of qualifications of entry-level public accountants.	166 CPA firm partners, primarily local firms, from 41 states	1. Partners are most willing to sacrifice accounting knowledge for training in writing (than any other non-accounting skill). 2. Writing skills are most frequently cited weakness (99/166) of entry-level accountants.

26

Exhibit 1.2 (continued)

Survey Reference	Research Topic	Participants	Selected Findings
Bean and Watanabe [1990]	Opinion of effectiveness of techniques for improving communication skills.	356 accounting graduates of 13 universities; 287 accounting students of 5 universities	1. Accounting graduates rate all techniques higher than students. 2. Communications courses, case studies, and oral presentations are preferred training formats.
Hiemstra, Schmidt & Madison [1990]	Report of communication skills used. Opinion of importance of and training in communication.	269 CMAs	Communication skills become more important as CMAs advance.
Novin, Pearson & Senge [1990]	Opinion of qualifications of entry-level management accountants. Opinion of preferred academic preparation of entry-level accountants.	233 CMAs-corporate controllers	1. 92% of CMAs rate writing skills as very or extremely important and 49% would sacrifice technical content for its coverage. 2. Writing skills are most commonly mentioned weakness of entry-level management accountants.
Deppe, et al. [1991]	Report of competencies of accountants and where skills are developed.	501 practicing accountants, primarily in California, Oklahoma, Maryland, Michigan, and Utah	1. Writing is one of the most important competencies learned in undergraduate and graduate programs and on the job. 2. Writing competency obtained by plurality on the job (31%).

Source: B. W. Scofield, "Double Entry Journals: Writer-Based Prose in the Intermediate Accounting Curriculum," *Issues in Accounting Education* 9 (Fall 1994): 334-336. Reprinted with permission from the American Accounting Association and the author.

ond, there has been a conspicuous lack of empirical support for proposals aimed at reducing or eliminating these problems.[107] In this paper, Haried develops a semantic structure, in the form of a multidimensional semantic space. First, a technique known as the *triad procedure* is used to generate 30 bipolar adjective pairs for possible use in the semantic differential. Then a factor analysis was undertaken to identify seven independent dimensions to the meaning of this report terminology. In this, he reported on the use of this refined semantic differential for measuring differences in meaning associated with terms used in financial reports. In a second paper, he reported on an adoption of a second technique— the antecedent-consequent method—for measuring differences in meaning, a method that permits a study of controlled word associations.[108] Using five groups with different backgrounds to measure the meaning of selected statement terms and to study any semantic difficulties regarding financial statement on terminology, he showed the antecedent-consequent method to be adaptable to financial report terminology and useful in systematically gathering and analyzing empirical evidence relevant to the hypothesis about semantic problems in external accounting communication.[109] The semantic differential as proposed by Osgood et al.[110] was found, however, to be less capable. These results were reanalyzed by Houghton,[111] providing new results that are consistent with Haried's and showing that "(1) the structure within which accounting meaning is held is, largely, consistent with the seminal work of Osgood et al. (1975); and (2) the measured meaning of accounting concepts within that structure is consistent with expectations."[112]

Oliver also used the semantic differential technique to measure the semantic meaning of eight selected important accounting concepts, using seven selected professional groups involved in the production and use of accounting data.[113] While Haried's studies focus on the meaning of accounting terms used within financial reports, Oliver's study is directed toward the basic, underlying accounting concepts. The results indicate (a) the nonconformance of accounting educators' perceptions from the other groups and (b) the conformance of certified public accountants (CPAs) with the other groups. A clear implication of these findings is:

If accounting educators sincerely desire an influential role in the continuing development and utilization of accounting information, it appears they should structure their future attempts to interject their positions within a communication network in phase with the nonacademics. This does not mean that abstract or theoretical positions must be altered. What does need attention is the presentation mode. To become an integral component of the existing decision network, the educators must learn to send and to receive accounting messages which are reasonably accurate communications.[114]

Dupree investigated whether four user groups possessing various levels of accounting sophistication differed in the terminology preferred in accounting reports.[115] Subjects came from four groups of users of accounting reports defined as follows:

1. American Institute of Certified Public Accountants (AICPA): preparers who function primarily externally to the corporate reporting entity;

2. Financial Executive Institute (FEI): preparers who function within the reporting entity;

3. Chartered Financial Analyst (CFA) members of the Financial Analysts Federation (FAF): professional report users who are not preparers;

4. Graduates of Emory University, Atlanta, Georgia: a surrogate group for college-educated non-professional users of financial reports.[116]

They were asked to select preferences from a list of synonyms for a number of accounting terms. The results showed that the four groups disagreed as to preferences for technical versus descriptive accounting terms, and that the AICPA members were the most likely to disagree with the others but that different combined groups, with the exception of the group of AICPA and financial professionals, had similar preferences for income statement variables.

Houghton examined the annotative meaning of the concept of "true and fair view."[117] Although the concept is assumed to imply the consistent application of generally accepted accounting principles, it is the subject of a debate as to its meaning.[118] Houghton relied on the semantic differential to investigate the differential meaning of *true* and *fair view* that may be held by both accountants and shareholders. More precisely, the study measured three meanings: "accountant's own meaning, accountant's perception of shareholders' meaning, and shareholders' own meaning."[119] The results showed (a) significant differences between the responses held by accountants and private shareholders as to the meaning of *true* and *fair* and (b) the factor or cognitive structure of the expert accountants' group to be more complex than lay private shareholders.

Adelberg examined the readability of narrative disclosure contained in financial reports by measuring the understandability of narrative disclosures by sophisticated users and correlating the level of understandability with the change in earnings per share.[120] The understandability of narrative disclosure was measured by the Cloze readability procedure. As defined by Taylor, the Cloze procedure is a "method of intercepting a message from a transmitter (writer or speaker), mutilating its language patterns by deleting parts, and so administering it to receivers (readers or listeners) that their attempts to make patterns whole again potentially yield a considerable number of Cloze units."[121] Adelberg used four different types of narrative disclosures for testing:

The first type of message, designated "A," was a footnote whose format has become standardized (i.e., the footnote required by Accounting Principles Board *Opinion No. 22* "Accounting Policies").

The second type of message, designated "B," was a footnote whose format has not become standardized (i.e., the footnote required by Financial Accounting Standards Board *Statement of Financial Accounting Standards No. 5* "Accounting for Contingencies").

The third type of message, designated "C," was a management's analysis of operations required by the Securities and Exchange Commission in *Accounting Series Release No. 159*; its format has become standardized.

The fourth type of message, designated "D," was a qualified auditor's report required by the American Institute of Certified Public Accountants' fourth standard of reporting.[122]

The subjects selected were from a certified public accountant group of a chartered financial analyst group. The results show that both standard format footnotes and management's analysis of operations, which were the most technical, contained the most numbers, and made reference to specific financial statement items and amounts, were not well understood by the sophisticated users, while nonstandard format footnotes and qualified auditor's reports were. The results also show that the level of understandability of the type of message varied directly with the change in earnings per share. The first results indicate that even sophisticated users have difficulties understanding technical accounting terms. The second results indicate the potential of management manipulation, prompting the following advice:

Given human behavior, the placing of managers in complete control of the accounting communication process which monitors their performance breeds a situation wherein it is perfectly natural to expect that some managers would obfuscate their failures and underscore their successes. To partially satisfy the requirements for objective and impartial reporting on the performance of management, the understandability of narrative disclosures must be free as possible from the manipulations of management.[123]

Similar results were reported in another paper.[124]

Adelberg also examined the understandability of authoritative pronouncements.[125] The quality of the language of these pronouncements is deemed important:

To properly prepare financial statements, private accountants must completely understand the authoritative pronouncements that underlie their formulation. To successfully perform the attest function, certified public accountants must completely understand both the authoritative pronouncements that underlie auditing and the authoritative pronouncements that underlie the preparation of an entity's financial statements. To effectively (1) educate prospective certified public accountants and private accountants and (2) engage in scholarly research, academic accountants must also completely understand authoritative pronouncements. It is inconceivable that authoritative pronouncements could be properly implemented by private, public, and academic accountants without a full understanding of their contents.[126]

The study used a psycholinguistic technique, the Cloze procedure, in an experiment involving three groups of certified public accountants, academic accountants, and private accountants to evaluate the communication of authoritative pronouncements in accounting. The results indicated that communication problems did not exist at either the source (authoritative body) level or the destination (accountant) level. However, a serious communication problem was found to exist at the message (authoritative pronouncement) level.

Adelberg and Farrelly examined the measurement of both the denotative and connotative meaning of financial statement terminology between and among producers (certified public accountants, academic accountants, and private accountants) and users (chartered financial analysts, commercial bank loan officers, and shareholders) of financial statements.[127] Two psycholinguistic approaches, classification analysis (for denotative meaning) and association analysis (for connotative meaning), were used. The following 25 terms were used as the financial statement terms:

Income	net sales
	expense
	depreciation and amortization
	revenue
	extraordinary credit
	net income
	cost of products sold
Balance Sheet	goodwill
	unearned revenue
	stockholders' equity
	allowance for doubtful accounts
	accrued expense
	asset
	deferred charge
	additional paid-in capital

Statement of Change in
  Financial Position

preferred stock

retained earnings liability

retirement of long-term debt

uses of working capital

declaration of dividends

issuance of common stock

disposal of fixed assets

sources of working capital

capital expenditure

long-term borrowing[128]

As expected, the results showed no significance of either an intergroup or intragroup nature on denotative meaning. With regard to connotative meanings, the results showed significant differences between producers and users for the selected financial statement terms as measured by association analysis. The following alternative explanations were proposed:

Those attracted to the "producer" occupations vs. the "user" occupations could have basically different personalities and/or innate cognitive structures that account for the different processing of information. Or, their educational backgrounds may account for the differences. We tend to think, however, that the most plausible explanation is that producers via their professional affiliations are continually exposed to, and are therefore intimately familiar with, financial statement terms whether the terms are audited by them (certified public accountants), taught by them (academic accountants), or prepared for them (private accountants). On the other hand, users via their professional affiliations probably need not be as competent in the technical complexities of financial reporting as producers in order to advise (chartered financial analysts), make loan decisions (commercial bank loan officers), or make security purchase/sale decisions (shareholders).[129]

Flamholtz and Cook examined the connotative meaning of three accounting constructs: human resources accounting and related constructs, other recently developed accounting constructs (such as social accounting), and well-established accounting constructs (i.e., financial accounting).[130] The semantic differential was the methodology used. The subjects were from two professional groups (accountants and managers). The results show that there are three or four dimensions underlying the accounting constructs, there are significant differences in the connotative meaning of the constructs to accountants and managers, and there is a "semantic halo effect" differentiating between the connotative meaning of traditional and nontraditional accounting constructs.[131] The third finding is explicated as follows:

Exhibit 1.3
Analysis of Empirically Based Thematic Content Analysis Studies

Researchers Publication Date & Country	Purpose	Recording Unit	Coding Method	Measurement Model	Findings
Bowman and Haire [1976] USA	To measure social disclosures as surrogates for social responsibility activity.	lines of text in annual reports	authors counted lines of social disclosures	raw line counts—proportions	Line-by-line prose in annual reports serves as an indicator to investors of corporate social responsibility.
Chan [1979] USA	To determine social disclosure practices in the area of employee occupational safety and health.	annual reports	author coded presence or absence of social disclosures, and their nature	raw counts qualitative analysis	Social disclosure reporting was not uniform among firms. There were more disclosures about efforts to increase occupational safety and health than of the results achieved.
Madeo [1979] USA	To classify tax court decisions regarding the accumulated earnings tax.	themes developed from Treasury Regulations and IRS audit guidelines	author identified presence or absence of 18 themes	discriminant analysis	Themes drawn from Treasury Regulations and IRS Audit Guidelines successfully discriminated outcomes (winners and losers) of tax court cases.
Ingram and Frazier [1980] USA	To determine the correlation between environmental performance and environmental disclosure of firms.	sentences of annual report narratives to identify content categories	authors coded sentences and tested agreement correlations	product-moment correlations multiple regression	There was no statistical relationship between environmental performance and environmental disclosure.
Kelly-Newton [1980] USA	To determine managements' attitudes towards forced implementation of the SEC's ASR No. 190.	themes within each sentence in footnote disclosures of annual reports	author coded sentences for the presence or absence of 16 pre-determined themes	factor analysis	Seven underlying attitudes were revealed towards ASR 190. Management appeared to question the relevance and reliability of mandated replacement cost disclosures.

Exhibit 1.3 (continued)

Researchers Publication Date & Country	Purpose	Recording Unit	Coding Method	Measurement Model	Findings
Whittington & Whittenburg [1980] USA	To classify debt versus equity in closely held corporations.	themes established by the Internal Revenue Code, court cases and other literature	authors identified presence or absence of 12 themes	factor analysis and discriminant analysis	Four of twelve themes accurately predicted the outcome of tax court cases; however, the overall decision process of classifying debt versus equity changed over time.
Karlinsky [1981] USA	To measure tax complexity of capital gain and loss taxation.	paragraphs—percentage of paragraphs containing references to capital gain and/or loss	author counted number of paragraphs containing capital gain or loss theme	tax expenditure/complexity index (TEC)	Capital gain and loss legislation complicates income tax law both absolutely and relatively. A low TEC index indicates an inefficient tax law which is unjustified under the Smithian model.
Wallace [1981] USA	To identify consistencies (inconsistencies) of internal reporting in the municipal sector.	themes of internal control disclosures within government reports	interpretation of author	qualitative analysis	The municipal reports do not adequately address risk exposure due to internal control weaknesses. The effects of the reports on cost—benefit analyzes are contrary to that stated in SAS pronouncements.
Kramer [1982] USA	To model tax court decision criteria regarding blockage.	themes established by court cases and tax literature	author identified 13 themes—continuous, dichotomous, categorical	multiple regression	Model had limited success in discriminating court cases outcomes. The Tax Court, Court of Claims, and district courts modeled their decisions differently.
Bettman & Weitz [1983] USA	To test attribution theory in letters to shareholders.	themes of causal reasoning	two graduate students identified themes and coded their outcomes (favorable or unfavorable)	log-linear Chi-square ANOVA	Self-serving patterns of attributions were found in Letters to Shareholders. Unfavorable outcomes were attributed more to external and uncontrollable causes than were favorable outcomes.

Exhibit 1.3 (continued)

Researchers Publication Date & Country	Purpose	Recording Unit	Coding Method	Measurement Model	Findings
Burns & Groomer [1983] USA	To discriminate between tax case outcomes for profit and not-for-profit activities.	themes established by court cases, Treasury Regulations, and tax literature	one author coded 38 themes and recoded a subset for validation	discriminant analysis	Salient tax classification variables were identified. There appears to be an increased emphasis on the importance of variables contained in the Treasury Regulations.
Committe [1983] USA	To develop a structure for the theory of auditor independence.	themes developed from participant testimonies at Congressional hearings	author identified the themes	qualitative analysis only	Defined ''independence'' as acting only on behalf of the public and having no association or relationship with the auditee organization which would influence auditor judgment.
Dillard & Jensen [1983] USA	To evaluate the effects of comment letters on proposed changes to the standard audit report. Observed differences of letters between industries.	letters	authors coded the letters by general reaction to exposure draft (favorable or unfavorable) and by reactions to six proposed audit report changes	descriptive statistics and graphical analyzes	Three types of business entities reacted differently to proposed changes in the language of the standard audit report.
Degnan [1983] USA	To validate computer coding by replicating Kramer's [1979] study.	words	computer counted word occurrences and co-occurrences	factor analysis and discriminant analysis	Computer results were different than Kramer's manually coded results but the author could not substantiate that the computer results were statistically superior.
Ingram & Frazier [1983] USA	To associate the content of narrative disclosures with financial results in annual reports.	words and financial ratios	computer coding of narrative disclosures and established financial ratios	factor analysis and stepwise regression	Consistent with attribution theory, the narratives associate good financial performance with management skills and poor financial performance with external factors.

Exhibit 1.3 (continued)

Researchers Publication Date & Country	Purpose	Recording Unit	Coding Method	Measurement Model	Findings
Neimark [1983] USA	To measure the process of social change through company annual reports.	characters	author coding of each character in the annual report narrative	dialectical theme index— proportions	The article illustrates the interaction of resolutions and impediments to capital accumulation and their traceability in annual reports.
Robison [1983] USA	To classify profit versus not-for-profit tax cases.	themes established by court cases and Treasury Regulations	two coders identified the presence or absence of 40 themes	probit analysis	Five themes adequately served as a prediction model for court cases. The prediction model was stable over time and across lines of business.
Staw et al. [1983] USA	To test attribution theory in letters to shareholders.	themes of causal reasoning	two independent coders identified locus of causality and outcomes	t-test of differences	The existence of self-serving attributions in annual reports was demonstrated. Positive (negative) attributions were correlated with increases (decreases) in stock prices.
Frazier et al. [1984] USA	To examine the differences in narrative disclosures of annual reports between management-controlled and owner-controlled firms.	words	computer coding of disclosures in annual reports	factor analysis MANOVA discriminant analysis	Results were not significant that management-controlled firms would be motivated to misrepresent narrative reports relative to owner controlled firms. Results were significant that narrative data could be used to predict future performance.
Lewis et al. [1984] AUST	To correlate socio-economic environments to financial reporting to employees.	themes (issues) of narrative reports	authors identified and coded themes	raw frequency counts	Four socio-economic factors correlated with four reporting categories. Seven distinct periods between 1919 and 1979 in which reporting frequencies increased were identified.

Exhibit 1.3 (continued)

Researchers Publication Date & Country	Purpose	Recording Unit	Coding Method	Measurement Model	Findings
Puro [1984] USA	To explain lobbyist behavior towards additional disclosure requirements.	comment letters to exposure drafts	author classified letters as favorable, unfavor-able, or neutral	probit analysis	Responses to additional disclosure rules were best explained by the economics of regulation theory. Agency theory best explained the lobbying behavior towards standardization.
Salancik & Meindl [1984] USA	To test differences in attribution theory between stable and unstable firms as evidenced in letters to shareholders.	themes of causal reasoning	twenty-three students coded causal themes based on criteria established by authors	correlations and multiple regression	Unstable firms were more likely to take responsibility for good and bad performance than stable firms. Stable firms were more likely to take credit for good performance and blame external forces for bad performance.
Taylor and Ingram [1984] USA	To discriminate between tax court case outcomes in real estate transactions.	words	computer coding of court case narratives	factor analysis and logistic regression	Seven of fifteen variables were significant in a computer model which accurately predicted court case determinations between capital gains and ordinary income.
McConnell et al. [1986] USA	To test for differences in Presidents' Letters between good and poor performance firms.	words and themes	computer coding of Presidents' Letters	t-test for differences discriminant analysis	Nine recurring themes were found in a sample of 100 Presidents' Letters. Five of the nine themes were significantly different between "gainer" and "loser" firms based on word counts devoted to each theme.
Neimark & Tinker [1986] USA	To identify internation-alization of markets as resolutions to capital accumulation impediments.	characters	author coding of characters in annual report narratives	raw data counts - proportions	Three distinct periods of capital accumulation impediment resolutions were analyzed for the period 1916-1976.

37

Exhibit 1.3 (continued)

Researchers Publication Date & Country	Purpose	Recording Unit	Coding Method	Measurement Model	Findings
MacArthur [1988] UK	To identify economic and political reasons for comments to exposure drafts.	comment letters to drafts	author coded for presence or absence of economic and political referents	no statistical analysis	The most frequent exposure draft comments related to economic or political impacts on corporations. The relative importance of the arguments was identified.
Garrison & Michaelsen [1989] USA	To evaluate models for analysis of court cases.	themes established by decision rule algorithms	interactive computer coding of answers to questions	raw comparisons of predictive success against other models	The ACLS computer model predicted court case outcomes better than alternative models.
Geiger [1989] USA	To determine the influence of comment letters to an exposure draft on SAS 58.	themes established by the predetermined respondent concerns	author coded presence or absence of 182 themes—six individuals coded a subsample for validation	descriptive statistics based on theme counts	Actual changes from an exposure draft to final SAS 58 were correlated to comment letters but no statistical inferences were drawn.
Guthrie and Parker [1989] AUST	To determine if legitimacy theory explained corporate social reporting (CSR).	six predetermined themes	one researcher measured amount of page space devoted to each theme	graphical analysis	Fluctuations in CSR did not correlate well with socioeconomic events, dispelling legitimacy theory.
Buckmaster & Hall [1990] USA	To determine if lobbying efforts in response to an exposure draft affected the final pronouncement for SFAS 88.	themes of 14 paragraphs in the exposure draft	author coding of 14 themes—support, opposition, no position	no statistical analysis—used raw theme count	Lobbying efforts did not result in significant changes in the final SFAS 88.

Exhibit 1.3 (continued)

Researchers Publication Date & Country	Purpose	Recording Unit	Coding Method	Measurement Model	Findings
Tennyson et al. [1990] USA	To find information content in narrative disclosures regarding bankruptcy.	words	computer coding of President's Letter and MD&A	factor analysis and logistic regression	The nature of narrative disclosures was successful in predicting financial distress. The computer model identified key themes useful in predicting bankruptcy.
McKee et al. [1991] USA	To test for differences between Big 8 and corresponding client comment letters to the FASB.	words and letters	two independent judges coded letters to SFAS 86 and computer coded words	chi-square	No similarities were found in comment letters to SFAS 86 between Big 8 firms and their clients. but the size of the clients appeared to influence accounting firms' positions regarding exposure drafts.
Wallace [1991] USA	To assess self-regulation process of peer review by observing differences between peer review reports and peer review standards.	themes developed from AICPA peer review training manual	three research assistants coded letters on 10 themes	logit regression and chi-square	No statistical relationship was found between AICPA review team and Big 15 review team in terms of which categories appeared most often as violations in their reports.
Collins et al. [1993] UK	To observe differences between U.K. and U.S. MD&A reports.	lines	authors counted number of lines devoted to each reporting guideline	chi-square	The content of MD&A's of U.S. and U.K. firms was significantly different.

Exhibit 1.3 (continued)

Researchers Publication Date & Country	Purpose	Recording Unit	Coding Method	Measurement Model	Findings
Hooks and Moon [1993] USA	To develop a classification scheme for annual report disclosures and test changes in SEC mandate.	themes—disclosures from SEC Regulation S-K and FRR 36	authors coded presence or absence of disclosure themes	McNemar test	The issuance of FRR 36 resulted in increased disclosure beginning one year after the implementation date.
McEnroe [1993] USA	To determine if the incorporation of exposure draft comments into final SAS 54 was politically driven.	themes and letters	author coded letters and themes with a sub-sample of themes coded by an assistant for agreement verification	logit regression and chi-square	No systematic classification scheme was found. The incorporation of exposure draft comments into the final SAS was not found to be politically driven.

Source: M. J. Jones and P. A. Shoemaker, "Accounting Narratives: A Review of Empirical Studies of Content and Readability," *Journal of Accounting Literature* 13 (1994): 145–152. Reprinted with permission from the *Journal of Accounting Literature*.

As used in psychology, the term "halo effect" refers to a tendency to generalize an overall impression of a person to specific traits or characteristics. As used in this article, the semantic halo effect refers to a tendency to generalize to specific characteristics of a construct based upon whether the construct is perceived as traditional or nontraditional.[132]

CONCLUSIONS

Accounting is first a communication tool. The communication is accomplished by the use of a special language, leading to the labeling of accounting as the language of business. The success of accounting as a language in general and the success of the communication in particular rest in both the readability of accounting messages and the understandability of the meaning of accounting messages of users. This chapter shows that in general the level of readability of accounting messages is difficult, and the level of understandability of the meaning of accounting messages is less than perfect. All the studies reviewed in this chapter focused on readability rather than thematic content analysis. Studies using thematic analysis to extract and analyze themes inherent within the message are summarized in Exhibit 1.3. The next chapter provides an explanation of both phenomena by using the linguistic relativity thesis (Chapter 2), the sociolinguistic thesis (Chapter 3), and the bilingual thesis (Chapter 4).

NOTES

1. S. Lawrence, "How Accountants Do It: The Social Creation of Objective Reality," *Asian Review of Accounting* (December 1992): 1–15.

2. D. Laudie, "The Accounting of Interpretations and the Interpretation of Accounts: The Communicative Function of 'The Language of Business,'" *Accounting Organizations and Society* (June 1987): 579–604.

3. Ibid., 580.

4. C. T. Horngren, *Accounting for Management Control* (Englewood Cliffs, NJ: Prentice-Hall, 1974), 70.

5. R. N. Anthony, and J. S. Reece, *Management Accounting: Text and Cases* (Homewood, IL: Irwin, 1975), 12.

6. Y. Ijiri, *Theory of Accounting Measurement* (Sarasota, FL: American Accounting Association, 1975), 14.

7. P. A. Mills, "Words and the Study of Accounting History," *Accounting, Auditing and Accountability Journal* (January 1990): 21–35.

8. F. Brandel, *The Wheels of Commerce (Civilization and Capitalism, 15th-18th Century)* (New York: Harper and Row, 1979).

9. Ibid., 232.

10. Mills, "Words and the Study of Accounting History," 33.

11. Ibid.

12. D. L. Scott, and G. Fiebelkorn, *Dictionary of Accounting* (New York: Rowman & Allanheld, 1985).

13. J. K. Shim, and J. G. Siegel, *Encyclopedic Dictionary of Accounting and Finance* (Englewood Cliffs, NJ: Prentice-Hall, 1989).

14. W. W. Cooper, and Y. Ijiri, *Kohler's Dictionary for Accountants* (Englewood Cliffs, NJ: Prentice-Hall, 1982).

15. R. H. Parker, *Macmillan Dictionary of Accounting* (New York: Macmillan, 1984).

16. R. P. Brief, *Selections from Encyclopedia of Accounting 1903* (New York: Arno Press, 1978).

17. D. Wasson, *English/Spanish Glossary of Basic Accounting Terms* (Homewood, IL: Irwin, 1994).

18. D. French, *Dictionary of Accounting Terms* (London: Financial Training, 1985).

19. D. Houghton, and R. G. Wallace, *Students' Accounting Vocabulary* (Farnborough: Gower, 1980).

20. A. J. Robb, with R. W. Wallis, *Accounting Terms Dictionary* (London: Pitman, 1985).

21. D. A. R. Forrester, and C. M. Grant, "New Vocabularies Reviewed in the Light of No Syntax of Accounting—A Review Article," *British Accounting Review* (Autumn 1966): 90–98.

22. Ibid., 97.

23. Financial Accounting Standards Board, *Statement of Financial Accounting Concepts No. 1: Objectives of Financial Reporting by Business Enterprises* (Stanford, CT: FASB, 1986), 16.

24. A. Belkaoui, "Linguistic Relativity in Accounting," *Accounting, Organizations and Society* 2 (1978): 97–104.

25. L. C. Hawes, *Pragmatics of Analoguing* (Reading, MA: Addison-Wesley, 1975), 3–4.

26. G. Zaltman, C. R. A. Dison, and R. Angelman, *Metatheory and Consumer Research* (New York: Holt, Rinehart & Winston, 1973), 22–23.

27. D. McDonald, *Comparative Accounting Theory* (Reading, MA: Addison-Wesley, 1972), 6.

28. T. N. Jain, "Alternative Networks of Accounting and Decision Making: A Psycholinguistic Analysis," *Accounting Review* (January 1973): 98.

29. Ibid., 99.

30. Committee to Prepare a Statement of Basic Accounting Theory, *A Statement of Basic Accounting Theory* (Evanston, IL: American Accounting Association, 1966), 7.

31. K. Most, *Accounting Theory* (Columbus, OH: Grid, 1989), 43.

32. L. Kelly-Newton, *Accounting Policy Formulation* (Reading, MA: Addison-Wesley, 1980), 105.

33. E. B. Swanson, "Management Information Systems: Appreciation and Involvement," *Management Science* 2 (1974): 178–188.

34. R. W. Zmud, "An Empirical Investigation of the Dimensionality of the Concept of Information," *Decision Sciences* 2 (1978): 187–195.

35. M. Smith, and R. Taffler, "Improving the Communication Function of Pub-

lished Accounting Statements," *Accounting and Business Research* (Spring 1984): 139–146.

36. D. F. Larcker, and V. P. Vessig, "Perceived Usefulness of Information: A Psychometric Examination," *Decision Sciences* (January 1980): 121–134.

37. J. Smith, and N. P. Smith, "Readability: A Measure of the Performance of the Communication Function of Financial Reporting," *Accounting Review* (July 1971): 354.

38. Ibid., 352.

39. C. Harrison, *Readability in the Classroom* (Cambridge: Cambridge University Press, 1980).

40. R. Flesch, "A New Readability Yardstick," *Journal of Applied Psychology* (June 1948): 221–233.

41. Harrison, *Readability in the Classroom*, 74.

42. J. P. Kincaid, R. P. Fishbourne, R. L. Rogers, and B. S. Chisson, *Derivation of New Readability Formulas (Automated Readability Index Fog Count and Flesch Reading Ease Formula for Navy Enlisted Personnel)* (CNTT Research Branch Report 8–75) (Memphis, TN: Chief of Naval Technical Training, Naval Air Station, 1975).

43. R. Gunning, *The Technique of Clear Writing* (New York: McGraw-Hill, 1952).

44. Harrison, *Readability in the Classroom*, 79.

45. W. F. Kwolek, "Readability Survey of Technical and Popular Literature," *Journalism Quarterly* (Summer 1973): 255–264.

46. Ibid., 256–257.

47. J. Anderson, "Analyzing the Readability of English and Non-English Texts in the Classroom with Lix" (paper presented at the Seventh Australian Reading Association Conference, Darwin, August 1981), 1–12.

48. Ibid., 5.

49. R. Gunning, *The Technique of Clear Writing*, 2d ed. (New York: McGraw-Hill, 1968), 40.

50. N. R. Lewis, L. D. Parker, G. D. Pound, and P. Sutcliffe, "Accounting Report Readability: The Use of Readability Techniques," *Accounting and Business Research* (Summer 1986): 201.

51. K. B. Frazier, R. W. Ingram, and B. M. Tennyson, "A Methodology for the Analysis of Narrative Accounting Disclosures," *Journal of Accounting Research* (Spring 1984): 318–331.

52. Ibid., 319.

53. H. P. Isler, "A Historical Note on the Use of Word-Frequency Contiguities in Content Analysis," *Computers and the Humanities* 8 (1974): 95–96.

54. Lewis et al., "Accounting Report Readability: The Use of Readability Techniques," 199–213.

55. Ibid., 208.

56. S. Pashalian, and W. J. E. Crissy, "How Readable Are Corporate Annual Reports?" *Journal of Applied Psychology* (August 1980): 244–248.

57. R. F. Flesch, *The Art of Plain Talk* (New York: Harper and Brothers, 1946).

58. Flesch, "A New Readability Yardstick."

59. The same results are reported in S. Pashalian, and W. J. E. Crissy, "Corporate Annual Reports Are Difficult, Dull Reading, Human Interest Value Low, Survey Shows," *Journal of Accounting* (August 1952): 215–219.

60. F. J. Soper, and R. Dolphin, Jr., "Readability and Corporate Annual Reports," *Accounting Review* (April 1964): 358–362.

61. C. L. Holley, and J. Early, "Are Financial Statements Easy to Read?" *Woman CPA* (August 1980): 9–13.

62. Ibid., 13.

63. R. A. Wagley, and R. Dolphin, Jr., "Reading the Annual Report," *Financial Executive* (June 1977): 20–22.

64. Smith and Smith, "Readability: A Measure of the Performance of the Communication Function of Financial Reporting."

65. L. D. Parker, "Corporate Annual Reporting: A Mass Communication Perspective," *Accounting and Business Research* (Autumn 1982): 279–286.

66. Ibid., 284.

67. R. Hoskins, "Annual Reports I: Difficult Reading and Getting More So," *Public Relations Review* (Summer 1984): 49–55.

68. R. L. Heath, and G. Phelps, "Annual Reports II: Readability of Reports vs. Business Press," *Public Relations Review* (Summer 1984): 56–62.

69. Ibid., 61.

70. J. K. Courtis, "An Investigation into Annual Report Readability and Corporate Risk-Return Relationships," *Accounting and Business Research* (Fall 1986): 285–294.

71. Ibid., 292.

72. M. J. Jones, "A Longitudinal Study of the Readability of the Chairman's Narrative in the Corporate Reports of a UK Company," *Accounting and Business Research* 18 (1988): 297–305.

73. Ibid., 297.

74. Ibid., 303.

75. N. Schroeder, and C. Gibson, "Readability of Management's Discussion and Analysis," *Accounting Horizons* (December 1990): 78–87.

76. Ibid., 87.

77. N. Schroeder, R. Aggarwal, and C. Gibson, "Financial Reporting by Japanese Firms on the NYSE: An Analysis of Linguistic Contact," *Management International Review* 31, no. 3 (1991): 233–251.

78. Ibid., 247.

79. C. H. Gibson, and N. W. Schroeder, "U.K. Firms on the NYSE: An Analysis of Readability Traits," *Journal of International Accounting Auditing and Taxation* 3 (1994): 27–40.

80. Ibid., 37.

81. N. W. Schroeder, and C. H. Gibson, "A Readability Comparison of Financial Statement Footnotes of International Banks," *Advances in International Accounting* 7 (1994): 121–134.

82. Ibid., 123.

83. Kincaid et al., *Derivation of New Readability Formulas*.

84. Schroeder and Gibson, "A Readability Comparison of Financial Statement Footnotes of International Banks," 129.

85. P. Healy, "Can You Understand the Footnotes to Financial Statements?" *Accountants' Journal* (July 1977): 219–222.

86. M. D. Still, "The Readability of Chairman's Statement," *Accounting and Business Research* (Winter 1972): 36–39.

87. G. D. Pound, "Employee Reports: Readability," *Australian Accountant* (December 1980): 775–779.

88. G. D. Pound, "A Note on Audit Report Readability," *Accounting and Finance* (May 1981): 45–55.

89. A. H. Adelberg, "Narrative Disclosures Contained in Financial Reports: Means of Communication or Manipulation?" *Accounting and Business Research* (Summer 1979): 179–190.

90. Courtis, "An Investigation into Annual Report Readability and Corporate Risk-Return Relationships."

91. Jones, "A Longitudinal Study of the Readability of the Chairman's Narrative in the Corporate Reports of a UK Company."

92. H. E. Baker III, and D. D. Klare, "Relationship Between Annual Report Readability and Corporate Financial Performance," *Management Research News* 4 (1992): 1–4.

93. M. Smith, and R. Taffler, "The Chairman's Statement and Corporate Financial Performance," *Accounting and Finance* 1 (1992): 75–90.

94. R. Subramarian, R. G. Insley, and R. D. Blackwell, "Performance and Readability: A Comparison of Annual Reports of Profitable and Unprofitable Operations," *Journal of Business Communication* 30 (1993): 49–61.

95. Ibid., 59.

96. D. McConnell, J. A. Haslem, and V. R. Gibson, "The President's Letter to Stockholders: A New Look," *Financial Analysts Journal* 5 (1986): 67–70.

97. F. A. Fisher, and M. Y. Yu, "Does the CEO's Letter to the Shareholders Have Predictive Value?" *Business Forum* 1 (1989): 22–24.

98. Courtis, "An Investigation into Annual Report Readability and Corporate Risk-Return Relationships."

99. T. A. Lee, and D. P. Tweedie, "Accounting Information: An Investigation of Private Shareholder Usage," *Accounting and Business Research* (Autumn 1975): 280–291.

100. Smith and Taffler, "Improving the Communication Function of Published Accounting Statements."

101. Ibid., 146.

102. B. W. Scofield, "Double Entry Journals: Writer-Based Prose in the Intermediate Accounting Curriculum," *Issues in Accounting Education* (Fall 1994): 330–352.

103. American Institute of Certified Public Accountants, *Education Requirements for Entry in the Accounting Profession* (New York: AICPA, 1988), 17.

104. *Perspective on Education: Capabilities for Success in the Accounting Profession* (New York: Arthur Andersen & Co.; Arthur Young, Coopers and Lybrand, Deloitte Haskings & Sells, Ernst and Whinney, Peat Marwick Main & Co., Price Waterhouse, and Touche Ross, 1989), 6.

105. Accounting Education Change Commission, "Objectives of Education for Accountants: Position Statement Number One," *Issues in Accounting Education* (Fall 1990): 7.

106. H. H. Haried, "The Semantic Dimensions of Financial Statements," *Journal of Accounting Research* (Autumn 1972): 379–391.

107. Ibid., 379.

108. A. Haried, "Measurement of Meaning in Financial Reports," *Journal of Accounting Research* (Spring 1993): 117–145.

109. Ibid., 143.

110. C. E. Osgood, G. J. Suci, and P. H. Tannenbaum, *The Measurement of Meaning* (Champaign: University of Illinois Press, 1957).

111. K. A. Houghton, "The Measurement of Meaning in Accounting: A Critical Analysis of the Principal Evidence," *Accounting, Organizations and Society* 3 (1988): 263–280).

112. Ibid., 263.

113. B. L. Oliver, "The Semantic Differential: A Device for Measuring the Interprofessional Communication of Selected Accounting Concepts," *Journal of Accounting Research* (Autumn 1974): 299–316.

114. Ibid., 312.

115. J. M. Dupree, "Users' Preferences for Descriptive Versus Technical Accounting Terms," *Accounting and Business Research* (Fall 1985): 281–290.

116. Ibid., 282.

117. K. A. Houghton, "True and Fair View: An Empirical Study of Connotative Meaning," *Accounting, Organizations and Society* 12, no. 2 (1987): 143–152.

118. T. K. Cowan, "Are Truth and Fairness Generally Acceptable?" *Accounting Review* (October 1965): 788–794.

119. Houghton, "True and Fair View: Am Empirical Study of Connotative Meaning."

120. Adelberg, "Narrative Disclosures Contained in Financial Reports: Means of Communication or Manipulation?"

121. W. Taylor, "Cloze Procedure: A New Tool for Measuring Readability," *Journalism Quarterly* (Fall 1953): 46.

122. Adelberg, "Narrative Disclosures Contained in Financial Reports: Means of Communication or Manipulation?" 182.

123. Ibid., 187.

124. A. H. Adelberg, "A Methodology for Measuring the Understandability of Financial Report Messages," *Journal of Accounting Research* (Autumn 1979): 565–592.

125. A. H. Adelberg, "An Empirical Evaluation of the Communication of Authoritative Pronouncements in Accounting," *Accounting and Finance* (November 1982): 73–94.

126. Ibid., 75–85.

127. A. H. Adelberg, and G. E. Farrelly, "Measuring the Meaning of Financial Statement Terminology: A Psycholinguistic Approach," *Accounting and Finance* (May 1989): 33–61.

128. Ibid., 44–45.

129. Ibid., 49.

130. E. Flamholtz, and E. Cook, "Connotative Meaning and Its Role in Accounting Change: A Field Study," *Accounting, Organizations and Society* 8 (1978): 125–139.

131. Ibid., 132, 134, 135.

132. Ibid., 139.

REFERENCES

Accounting Education Change Commission. "Objectives of Education for Accountants: Position Statement Number One." *Issues in Accounting Education* (Fall 1990): 7.

Addams, H. L. "Should the Big 8 Teach Communication Skills?" *Management Accounting* (May 1981): 37–40.

Adelberg, A. H. "Narrative Disclosures Contained in Financial Reports: Means of Communication or Manipulation?" *Accounting and Business Research* (Summer 1979): 179–190.

Adelberg, A. H. "A Methodology for Measuring the Understandability of Financial Report Messages." *Journal of Accounting Research* (Autumn 1979): 565–592.

Adelberg, A. H. "An Empirical Evaluation of the Communication of Authoritative Pronouncements in Accounting." *Accounting and Finance* (November 1982): 73–94.

Adelberg, A. H., and G. E. Farrelly. "Measuring the Meaning of Financial Statement Terminology: A Psycholinguistic Approach." *Accounting and Finance* (May 1989): 33–61.

American Institute of Certified Public Accountants. *Restructuring Professional Standards to Achieve Professional Excellence in a Changing Environment.* New York: AICPA, 1986.

American Institute of Certified Public Accountants. *Education Requirements for Entry in the Accounting Profession.* New York: AICPA, 1988.

Anderson, J. "Analyzing the Readability of English and Non-English Texts in the Classroom with Lix." Paper presented at the Seventh Australian Reading Association Conference, Darwin, August 1981, 1–12.

Andrews, J. D., and R. J. Koester. "Communication Difficulties as Perceived by the Accounting Profession and Professors of Accounting." *Journal of Business Communication* (Winter 1979): 33–42.

Anthony, R. N., and J. S. Reece. *Management Accounting: Text and Cases.* Homewood, IL: Irwin, 1975.

Avard, S. L., and J. H. White. "Readability Study of Principles of Financial Management Text Books." *Journal of Financial Education* (Fall 1986): 53–63.

Baker III, H. E., and D. D. Kare. "Relationship Between Annual Report Readability and Corporate Financial Performance." *Management Research News* 4 (1992): 1–4.

Barnett, A., and K. Leoffler. "Readability of Accounting and Auditing Messages." *Journal of Business Communication* 3 (1979): 49–59.

Bean, V. L., and J. E. Watanabe. "Techniques for Improvement of Communication Skills: Accounting Students and Graduates Rate Effectiveness." *Accounting Educators' Journal* (Summer 1990): 36–45.

Bedford, N., and V. Baladouni. "A Communication Theory Approach to Accounting." *Accounting Review* (1962): 650–659.

Belkaoui, A. "Linguistic Relativity in Accounting." *Accounting, Organizations and Society* 2 (1978): 97–104.

Bettman, J. R., and B. A. Weitz. "Attributions in the Board Room: Causal Reasoning in Corporate Annual Reports." *Administrative Science Quarterly* (June 1983): 165–183.

Borthick, A. F., and R. L. Clark. "Improving Accounting Majors' Writing Quality: The Role of Language Analysis in Attention Directing." *Issues in Accounting Education* (Spring 1987): 13–27.

Bowman, E. G., and M. Haire. "Social Impact Disclosure and Corporate Annual Reports." *Accounting, Organizations and Society* 1 (1976): 11–21.

Brandel, F. *The Wheels of Commerce (Civilization and Capitalism, 15th-18th Century.* New York: Harper and Row, 1979.

Brief, R. P. *Selections from Encyclopedia of Accounting 1903*. New York: Arno Press, 1978.

Briloff, A. *The Effectiveness of Accounting Communication*. New York: Frederick A. Praeger, 1967.

Buckmaster, D., and D. Hall. "Lobbying with the FASB: The Case of Accounting for Pension Terminations and Curtailments." *Journal of Applied Business Research* (Spring 1990): 23–31.

Burns, J. O., and S. M. Groomer. "An Analysis of Tax Court Decisions that Assess the Profit Motive of Farming-Oriented Operations." *Journal of the American Taxation Association* 5 Fall 1983): 23–29.

Chan, J. L. "Corporate Disclosure in Occupational Safety and Health: Some Empirical Evidence." *Accounting, Organizations and Society* 4 (1979): 273–281.

Collins, W., E. S. Davie, and P. Weetman. "Management Discussion and Analysis: An Evaluation of Practice in UK and US Companies." *Accounting and Business Research* (Spring 1993): 123–127.

Committe, B. E. "Structuring a Public Accounting Audit Independence Theory from a Document Study of U.S. Congressional Testimony." Ph.D. diss., University of Alabama, 1983.

Committee to Prepare a Statement of Basic Accounting Theory. *A Statement of Basic Accounting Theory*. Evanston, IL: American Accounting Association, 1966.

Cooper, W. W., and Y. Ijiri. *Kohler's Dictionary for Accountants*. Englewood Cliffs, NJ: Prentice-Hall, 1982.

Courtis, J. K. "An Investigation into Annual Report Readability and Corporate Risk-Return Relationships." *Accounting and Business Research* (Fall 1986): 285–294.

Courtis, J. K. "Fry, Smug, Lix and Risk: Insinuations About Corporate Communication." *Journal of Business Communication* (Spring 1987): 19–27.

Cowan, T. K. "Are Truth and Fairness Generally Acceptable?" *Accounting Review* (October 1965): 788–794.

Cunningham, B. M. "Classroom Research and Experiential Learning: Three Successful Experiences—The Impact of Student Writing in Learning Accounting." *Community/Junior College Quarterly of Research and Practice* (July-September 1991): 317–325.

Degnan, T. "A Computer Coded Content Analysis Study of Tax Cases Involving Valuations of Large Holdings of Publicly Traded Stocks." Ph.D. diss., University of South Carolina, 1983.

Deitrick, J. W., and R. H. Tabor. "Improving the Writing Skills of Accounting Majors: One School's Approach." *Advances in Accounting* (1987): 97–110.

Deppe, L. A., E. O. Sondereger, J. D. Stice, D. C. Clark, and G. F. Streuling. "Emerging Competencies for the Practice of Accountancy." *Journal of Accounting Education* (Fall 1991): 257–290.

Dillard, J. F., and D. L. Jensen. "The Auditor's Report: An Analysis of Opinion." *The Accounting Review* 58 (October 1983): 787–798.

Dolphin, R., and R. .A. Wagley. "Reading the Annual Report." *Financial Executive* (June 1977): 2–22.

Dorrell, J. T., and N. S. Darsey. "An Analysis of the Readability and Style of Letters to Stockholders." *Journal of Technical Writing and Communication* 21 (1991): 73–83.

Dupree, J. M. "Users' Preferences for Descriptive Versus Technical Accounting Terms." *Accounting and Business Research* (Fall 1985): 281–290.

Estes, R. "The Profession's Changing Horizons: A Survey of Practitioners on the Present and Future Importance of Selected Knowledge and Skills." *International Journal of Accounting Education and Research* (Spring 1979): 47–70.

Financial Accounting Standards Board. *Statement of Financial Accounting Concepts No. 1: Objectives of Financial Reporting by Business Enterprises.* Stanford, CT: FASB, 1986.

Fisher, F. A., and M. Y. Yu. "Does the CEO's Letter to the Shareholders Have Predictive Value?" *Business Forum* 1 (1989): 22–24.

Flamholtz, E., and E. Cook. "Connotative Meaning and Its Role in Accounting Change: A Field Study." *Accounting, Organizations and Society* 8 (1978): 125–139.

Flesch, R. "A New Readability Yardstick." *Journal of Applied Psychology* (June 1948): 221–233.

Flesch, R. F. *The Art of Plain Talk.* New York: Harper and Brothers, 1946.

Flory, S. M., T. J. Phillips, Jr., and M. F. Tassin. "Measuring Readability: A Comparison of Accounting Textbooks." *Journal of Accounting Education* 10 (1992): 51–62.

Forrester, D. A. R., and C. M. Grant. "New Vocabularies Reviewed in the Light of No Syntax of Accounting—A Review Article." *British Accounting Review* (Autumn 1966): 90–98.

Frazier, K. B., R. W. Ingram, and B. M. Tennyson. "A Methodology for the Analysis of Narrative Accounting Disclosures." *Journal of Accounting Research* (Spring 1984): 318–331.

French, D. *Dictionary of Accounting Terms.* London: Financial Training, 1985.

Garrison, L. R., and R. H. Michaelsen. "Symbolic Concept Acquisition: A New Approach to Determining Underlying Tax Law Constructs." *Journal of the American Taxation Association* 11 (Fall 1989): 77–91.

Geiger, M. A. "The New Audit Report: An Analysis of Exposure Draft Comments." *Auditing: A Journal of Practice and Theory* (Spring 1989): 40–63.

Gibson, C. H., and N. W. Schroeder. "U.K. Firms on the NYSE: An Analysis of Readability Traits." *Journal of International Accounting Auditing and Taxation* 3 (1994): 27–40.

Gingras, R. T. "Writing and the Certified Public Accountant." *Journal of Accounting Education* (Spring 1987): 127–137.

Gunning, R. *The Technique of Clear Writing*. New York: McGraw-Hill, 1952.

Gunning, R. *The Technique of Clear Writing*, 2d. ed. New York: McGraw-Hill, 1968.

Guthrie, J., and L. D. Parker. "Corporate Social Reporting: A Rebuttal of Legitimacy Theory." *Accounting and Business Research* 19 (1989): 343–352.

Haried, A. "Measurement of Meaning in Financial Reports." *Journal of Accounting Research* (Spring 1993): 117–145.

Haried, H. H. "The Semantic Dimensions of Financial Statements." *Journal of Accounting Research* (Autumn 1972): 379–391.

Harrison, C. *Readability in the Classroom*. Cambridge: Cambridge University Press, 1980.

Hawes, L. C. *Pragmatics of Analoguing*. Reading, MA: Addison-Wesley, 1975.

Healy, P. "Can You Understand the Footnotes to Financial Statements?" *Accountants' Journal* (July 1977): 219–222.

Heath, R. L., and G. Phelps. "Annual Reports II: Readability of Reports vs. Business Press." *Public Relations Review* (Summer 1984): 56–62.

Henry, L. B., and N. Y. Razzouk. "The CPA's Perception of Accounting Education: Implications for Curriculum Development." *Accounting Educators' Journal* (Spring 1988): 105–117.

Hiemstra, K. M., J. J. Schmidt, and R. L. Madison. "Certified Management Accountants: Perceptions of the Need for Communication Skills in Accounting." *Bulletin of the Association for Business Communication* (December 1990): 5–9.

Hoff, K. T., and D. E. Stout. "Practical Accounting/English Collaboration to Improve Student Writing Skills: The Use of Informal Journals and the Diagnostic Reading Technique." *Accounting Educators' Journal* (Winter 1989–1990): 83–96.

Holley, C. L., and J. Early. "Are Financial Statements Easy to Read?" *Woman CPA* (August 1980): 9–13.

Hooks, K. L., and J. E. Moon. "A Classification Scheme to Examine Management Discussion and Analysis Compliance." *Accounting Horizons* 7 (June 1993): 41–59.

Horngren, C. T. *Accounting for Management Control*. Englewood Cliffs, NJ: Prentice-Hall, 1974.

Hoskins, R. "Annual Reports I: Difficult Reading and Getting More So." *Public Relations Review* (Summer 1984): 49–55.

Houghton, D., and R. G. Wallace. *Students' Accounting Vocabulary*. Farnborough: Gower, 1980.

Houghton, K.A. "The Development of Meaning in Accounting: An Intertemporal Study." *Accounting and Finance* (November 1987): 25–40.

Houghton, K. A. "True and Fair View: An Empirical Study of Connotative Meaning." *Accounting, Organizations and Society* 12, no. 2 (1987): 143–152.

Houghton, K. A. "The Measurement of Meaning in Accounting: A Critical Analysis of the Principal Evidence." *Accounting, Organizations and Society* 3 (1988): 263–280.

Hussey, R., and H. Everitt. *Summary and Simplified Financial Reporting*. London: Butterworths, 1991.

Ijiri, Y. *Theory of Accounting Measurement*. Sarasota, FL: American Accounting Association, 1975.

Ingram, R. W., and F. B. Frazier. *Developing Communications Skills for the Accounting Profession.* Sarasota, FL: American Accounting Association, 1980.

Ingram, R. W., and F. B. Frazier. "Environmental Performance and Corporate Disclosure." *Journal of Accounting Research* 18 (Autumn 1980): 614–622.

Ingram, R. W., and F. B. Frazier. "Narrative Disclosures in Annual Reports." *Journal of Business Research* (March 1983): 49–60.

Isler, H. P. "A Historical Note on the Use of Word-Frequency Contiguities in Content Analysis." *Computers and the Humanities* 8 (1974): 95–96.

Jain, T. N. "Alternative Networks of Accounting and Decision Making: A Psycholinguistic Analysis." *Accounting Review* (January 1973): 95–104.

Jones, M. J. "A Longitudinal Study of the Readability of the Chairman's Narrative in the Corporate Reports of a UK Company." *Accounting and Business Research* 18 (1988): 297–305.

Jones, M. J., and P. A. Shoemaker. "Accounting Narratives: A Review of Empirical Studies of Content and Readability." *Journal of Accounting Literature* 13 (1994): 142–184.

Karlinsky, S. S. "Complexity in the Federal Income Tax Law Attributable to the Capital Gain and Loss Preference: A Measurement Model." Ph.D. diss., New York University, 1981.

Karlinsky, S. S. "Readability Is in the Mind of the Reader." *Journal of Business Communication* 20 (1983): 57–69.

Karlinsky, S. S., and B. S. Koch. "Impact of Tax Law Complexity on Professionals." *Journal of the American Taxation Association* 9 (Fall 1987): 24–34.

Kelly-Newton, L. *Accounting Policy Formulation.* Reading, MA: Addison-Wesley, 1980.

Kelly-Newton, L. "A Sociological Investigation of the U.S.A. Mandate for Replacement Cost Disclosures." *Accounting, Organizations and Society* 5 (1980): 311–321.

Kincaid, J. P., R. P. Fishbourne, R. L. Rogers, and B. S. Chisson. *Derivation of New Readability Formulas (Automated Readability Index Fog Count and Flesch Reading Ease Formula for Navy Enlisted Personnel)* (CNTT Research Branch Report 8–75). Memphis, TN: Chief of Naval Technical Training, Naval Air Station, 1975.

Kramer, S. "Blockage: Valuation of Large Blocks of Publicly Traded Stocks for Tax Purposes." *Accounting Review* 57 (January 1982): 70–87.

Kwolek, W. F. "Readability Survey of Technical and Popular Literature." *Journalism Quarterly* (Summer 1973): 255–264.

Larcker, D. F., and V. P. Vessig. "Perceived Usefulness of Information: A Psychometric Examination." *Decision Sciences* (January 1980): 121–134.

Laudie, D. "The Accounting of Interpretations and the Interpretation of Accounts: The Communicative Function of 'The Language of Business,' " *Accounting, Organizations and Society* (June 1987): 579–604.

Lawrence, S. "How Accountants Do It: The Social Creation of Objective Reality." *Asian Review of Accounting* (December 1992): 1–15.

Lee, T. A., and D. P. Tweedie. "Accounting Information: An Investigation of Private Shareholder Usage." *Accounting and Business Research* (Autumn 1975): 280–291.

Lewis, N. R., L. D. Parker, G. D. Pound, and P. Sutcliffe. "Accounting Report

   Readability: The Use of Readability Techniques." *Accounting and Business
   Research* (Summer 1986): 199–213.

Lewis, N. R., L. D. Parker, and P. Sutcliffe. "Financial Reporting to Employees:
   The Pattern of Development 1919 to 1979." *Accounting, Organizations and
   Society* 9 (1984): 275–289.

Li, D. "The Semantic Aspect of Communication Theory and Accounting." *Journal
   of Accounting Research* (1963): 102–107.

Libby, R. "Bankers' and Auditors' Perceptions of the Message Communicated by
   the Audit Report." *Journal of Accounting Research* (1979): 99–122.

MacArthur, J. B. "An Analysis of the Content of Corporate Submissions on Proposed Accounting Standards in the UK." *Accounting and Business Research*
   (Summer 1988): 213–266.

Madeo, S. A. "An Empirical Analysis of Tax Court Decision in Accumulated
   Earnings Cases." *Accounting Review* 54 (July 1979): 538–553.

Martindale, B. C., B. S. Koch, and S. S. Karlinsky. "Tax Law Complexity: The
   Impact of Style." *Journal of Business Communication* 29 (1992): 383–400.

May, G. S., and C. B. May. "Communication Instruction: What Is Being Done to
   Develop the Communication Skills of Accounting Students?" *Journal of
   Accounting Education* (Fall 1989): 233–244.

McConnell, D., J. A. Haslem, and V. R. Gibson. "The President's Letter to Stockholders: A New Look." *Financial Analysts Journal* 5 (1986): 67–70.

McDonald, D. *Comparative Accounting Theory.* Reading, MA: Addison-Wesley,
   1972.

McEnroe, J. E. "An Analysis of Comment Integration Involving SAS 54." ABA-
   CUS (September 1993): 160–175.

McKee, A. J., P. F. Williams, and K. B. Frazier. "A Case Study of Accounting Firm
   Lobbying: Advice or Consent." *Critical Perspectives on Accounting* 2 (September 1991): 273–294.

Means, T. L. "Readability: An Evaluative Criterion of Stockholder Reactions to
   Annual Reports." *Journal of Business Communication* 24 (1981): 19–27.

Mills, P. A. "Words and the Study of Accounting History." *Accounting, Auditing
   and Accountability Journal* (January 1990): 21–35.

Mohrweis, L. C. "The Impact of Writing Assignments on Accounting Students'
   Writing Skills." *Journal of Accounting Education* (Fall 1991): 309–325.

Monti-Belkaoui, J., and A. Belkaoui. "Bilingualism and the Perception of Professional Concepts." *Journal of Psycholinguistic Research* 12 (1983): 111–127.

Most, K. *Accounting Theory.* Columbus, OH: Grid, 1989.

National Commission on Fraudulent Financial Reporting. *Report of the National
   Commission on Fraudulent Financial Reporting.* Washington, DC: National
   Commission on Fraudulent Financial Reporting, 1987.

Neimark, M. "How to Use Content Analysis in Historical Research." *Accounting
   Historians Notebook* (Fall 1983): 19–23.

Neimark, M., and T. Tinker. "The Social Construction of Management Control
   Systems." *Accounting, Organizations and Society* 11 (1986): 369–395.

Novin, A. M., and M. A. Pearson. "Non-Accounting-Knowledge Qualifications
   for Entry-Level Public Accountants." *Ohio CPA Journal* (Winter 1989): 12–
   17.

Oliver, B. L. "The Semantic Differential: A Device for Measuring the Interprofessional Communication of Selected Accounting Concepts." *Journal of Accounting Research* (Autumn 1974): 299–316.

Osgood, C. E., G. J. Suci, and P. H. Tannenbaum. *The Measurement of Meaning.* Champaign: University of Illinois Press, 1957.

Parker, L. D. "Corporate Annual Reporting: A Mass Communication Perspective." *Accounting and Business Research* (Autumn 1982): 279–286.

Parker, R. H. *Macmillan Dictionary of Accounting.* New York: Macmillan, 1984.

Pashalian, S., and W. J. E. Crissy. "Corporate Annual Reports Are Difficult, Dull Reading, Human Interest Value Low, Survey Shows." *Journal of Accounting* (August 1952): 215–219.

Pashalian, S., and W. J. E. Crissy. "How Readable Are Corporate Annual Reports?" *Journal of Applied Psychology* (August 1980): 244–248.

Perspective on Education: Capabilities for Success in the Accounting Profession. New York: Arthur Andersen & Co.; Arthur Young, Coopers and Lybrand, Deloitte Haskings & Sells, Ernst and Whinney, Peat Marwick Main & Co., Price Waterhouse, and Touche Ross, 1989.

Pound, G. D. "Employee Reports: Readability." *Australian Accountant* (December 1980): 775–779.

Pound, G. D. "A Note on Audit Report Readability." *Accounting and Finance* (May 1981): 45–55.

Puro, M. "Audit Firm Lobbying Before the Financial Accounting Standards Board: An Empirical Study." *Journal of Accounting Research* 22 (Autumn 1984): 624–646.

Razek, J. R., G. A. Hosch, and D. Pearl. "Readability of Accounting Textbooks." *Journal of Business Education* (October 1982): 23–26.

Rebele, J. E. "An Examination of Accounting Students' Perceptions of the Importance of Communication Skills in Public Accounting." *Issues in Accounting Education* (1985): 41–50.

Robb, A. J., with R. W. Wallis. *Accounting Terms Dictionary.* London: Pitman, 1985.

Robinson, J. "Tax Court Classification of Activities Not Engaged in for Profit: Some Empirical Evidence." *Journal of the American Taxation Association* 5 (Fall 1983): 7–22.

Salancik, G. R., and J. R. Meindl. "Corporate Attributions as Strategic Illusions of Management Control." *Administrative Science Quarterly* (June 1984): 238–254.

Schroeder, N. "Are Summary Annual Reports Successful?" *Accounting Horizons* 6 (June 1992): 28–37.

Schroeder, N., R. Aggarwal, and C. Gibson. "Financial Reporting by Japanese Firms on the NYSE: An Analysis of Linguistic Content." *Management International Review* 31, no. 3 (1991): 233–251.

Schroeder, N., and C. Gibson. "Readability of Management's Discussion and Analysis." *Accounting Horizons* (December 1990): 78–87.

Schroeder, N. W., and C. H. Gibson. "A Readability Comparison of Financial Statement Footnotes of International Banks." *Advances in International Accounting* 7 (1994): 121–134.

Scofield, B. W. "Double Entry Journals: Writer-Based Prose in the Intermediate Accounting Curriculum." *Issues in Accounting Education* (Fall 1994): 330–332.

Scott, D. L., and G. Fiebelkorn. *Dictionary of Accounting.* New York: Rowman & Allanheld, 1985.

Shim, J. K., and J. G. Siegel. *Encyclopedic Dictionary of Accounting and Finance.* Englewood Cliffs, NJ: Prentice-Hall, 1989.

Smith, J. E., and N. P. Smith. "Readability: A Measure of the Performance of the Communication Function of Financial Reporting." *Accounting Review* (July 1971): 352–361.

Smith, M. "Readability and Understandability: Different Measures of the Textual Complexity of Accounting Narrative." *Accounting, Auditing and Accountability Journal* 5 (1992): 84–98.

Smith, M., and R. Taffler. "Improving the Communication Function of Published Accounting Statements." *Accounting and Business Research* (Spring 1984): 139–146.

Smith, M., and R. Taffler. "The Chairman's Statement and Corporate Financial Performance." *Accounting and Finance* 1 (1992): 75–90.

Soper, F. J., and R. Dolphin, Jr. "Readability and Corporate Annual Reports." *Accounting Review* (April 1964): 358–362.

Staw, B. M., P. I. McKechnie, and S. M. Puffer. "The Justification of Organizational Performance." *Administrative Science Quarterly* (December 1983): 582–600.

Stevens, W. P., K. L. Stevens, and W. A. Raabe. "FASB Statement in the Classroom: A Study of Readability." *Advances in Accounting* 2 (1985): 32–48.

Still, M. D. "The Readability of Chairman's Statement." *Accounting and Business Research* (Winter 1972): 36–39.

Stout, D. E., A. R. Smutka, and D. E. Wygal. "Experiential Evidence on the Use of Writing Assignments in Upper-Level Accounting Courses." *Advances in Accounting* (1991): 125–141.

Stout, D. E., D. E. Wygal, and K. T. Hoff. "Writing Across the Disciplines: Applications to the Accounting Classroom." *Bulletin of the Association for Business Communication* (December 1990): 10–16.

Subramanian, R., R. G. Insley, and R. D. Blackwell. "Performance and Readability: A Comparison of Annual Reports of Profitable and Unprofitable Operations." *Journal of Business Communication* 30 (1993): 49–61.

Swanson, E. B. "Management Information Systems: Appreciation and Involvement." *Management Science* 2 (1974): 178–188.

Taylor, R. L., and R. W. Ingram. "WORDS: A New Approach to Determining the Factors Affecting Tax Court Decisions Involving Real Estate Transactions." *The Journal of American Taxation Association* 30 (1984): 49–61.

Taylor, W. "Cloze Procedure: A New Tool for Measuring Readability." *Journalism Quarterly* (Fall 1953): 415–433.

Tennyson, B. M., R. W. Ingram, and M. T. Dugan. "Assessing the Information Content of Narrative Disclosures in Explaining Bankruptcy." *Journal of Business Finance and Accounting* (Summer 1990): 391–410.

Urbancic, F. R. "An Analysis of Tax Instruction Readability for Individuals in the North Eastern States." *Journal of Business and Economic Studies* 2 (1993): 59–63.

Wagley, R. A., and R. Dolphin, Jr. "Reading the Annual Report." *Financial Executive* (June 1977): 20–22.

Wallace, W. "Internal Control Reporting Practices in the Municipal Sector." *Accounting Review* (July 1981): 666–689.

Wallace. W. "Peer Review Filings and Their Implications in Evaluating Self-Regulation." *Auditing: A Journal of Practice and Theory* (Spring 1991): 53–68.

Wasson, D. *English/Spanish Glossary of Basic Accounting Terms*. Homewood, IL: Irwin, 1994.

Whittington, R., and G. Whittenburg. "Judicial Classification of Debt Versus Equity—An Empirical Study." *Accounting Review* 55 (July 1980): 409–418.

Worthington, J. S. "Making Financial Statement Footnotes More Readable." *CA Magazine* (September 1977): 34–37.

Worthington, J. S. "Footnotes: Readability or Liability." *CPA Journal* (1978): 27–32.

Worthington, J. S. "More Understanding with Simpler Footnotes." *CA Magazine* (July 1979): 44–47.

Wygal, D. E., and D. E. Stout. "Incorporating Writing Techniques in the Accounting Classroom: Experience in Financial, Managerial and Cost Courses." *Journal of Accounting Education* (Fall 1989): 245–252.

Zaltman, G., C. R. A. Dison, and R. Angelman. *Metatheory and Consumer Research*. New York: Holt, Rinehart & Winston, 1973.

Zmud, R. W. "An Empirical Investigation of the Dimensionality of the Concept of Information." *Decision Sciences* 2 (1978): 187–195.

2

LINGUISTIC RELATIVITY IN ACCOUNTING

INTRODUCTION

Accounting is the language of business. It represents phenomena in the business world as language represents phenomena in the real world. Both linguistics and accounting have a great number of similarities. Jain, for example, considered accounting rules as analogous to financial grammar and, based on this analogy, used the effect of grammatical structure on the perceptions of listeners to support the hypothesis that accounting methods affect decision making.[1] However, as a language, accounting includes both lexical and grammatical characteristics. They both play a role in our conception of the world, or Weltanschauung. More explicitly, they shape the perception and thoughts of those who have assimilated the accounting discipline. Accounting as a language predisposes "users" to a given method of perception and behavior. This thesis is derived from the linguistic relativity school in the study of language, which emphasizes the role of language as a mediator and shaper of the environment. This thesis is better known as the *Sapir-Whorf hypothesis*. This chapter will conceptually evaluate this thesis in an accounting context. The focus is on accounting as a language and consequently on accounting as a mediator of the cognitive perceptual process. First, a survey of the developments in the study of language are presented, with particular emphasis on the Sapir-Whorf hypothesis, also referred to as the linguistic relativity and determinism hypothesis. This is followed by an analysis of accounting as a language. Finally, an attempt is made to systematize the Sapir-Whorf hypothesis in accounting, that is, the hypothesis that the lexical and grammatical characteristics of accounting shape users' perceptions.

A STUDY OF LANGUAGE—A DIFFERENTIATED FIELD

The study of language has focused primarily on four areas: structural linguistics, developmental psycholinguistics, linguistic relativity, and sociolinguistics.

Structural linguistics deals with the process of acquisition of language and the identification of formal structural properties. In developmental psycholinguistics, efforts are directed toward formulating language acquisition and use as a special instance of a more general cognitive functioning.[2, 3, 4] Researchers attempt to acquire a better understanding of the human thinking process by an examination of grammatical organization and transformation. The third area, dealing with linguistic relativity, focuses on the role that language plays in our conception of the world. In brief, our worldview, or Weltanschauung, as speakers of one language is said to be different from that of speakers of another language. Finally, the fourth area, sociolinguistics, or the sociology of language, deals with the existence of different linguistic codes in a single language associated with different social strata and corresponding to different social behaviors. Sociolinguistics examines the interaction between two aspects of human behavior: the use of language and the social organization of behavior. One part of its domain is concerned with describing the generally accepted social organization of language usage with speech communities. This area is known as the descriptive sociology of language; it attempts to discover who speaks or writes what linguistic code, to whom, when, and why. Another area of the sociology of language is concerned with discovering the determinants of the changes in the social organization of language use and behavior. It is known as the dynamic sociology of language.

This chapter focuses on linguistic relativity within accounting. Accordingly, the "linguistic relativity hypothesis" is examined to support the hypothesis that accounting shapes users' perceptions.

LINGUISTIC RELATIVITY HYPOTHESIS

The linguistic relativity hypothesis simply implies that diverse languages influence the thoughts of their speakers. Formulations of this thesis can be traced to eighteenth-century Germany. The thesis relates linguistic diversity to thought and therefore to human behavior if we subscribe to the view that thought is the immediate cause of or guide for overt behavior.[5] The thesis has been expressed in one of two ways: (1) the thesis that the specific structure of a language *determines* thought, binding any self-conscious speaker to his language, and (2) the thesis that variable structures of specific languages *influence* thought, stipulating a link between certain cognitive correlates and particular languages. There is a general agreement that the second thesis is more tenable than the first one.

The development of the linguistic relativity hypothesis has gone through several research phases.

Boas's and Sapir's Contributions

Franz Boas and Edward Sapir were among the first anthropologists to be associated with the linguistic relativity hypothesis in the United States.

Boas argued that languages classify experience differently. A given experience would be expressed and classified differently by each language. He gave this famous example:

Another example of the same kind, the words for snow in Eskimo, may be given. Here we find one word, *aqut*, expressing SNOW ON THE GROUND; another one, *qana*, FALLING SNOW; a third one, *pipsirqoq*, DRIFTING SNOW; and a fourth one, *qimuqsuq*, A SNOWDRIFT.[6]

Boas viewed the resulting thoughts as being influenced by these linguistic classifications or categories. His view of the linguistic relativity hypothesis was first formulated as follows:

It is another question in how far the categories of grammar and the general classification of experience may control thought. . . . [T]he obligatory categories of language differ fundamentally. . . . It is obvious that the mental picture aroused by a spoken sentence will be fundamentally different according to the categories. . . . The form of our grammar compels us to select a few traits of thought we wish to express and suppresses many other aspects which the speaker has in mind and which the hearer supplies according to his fancy. . . . There is little doubt that thought is thus directed in various channels. . . . Such a tendency pervading the language may well lead to a different reaction to the incidents of everyday life and it is conceivable that in this sense the mental activities of a people may be in/out directed by language.[7]

Sapir was a student of Boas. He agreed with the classification of experience in language with an emphasis on the social function of these shared formal classifications. Rather than linguistic classifications reflecting thought, as argued by Boas, Sapir argued that the classifications channel thought and are a more powerful factor in the shaping of thought.

Language is . . . a self-contained creative symbolic organization, which not only refers to experience largely acquired without its help but actually defines experiences for us by reason of its formal completeness and because of our unconscious projection of its implicit expectations into the field of experience. . . .

[Language] categories . . . are, of course, derivative of experience of last analysis, but, once abstracted from experience, they are systematically elaborated in language and are not so much discovered in experience as imposed upon it because of the tyrannical hold that linguistic form has upon our orientation in the world.[8]

His best statement of the linguistic relativity hypothesis goes as follows:

Language is a guide to "social reality." . . . It purposefully conditions all our thinking about social problems and processes. Human beings do not live in the objective world alone, nor alone in the world of social activity as ordinarily understood, but are very much at the mercy of the particular language which has become the medium of expression for their society. It is quite an illusion to imagine that one adjusts to reality essentially without the use of language and that language is merely an incidental means of solving specific problems of communication or reflection. The fact of the matter is that the "real world" is to a large extent unconsciously built upon the language habits of the group. No two languages are ever sufficiently similar to be considered as representing the same social reality. The worlds in which different societies live are distinct worlds, not merely the same world with different labels attached.[9]

It is a suggestion that language conditions our thinking. "The flow of language parallels that of the inner content of consciousness."[10]

Whorf's Contribution

Benjamin Lee Whorf was first self-taught in linguistics, then interacted with Sapir and his students. He agreed with the view of language as classifactory, isolating and organizing elements of experience, and put a special emphasis on the productive formal completeness of the linguistic system of classification.[11] He viewed language as a "connection of ideas,"[12] a "segmentation of nature,"[13] "organization, classification, or arrangement of experience,"[14] a "geometry of form principles characteristic of each language,"[15] and "metaphysics."[16] From these loose formulations emerged his direct formulation of the linguistic relativity principle:

The background linguistic system (in other words, the grammar) of each language is not merely a reproducing instrument for voicing ideas but rather is itself the shaper of ideas, the program and guide for the individual's mental activity, for his analysis of impressions, for his synthesis of his mental stock in task. . . . We dissect nature along lines laid down by our native language. The categories and types that we isolate from the world of phenomena we do not find there because they stare every observer in the fact; on the contrary, the world is presented in a kaleidoscopic flux of impressions which has to be organized by our minds—and this means largely by the linguistic systems in our mind. . . . We are thus introduced to a new principle of relativity, which holds that all observers are not led by the same physical evidence to the same picture of the universe, unless their linguistic backgrounds are similar, or can in some way be calibrated.[17]

Or:

Users of markedly different grammars are pointed by their grammars toward different types of observations and different evaluations of externally similar acts of observations, and hence are not equivalent as observers but must arrive at somewhat different views of the world. . . . The participants of a given world view are not aware of the idiomatic nature of the channels in which their talking and thinking run.[18]

Therefore, language has an influence in people's Weltanschauung of the universe, a form of conditioning of thought. Unfortunately, Whorf did not present a well-developed and -formulated theory of how language structure influences concepts. A reading of his writing allowed the deduction of at least ten distinct propositions.

1. Languages embody "integrated fashions of speaking" or *"background linguistic system,"* consisting of prescribed modes of expressing thought and experience.

2. A native speaker has a distinctive *"conceptual system"* for organizing experience; and

3. a distinctive "world view" concerning the universe and his relations to it.

4. The background linguistic system partially determines the associated conceptual system; and

5. partially determines the associated world view.

6. Reality consists of a "kaleidoscopic flux of impressions."

7. The "facts" said to be perceived are a function of the language in which they are expressed; and

8. the "nature of the universe" is a function of the language in which it is stated.

9. Grammar does not reflect reality, but varies arbitrarily with language.

10. Logic does not reflect reality, but varies arbitrarily with language.[19]

Anthropological Studies on Linguistic Relativity

Anthropological linguistics research began from Whorf's formulation of linguistic relativity to investigate the relation of a single language to an associated culture or cultural mode of thought. This research includes:

1. *Lee's examination of grammar as a direct reflection of a culture, and the worldview characteristic of a culture.*[20] Consider the following statement:

It has been said that a language will delineate and limit the logical concepts of the individual who speaks it. Conversely, a language is an organ for the expression of thought, of concepts and principles of classification. True enough, the thought of the individual must run along its grooves. They are heritage from individuals who laid them down in an unconscious effort to express their attitudes toward the world. Grammar contains in crystallized form the accumulated and accumulating experience, the Weltanschauung of a people.[21]

Lee examined the Wintu language to show a relation of language to thought, using both structural semantic analysis and analyses of myth.

2. *Mathiot's examination of grammar as a language, and vocabulary as culture.* She examined particularly the Papago language, both in terms of the relation between language and culture and the cognitive significance of the language. The cognitive significance analysis is explicated as follows:

In the cognitive analysis of a given aspect of language, the semantic distinctive features of that aspect are the basis for inferring its cognitive content as follows: the cognitive content of a given language is ascertained by relating the semantic distinctive features of that aspect to the concept assumed to correspond to the aspect of reality that is reflected in the aspect of language under investigation. This concept is called the *underlying concept*. The underlying concept relevant to a given aspect of a language is postulated on the basis of an examination of the range of meaning pertaining to that aspect as revealed by the naming of units of the universe of data.[22]

3. *Hoijer's examination of thematic parallels between language and culture.* He investigated the relationship between the Navaho language and culture. He explains:

The fashions of speaking peculiar to a people, like other aspects of their culture, are indicative of a view of life, a metaphysics of their culture, compounded of unquestioned, and mainly unstated, premises which define the nature of their universe and man's position within it. . . . It is this metaphysics, manifest to some degree in all the patterns of a culture, that channelizes the perceptions and thinking of those who participate in the culture and that predisposes them to certain modes of observation and interpretation. The metaphysics, as well, supplies the link between language as a cultural system and all other systems found in the same culture.[23]

Accordingly, he showed that the verbs in Navaho emphasize reporting motion and its nature, direction, and status, which were attributed to his parallels: "(1) the nomadic style of the Navaho, and (2) the motion of culture heroes in myths as they seek to perfect or repair the dynamic flux of the universe."[24]

Comparative Psycholinguistics on Linguistic Relativity

Studies on Lexical Properties. The studies in comparative psycholinguistics deal with the cognitive effects of lexical codability and aspects of grammar such as form, class, or logical relators. The studies of lexical codability dealt with the significance of color terms for cognition. They relied on the following methodology:

The basic procedure involves presenting speakers with samples of colors in two tasks. The first task involves naming or describing certain of the color samples. These responses are then used to construct a "linguistic" measure of each color, for example, a measure of how readily each color can be lexically encoded or described. In these studies, then, language is represented by lexical items functioning denotationally. The second task involves performing some other "nonlinguistic" activity with the same colors. Most often a perceptual recognition memory task has been used; typically this involves asking subjects to recognize from memory certain colors from within the large array of colors. Thought, then, is taken to involve a set of cognitive "processes" which can be examined by means of methodologically rigorous experiment assessment of individual nonlinguistic behavior. The cultural "context" of thought is not of concern.[25]

The two types of responses ("linguistic" or "nonlinguistic") are then analyzed to indicate the potential relationships between language and thought.

The studies in lexical codability in general and the research on color codability covered a first period (1953–1968) that supported language as determining thought and a second period (1969–1978) that supported language as reflecting thought. The first period research included a Brown and Lenneberg study on the concept of codability,[26] examining the relations within English between memory for those same colors; Lenneberg and Roberts's replication with Zuni speakers;[27] and extensions to relating codability to recognition memory using photographs of faces,[28] other pictures,[29] figures,[30] binary numbers,[31] and nonsense syllables.[32] Lexical encoding of colors in particular has been initiated by Lenneberg and his collaborators.[33, 34, 35]

Lenneberg's concern was with the effects of the structure of a given language on its speakers' cognitive processes, namely, thoughts, memory, perception, and learning ability. Unlike Wang, he was concerned by the "potential" rather than the "habitual" thought. The method of analysis suggested was the investigation within one language of the degree of codability of some referential domain, namely, the relation of color terminology to cognition. This "intra-cultural approach" was defined as follows:

Ethnolinguistic research based on cross-cultural comparison must endeavor to isolate data, both on codification and cognition, that are general enough to have comparable equivalents in at least two different languages and cultures; otherwise comparison would be meaningless. It is not infrequent, however, that a working hypothesis relates a certain cognitive datum to some phenomenon pertinent to codification which appears to be unique, lacking entirely a parallel in any other language. There is a simple way of studying this situation. I call it the intra-cultural approach because it reduces [the need for] cross-cultural comparison to a desirable but not indispensable expansion of investigations.[36]

This work is characterized by (1) the use of a new measure of codability communication accuracy, that called for the subjects to encode the colors using words they would use to name it to a friend so he/she could pick it out; and (2) the verification of the link between codability and recognition memory that is task and stimulus specific.

The second period of research (1969–1978) included the studies by Berlin and Kay[37] and Kay and McDaniel[38] on the basic color terms and focal colors; the study by Heider[39] on focality and recognition memory; the work of Lucy and Shweder[40] on focal color versus communication accuracy; and the work of Kay and Kempton[41] on category boundaries and perceptual judgment. The results in all these studies indicate that language is reflecting rather than determining thought by showing that language structure and cognitive structure (i.e., perceptual recognition memory) are not determinedly the underlying perceptual regularities— specifically by focal colors.[42]

Studies on Grammatical Properties. The studies focused on the cross-linguistic composition of grammatical differences and their impact on cognition. Four main types of studies may be identified.

First, there is the work of Brown[43, 44] showing that the meaning values of grammatical categories were psychologically real during language development.

Second, there are the works of Carroll and Casagrande[45] and Maclay[46] evaluating the functions of language classifications in behavior and showing correspondence between specific linguistic phenomena and specific nonlinguistic responses.

Third, there is the work of Bloom[47] on Chinese counterfactual reasoning, finding that English subjects outperformed Chinese subjects in their ability to correctly identify counterfactual statements in stories as counterfactual. He concluded:

The very fact that the English-speaking child from the outset hears thought expressed in an explicitly counterfactual way and by early adolescence is expected himself to become a master in both concrete and abstract contexts of explicit counterfactual speech, while his Chinese counterpart does not share this linguistic experience, must affect importantly the relative facility each develops for this mode of speech and thought—particularly so, moreover, for even though the rudiments of counterfactual thinking must predate language development, further development of a facility for counterfactual thought must take place within a language and hence the subject to whatever influence that language exerts.[48]

Finally, there is the work of Lucy[49] in grammatical categories and cognition, focusing on "whether differences in the grammatical treatment of nominal number (for example, pluralization) in Yucatec Maya and American English correspond with detectable differences in habitual thought as assessed through simple cognitive tasks involving attention, memory, and classification."[50] The Chicago student subjects showed more accurate memory for the numbers of implements in a scene, a finding used by Lucy to show an effect of a language form on nonlinguistic cognitive behavior.

SYSTEMATIZATION OF THE SAPIR-WHORF HYPOTHESIS

Linguistic Relativity Versus Alternative Explanations

To recapitulate, we have explained the study of the impact of language on cognition. Sapir referred to the linguistic symbolism of a given culture.[51] He perceived language as an instrument of thought and communication of thought. In other words, a given language predisposes its users to a distinct belief. All theses premises led to the formulation of the principle of linguistic relativity: that language is an active determinant of thought. Similarly, it is maintained that the ways of speaking are indicative of the metaphysics of a culture. Those metaphysics consist of unstated premises that shape the perception and thought of those who participate in that culture and predispose them to a given method of perception.

In its extreme position, the linguistic relativity hypothesis claims that cognitive organization is directly constrained by linguistic structure. Fishman explains:

Some languages recognize far more tenses than do others. Some languages recognize a gender of norms (and, therefore, also require markers of gender in the verb and adjective systems), whereas others do not. Some languages build into the verb system recognition of certainty or uncertainty of past, present, or future action. Other languages build into the very system a recognition of the size, shape and colors of norms referred to.[52]

This linguistic relativity hypothesis is usually contrasted with either a neutral tag view of language, a cultural relativity hypothesis, or a linguistic reflection hypothesis.

According to the neutral tag view, language provides a verbalized inventory of real items in the world. This inventory is always the same. Words are only referents that differ from one language to another. They are expressions of a common world of experiences shared by all people independently of language. In this school of thought, the Sapir-Whorf view maintains that the inventory is not given independently of language; it is determined by a given language. Consequently, the structure of a person's language is a kind of mode, fixing his cognitive function. Reality is not present in the same forms to all people. Human beings may be restricted because they only think what their language allows them to think.

According to the cultural relativity hypothesis, cultural patterns are the determinants of behavior. The Sapir-Whorf hypothesis differs from cultural relativity by prescribing the major role to linguistic patterns. These patterns affect to some degree the way of perceiving the world. Consequently, cultural experience is affected by linguistic categories. For example, Whorf holds that "[o]ur linguistically determined thought world not only collaborates with our cultural idols and ideas but engages even our unconscious personal relations in its patterns and gives them a certain character—characteristics."[53]

According to the linguistic reflection view, language primarily reflects rather than creates specific behavior and orientation. It originated to replace the rather strong claims of the linguistic relativity hypothesis as a restraint of sociocultural organizations. The differences between the linguistic relativity and the linguistic reflection view have been eloquently expressed:

One [the linguistic relativity hypothesis] posits that language structure and language usage are fundamental and "given" and that all behavior is influenced thereby. The other claims that social organization and behavior are prior and language merely reflects them.[54]

Both positions are important. Whether language is a mere reflection of the sociocultural structure or a constraint followed by particular behavior rests on the interpretation of the results of the empirical studies of the Sapir-Whorf hypothesis.

Formulations of Linguistic Relativity

Review of the empirical literature on linguistic relativity shows the following factors to be necessary for a real testing of the effect of natural language lexicon on thought.

(a) We must have at least two natural languages whose lexicons differ with respect to some domain of discourse—if languages are not different, there is no point in the investigation. (b) The domain must be one which can be measured by the investigator independently of the way it is encoded by the languages of concern (for example, color may be measured in independent physical units such as wavelength)—if that is not the case, (as, for example, in such domains as feelings or values), there is no objective way of describing how it is that the two languages differ. (c) The domain must not itself differ grossly between the cultures whose languages differ—if it does, then it may be differences in experience with the domain, and not language, which are affecting thought. (d) We must be able to obtain measures of specific aspects of cognition—such as perception, memory or classification—having to do with the domain which are independent of, rather than simply assumed from, the language. (e) We must have a cross-culturally meaningful measure of differences in the selected aspects of cognition—preferably we should be able to state the hypothesis in terms of an interaction between the linguistic and cognitive variables, rather than in terms of overall differences between speakers of the languages.[55]

In addition to these testing requirements, various attempts have been made to systematize the Sapir-Whorf hypothesis of linguistic relativism.
First, Brown suggested the following two Whorfian hypotheses:

1. Structural differences between language systems will, in general, be paralleled by non-linguistic cognitive differences, of an unspecified sort, in the native speakers of two languages.
2. The structure of anyone's native language strongly influences or fully determines the world-view he will acquire as he learns the language.[56]

Kay and Kempton suggested that these two hypotheses appear to have induced the following tacit postulation on Whorf's part: "III. The semantic systems of different languages vary without constraint."[57] Similarly, Schlesinger proposed that Whorf's thesis reflects a confluence of three standards of thought, which can be formulated in the form of the following three items:

Thesis 1. All thinking goes on in language.

Thesis 2. Language may distort thinking.

Thesis 3. Languages differ in the thoughts they afford to us.[58]

Exhibit 2.1
A Systematic Version of the Whorfian Hypothesis

	Data of user's behavior	
Data about language characteristics	Linguistic Data	Nonlinguistic Data
Lexical characteristics	1	2
Grammatical characteristics	3	4

Second, Fishman[59] has provided some order and systematization to the Sapir-Whorf hypothesis using a fourfold analytic scheme (see Exhibit 2.1). He distinguishes between the two levels of language—lexical and grammatical—and two types of behavior—linguistic and nonlinguistic. They may be described as follows:

The lexical level consists of all words composing a language. Languages differ in terms of the number of terms used to describe a phenomenon. The two words *financial leverage* in English are denoted by six words in French: *effet financier du coup de levier.*

The grammatical level of language refers primarily to the manner in which the structural units are organized. It is a syntactical arrangement procedure. *Double entry bookkeeping* is denoted in French as *compatibilite a partie double*, since noun and adjective are arranged differently in both languages.

Linguistic behavior refers to choices among *words*, whereas nonlinguistic behavior refers to choices among *objects*. This last distinction will become clearer with the explanation of each of the cells identified in Exhibit 2.1.

Cell 1 implies a relationship between the lexical properties of a language and the speaker's linguistic behavior. Phenomena are codified differently in each language. What requires a highly differentiated codification in one language is minimally codified in another language. So the linguistic behavior or choice of words for a particular phenomenon will be different from one language to another. For example, there are different terms for horses among speakers of Arabic and different terms for snow among speakers of Eskimo.

Cell 2 implies a relationship between lexical properties of a language and the nonlinguistic behavior of the users of a language. It assumes that speakers of a language that make certain lexical distinctions will be able to perform certain nonlinguistic tasks better and more rapidly than the speakers of languages that do not make these lexical distinctions. Brown and Lenneberg,[60] Lenneberg,[61] Lantz and Stefflre,[62] and others showed that the availability of labels for certain colors enabled the subjects to recognize them more readily than colors for which no labels were available. They also showed that the most highly codified colors in a given language are recognized and recalled more often by subjects. A highly codified color is described by a fewer number of words.

Cell 3 implies a relationship between the grammatical characteristics and linguistic behavior. The level of the hypothesis assumes that the speakers of one language that use specific grammatical rules are predisposed to a given worldview different from the speakers of other languages. Whorf bases his conclusions on an analysis of Hopi and comparing it with Standards Average European (SAE) language, which includes English. Hoijer[63] argued the same position by analyses of Navaho. The work of Ervin-Tripp[64] on bilingualism may also be used to support this level of the Sapir-Whorf hypothesis. He used bilingual Japanese women married to U.S. servicemen as subjects. When asked to converse in Japanese, the context of their conversation was more typical of women in Japan. Similarly, when asked to converse in English, the context was more typical of women in the United States.

Cell 4 implies a relationship between the grammatical characteristics and nonlinguistic behavior. Carroll and Casagrande[65] found some support for this level of the hypothesis. They attempted to evaluate whether the speakers of language that code for color, shape, and size in the same verb, as in the Navaho language, will classify objects differently from the speakers of language that only code for tense, person, and number in their verbs, as in English. They found that the Navaho-dominant Navahos made object choice as predicted by the grammatical verb more often than did the English-dominant Navahos.

From this discussion emerges the main paradigm of linguistic relativity: that cognitive organization may be directly influenced by linguistic structure. Accounting as a language is also a mediator of users' behavior.

APPLICATIONS OF LINGUISTIC RELATIVISM IN ACCOUNTING

Evidence in support of the Whorfian hypothesis exists at each of the levels identified by Fishman.[66] In order to assert that accounting as a language affects the user's cognitive behavior, a similar systematization is necessary as a guide for future accounting research on the subject. Similarly, the propositions derived from such a systematization may be used to justify conceptually some of the research findings on the impact of accounting information on decision making. Because the number of articles dealing with the impact of the informational content on decision

Exhibit 2.2
Propositions of Linguistic Relativism in Accounting

Data about accounting characteristics	Data of user's behavior	
	Linguistic behavior	Nonlinguistic behavior
Symbolic representations	1	2
Manipulation rules	3	4

making is quite large, only a few research findings will be used as an illustration of linguistic relativism in accounting.

To accomplish the systematization, a differentiation is made in terms of the different characteristics of accounting language and the different data of cognitive behavior. The characteristics of accounting language have already been defined as the symbolic representations and the manipulation rules. The data of cognitive behavior in accounting refer to the user's behavior, which could be either linguistic or nonlinguistic. For instance, a portfolio decision is an example of nonlinguistic behavior, whereas a similarity judgment between two stocks is linguistic behavior. This systematization leads to a four-fold analytical scheme, portrayed in Exhibit 2.2.

Cell 1 involves the relationship between the symbolic representations of accounting and the linguistic behavior of the user. For example, an accountant will find a business phenomenon easier to describe than a nonaccountant. It may be said that the codification structure in accounting is more differentiated than in ordinary English, leading to a different linguistic behavior of users. The first level of the Whorfian hypothesis in accounting may be expressed as:

The users that make certain lexical distinctions in accounting are enabled to talk and/or solve problems that cannot be easily solved by users that do not.

It may be used as conceptual justification for most studies evaluating the semantic meaning of accounting concepts or content.[67, 68, 69] For example, Oliver[70] used the semantic differential technique to measure the *semantic* meaning of eight selected important accounting concepts for seven selected professional groups involved in the production and use of accounting data. The results indicated the nonconformance of accounting educators' perceptions of the meaning of these concepts, when compared with the other six professional groups. In other words, following the first hypothesis, these results show that the accounting concepts had, first, an impact on the linguistic behavior of different professional users and, second, were understood differently by the different users.

Cell 2 involves the relationship between the symbolic representations of accounting and the nonlinguistic behavior of the user. It may be conjectured that phenomena or concepts that are highly codified in accounting will be recalled and responded to more often than those less highly codified concepts. This second level of the Whorfian hypothesis in accounting may be expressed as:

The users that make certain lexical distinctions in accounting are enabled to perform (nonlinguistic) tasks more rapidly or more completely than those users that do not.

This proposition may be used as a theoretical net for those studies evaluating the impact of accounting content (extent of codification) on the user's decision making.[71, 72] For example, Abdel-Khalik[73] reports on an empirical study concerning the stipulation that detailed financial information is more useful for lending decision-making. Although his results support imputing a higher utility for detailed data only under certain conditions, they are conceptually justifiable by the second Whorfian hypothesis in the sense that the extent of aggregation (or codification) of data implies a different utility and a different nonlinguistic behavior.

Cell 3 involves the relationship between the accounting manipulation rules and linguistic behavior. For example, the description of the financial position of a given firm will be different, depending on whether the firm had adopted LIFO (last in, first out) or FIFO (first in, first out). The third level of the Whorfian hypothesis in accounting may be expressed as:

The users that possess the accounting (grammatical) rules are predisposed to different managerial styles or emphases than those that do not.

Such a position could accommodate any findings on the differences of common stock perception and the preferences arising from the use of different alternative accounting techniques. More specifically, if subjects in a laboratory experiment were presented with different combinations of accounting information on different stocks and if an individual's stock perception may be assumed to be fully represented by his similarity judgments on all possible pairs of stocks, one could find axes in the multidimensional space of perceptual judgments. Green and Maheshwari[74] have adopted such a procedure and concluded that the axes or dimensions could be interpreted as the mean or variance of return advocated in the normative models of portfolio theory. They used two groups of subjects. Group A represented the "high international" group in that all subjects received a supplementary information sheet for each stock. Group B, representing the "low information" group, received only the industry classification of each company. The two groups' perceptual maps obtained by the use of the Torgeson and Young multidimensional scaling program were different. Following our second hypothesis, the results show that the accounting manipulation rules and results had an impact on the linguistic behavior of the subjects in Group A and Group B.

Finally, Cell 4 involves the relationship between the accounting manipulation rules and nonlinguistic behavior. For example, the adoption of LIFO or FIFO may affect the investment decision of a user. The fourth level of the Whorfian hypothesis in accounting may thus be expressed as:

The accounting techniques may tend to facilitate or render more difficult various (nonlinguistic) managerial behaviors on the part of the users.

Some behavioral accounting findings on the impact of alternative accounting methods on the user's decision making may be reconciled with this fourth accounting proposition of the Whorfian hypothesis.[75, 76, 77, 78] For example, Elias attempted to determine whether the investment decision would be made differently with the addition of information provided by a human resource accounting system. His participants came from several groups with different levels of sophistication in and orientations to accounting. They were asked to select one of the companies as the better investment on the basis of financial statements prepared in the conventional manner and financial statements including "human assets" treatment. One of the results of his study was that the company choice was associated with the experimental accounting treatment. Although exploratory, these results are in line with our fourth hypothesis and show the impact of accounting manipulation rules, that is, conventional versus human resource accounting on the nonlinguistic behavior of users—specifically, the selection of a portfolio.

SUMMARY AND CONCLUSIONS

Accounting is a *language*. According to the Sapir-Whorf hypothesis, its lexical characteristics and grammatical rules will affect the linguistic and nonlinguistic behavior of users. The resulting four propositions were introduced to conceptually integrate the research findings on the impact of accounting information on the user's behavior.

Accountants, managers, and the general public could make use of the knowledge that the lexical and grammatical rules of accounting affect choices among symbols and context in their application of accounting. That users' behavior is based on their relative understanding of certain lexical distinctions and grammatical rules in accounting may imply that a research attempt should be made in both practice and accounting academia to identify for each type of user the lexical and grammatical accounting distinctions most conducive to an efficient behavior. Accordingly, further research should be concerned with the testing of the four propositions presented in this chapter that apply the linguistic relativity paradigm to accounting as well as with the evaluation of the possible integration of accounting with the other areas of linguistics. An example of such a study is the Appendix to Chapter 2.

NOTES

1. T. N. Jain, "Alternative Methods of Accounting and Decision Making: A Psycholinguistic Analysis," *Accounting Review* (January 1973): 95–104.

2. N. Chomsky, *American Power and the New Mandarins* (New York: Pantheon Books, 1969).

3. N. Chomsky, *Aspects of the Theory of Syntax* (Cambridge, MA: MIT Press, 1965).

4. J. A. Fodor, "How to Learn to Talk: Some Simple Ways," in *The Genesis of Language: A Psycholinguistic Approach*, ed. F. Smith and G. Miller (Cambridge, MA: MIT Press, 1966).

5. J. A. Lucy, *Language, Diversity and Thought: A Reformulation of the Linguistic Relativity Hypothesis* (Cambridge: Cambridge University Press, 1992), 2.

6. F. Boas, ed., *Handbook of American Indian Languages* (Lincoln: University of Nebraska Press, 1966), 60.

7. F. Boas, "Language and Culture," in *Studies in the History of Culture: The Disciplines of the Humanities* (Menasha, WA: Banta, 1952) (published for the Conference of Secretaries of the American Council of Learned Societies), 181–183.

8. E. Sapir, "Conceptual Categories in Primitive Languages," in *Language in Culture and Society: A Reader in Linguistics and Anthropology*, ed. D. H. Hymes (New York: Harper and Row, 1964), 128.

9. E. Sapir, "The Status of Linguistics as a Science," in *The Selected Writings of Edward Sapir in Language, Culture, and Personality*, ed. D. G. Mandelbaum (Berkeley: University of California Press, 1949), 162.

10. E. Sapir, *Language: An Introduction to the Study of Speech* (New York: Harcourt Press, 1921), 14.

11. Lucy, *Language, Diversity and Thought: A Reformulation of the Linguistic Relativity Hypothesis*, 26.

12. B. L. Whorf, "On the Connection of Ideas," in *Language, Thought, and ·Reality: Selected Writings of Benjamin Lee Whorf*, ed. J. B. Carroll (Cambridge, MA: MIT Press, 1956), 35.

13. B. L. Whorf, "Languages and Logic," in *Language, Thought, and Reality*, 240.

14. B. L. Whorf, "The Punctual and Segmentative Aspects of Verbs in Hopi," in *Language, Thought, and Reality*, 55.

15. B. L. Whorf, "Language, Mind, and Reality," in *Language, Thought, and Reality*, 257.

16. B. L. Whorf, "An American Indian Model of the Universe," in *Language, Thought, and Reality*, 59.

17. B. L. Whorf, "Linguistics as an Exact Science," in *Language, Thought, and Reality*, 162.

18. Ibid., 221–222.

19. M. Black, "Linguistic Relativity: The Views of Benjamin Lee Whorf," *Philosophical Review* 68 (1959): 230.

20. D. Lee, "Conceptual Implications of an Indian Language," *Philosophy of Sciences* (1938): 89–102.

21. Ibid., 89.

22. M. Mathiot, "The Cognitive Significance of the Category of Nominal Numbers in Papago," in *Studies in Southwestern Ethnolinguistics*, ed. D. H. Hymes and W. Bittle (The Hague: Mouton, 1967), 201.

23. H. Hoijer, "The Relation of Language to Culture," in *Anthropology Today*, ed. A. L. Kroeber (Chicago: University of Chicago Press, 1953), 561.

24. Lucy, *Language, Diversity and Thought: A Reformulation of the Linguistic Relativity Hypothesis*, 79.

25. Ibid., 127–128.

26. R. W. Brown, and E. H. Lenneberg, "A Study in Language and Cognition," *Journal of Abnormal and Social Psychology* 49 (1954): 454–462.

27. E. H. Lenneberg, and J. M. Roberts, "The Language of Experience: A Study in Methodology," *International Journal of American Linguistics* 22 (1956).

28. N. H. Fryder, and J. P. Van der Ger, "Codability and Recognition: An Experiment with Facial Expressions," *Acta Psychologica* 18 (1961): 360–367.

29. D. Lantz, and V. Stefflre, "Language and Cognition Revisited," *Journal of Abnormal and Social Psychology* 69 (1964): 472–481.

30. R. Glanzer, and W. H. Clark, "Accuracy of Perceptual Recall: An Analysis of Organization," *Journal of Verbal Learning and Learning Behavior* 1 (1962): 225–242.

31. R. Glanzer, and W. H. Clark, "The Verbal Loop Hypothesis: Binary Numbers," *Journal of Verbal Learning and Learning Behavior* 3 (1963): 301–305.

32. Lantz and Stefflre, "Language and Cognition Revisited."

33. Brown and Lenneberg, "A Study in Language and Cognition."

34. Lenneberg and Roberts, "The Language of Experience: A Study in Methodology."

35. E. H. Lenneberg, "Cognitions in Ethnolinguistics," *Language* 29 (1953): 463–471.

36. Ibid., 468.

37. B. Berlin, and P. Kay, *Basic Color Terms: Their Universitality and Evolution* (Berkeley: University of California Press, 1969).

38. P. Kay, and C. K. McDaniel, "The Linguistic Significance of the Meanings of Basic Color Terms," *Language* 54 (1978): 610–646.

39. E. R. Heider, "Universals in Color Naming and Memory," *Journal of Experimental Psychology* 93 (1972): 10–20.

40. J. A. Lucy, and R. A. Shweder, "Whorf and His Critics: Linguistic and Nonlinguistic Influences on Color Memory," *American Anthropologist* 81 (1981): 581–615.

41. P. Kay, and W. Kempton, "What Is the Sapir-Whorf Hypothesis?" *American Anthropologist* 86 (1984): 65–79.

42. Lucy, *Language, Diversity and Thought: A Reformation of the Linguistic Relativity Hypothesis*, 184.

43. R. W. Brown, *Words and Things* (New York: Free Press, 1958).

44. R. W. Brown, "Linguistic Determinism and the Part of Speech," *Journal of Abnormal and Social Psychology* 55 (1958): 1–5.

45. J. B. Carroll, and J. B. Casagrande, "The Function of Language Classification on Behavior," in *Readings in Social Psychology*, 3d ed., ed. E. E. Maccoby, T. M. Newcomb, and E. L. Hartley (New York: Henry Holt, 1959), 18–31.

46. H. Maclay, "An Experimental Study of Language and Non-linguistic Behavior," *Southwestern Journal of Anthropology* 14 (1958): 220–229.

47. A. H. Bloom, *The Linguistic Shaping of Thought: A Study in the Impact of Language on Thinking in China and the West* (Hillsdale, NJ: Lawrence Erlbaum, 1981).

48. Ibid., 32–42.

49. J. A. Lucy, *Grammatical Categories and Cognition: A Case Study of the Linguistic Relativity Hypothesis* (Cambridge: Cambridge University Press, 1992).

50. Ibid., 3.

51. E. Sapir, "Culture," in *Language and Personality: Selected Essays*, ed. D. G. Mandelbaum (Berkeley: University of California Press, 1956).

52. J. A. Fishman, *The Sociology of Language* (Rowley, MA: Newbury House Publishers, 1972), 156.

53. B. L. Whorf, "The Relation of Habitual Thought and Behavior to Language," in *Language, Culture and Personality*, ed. L. Spier (Menasha: University of Wisconsin, 1941), 76.

54. Fishman, *The Sociology of Language*, 156.

55. E. Kosch, "Linguistic Relativity," in *Human Communication: Theoretical Explorations*, ed. A. Silverstein (Hillsdale, NJ: Lawrence Erlbaum, 1974), 107–108.

56. R. W. Brown, "Reference: The Memorial Tribute to Eric Lenneberg," *Cognition* 4 (1976): 130.

57. Kay and Kempton, "What Is the Sapir-Whorf Hypothesis?" 66.

58. I. M. Schlesinger, "The Wax and Ware of Whorfian Views," in *The Influence of Language on Culture and Thought* (Berlin: Mouton de Gruyter, 1991), 8.

59. J. A. Fishman, "A Systematization of the Whorfian Hypothesis," *Behavioral Science* 5 (1960): 323–339.

60. Brown and Lenneberg, "A Study in Language and Cognitions."

61. Lenneberg, "Cognitions in Ethnolinguistics."

62. Lantz and Stefflre, "Language and Cognition Revisited."

63. H. Hoijer, "Cultural Implications of the Navaho Linguistic Categories," *Language* (1951): 111–120.

64. S. Ervin-Tripp, "Sociolinguistic," *Advances in Experimental Social Psychology*, ed. L. Berkowitz (New York: Academic Press, 1969), 91–165.

65. Carroll and Casagrande, "The Function of Language Classification on Behavior."

66. Fishman, *The Sociology of Language*.

67. A. Belkaoui, and A. Cousineau, "Accounting Information, Nonaccounting

Information, and Common Stock Perception," *Journal of Business* (July 1977): 334–343.

68. A. A. Haried, "The Semantic Dimension of Financial Statements," *Journal of Accounting Research* (Autumn 1972): 376–391.

69. B. L. Oliver, "The Semantic Differential: A Device for Measuring the Interprofessional Communication of Selected Accounting Concepts," *Journal of Accounting Research* (Autumn 1974): 299–316.

70. Ibid.

71. E. J. Lusk, "Cognitive Aspects of Annual Reports: Field, Independence/Dependence," *Empirical Research in Accounting: Selected Studies* (1973): 191–202.

72. R. A. Abdel-Khalik, "The Effect of Aggregating Accounting Reports on the Quality of the Lending Decision: An Empirical Investigation," *Empirical Research in Accounting: Selected Studies* (1973): 104–138.

73. Ibid.

74. P. E. Green, and A. Maheshwari, "Common Stock Perception and Preference: An Application of Multidimensional Scaling," *Journal of Business* (October 1969): 439–457.

75. N. Elias, "The Effects of Human Asset Statements on the Investment Decision: An Experiment," *Empirical Research in Accounting: Selected Studies* (1972): 215–240.

76. T. R. Dyckman, "The Effects of Alternative Accounting Techniques on Certain Management Decisions," *Journal of Accounting Research* (Spring 1964): 91–107.

77. R. Jensen, "An Experimental Design for the Study of Effects of Accounting Variations in Decision Making," *Journal of Accounting Research* (Autumn 1966): 16–32.

78. J. Dickhaut, "Alternative Information Structures and Probability Revisions," *Accounting Review* (January 1973): 61–79.

REFERENCES

Abdel-Khalik, R. A. "The Effect of Aggregating Accounting Reports on the Quality of the Lending Decision: An Empirical Investigation." *Empirical Research in Accounting: Selected Studies* (1973): 104–138.

Alisjahbana, S. T. "The Relation of Language, Thought and Culture as Reflected in the Development of the Indonesian Language." *International Journal of the Sociology of Language* 62 (1986): 25–49.

Anthony, R. N., and J. S. Reece. *Management Accounting: Text and Cases.* New York: Irwin, 1975.

Au, T. K. "Chinese and English Counterfactuals: The Sapir-Whorf Hypothesis Revisited." *Cognition* 15 (1983): 155–187.

Belkaoui, A., and A. Cousineau. "Accounting Information, Nonaccounting Information, and Common Stock Perception." *Journal of Business* (July 1977): 334–343.

Berlin, B., and P. Kay. *Basic Color Terms: Their Universitality and Evolution.* Berkeley: University of California Press, 1969.

Bernstein, B. "Some Determinants of Perception: An Enquiry in Sub-Cultural Differences." *British Journal of Sociology* (1958): 159–174.

Bernstein, B. *Class, Codes, and Control*. Vol. 1, *Theoretical Studies Toward a Sociology of Language*. London: Routledge & Kegan Paul, 1971.

Berthoff, A. E. "Sapir and the Two Tasks of Language." *Semiotica* 71 (1988): 1–47.

Black, M. "Linguistic Relativity: The Views of Benjamin Lee Whorf." *Philosophical Review* 68 (1959): 228–238.

Bloom, A. H. *The Linguistic Shaping of Thought: A Study in the Impact of Language on Thinking in China and the West*. Hillsdale, NJ: Lawrence Erlbaum, 1981.

Boas, F. "Language and Culture." In *Studies in the History of Culture: The Disciplines of the Humanities*. Menasha, WA: Banta, 1952. Published for the Conference of Secretaries of the American Council of Learned Societies.

Boas, F. "The Methods of Ethnology." In *Race, Language, and Culture*, edited by F. Boas, 281–289. New York: Free Press, 1966.

Boas, F., ed. *Handbook of American Indian Languages*. Lincoln: University of Nebraska Press, 1976.

Bright, J. O., and W. Bright. "Semantic Structures in Northwestern California and the Sapir-Whorf Hypothesis." *American Anthropologist* 67 (1965): 249–258.

Brown, R. W. "Linguistic Determinism and the Part of Speech." *Journal of Abnormal and Social Psychology* 55 (1958): 1–5.

Brown, R. W. "How Shall a Thing Be Called?" *Psychological Review* 65 (1958): 14–21.

Brown, R. W. *Words and Things*. New York: Free Press, 1958.

Brown, R. W. *Social Psychology*. New York: Free Press, 1965.

Brown, R. W. "Reference: The Memorial Tribute to Eric Lenneberg." *Cognition* 4 (1976): 125–153.

Brown, R. W., and D. Fish. "The Psychological Causality Implicit in Language." *Cognition* 14 (1983): 237–273.

Brown, R. W., and E. H. Lenneberg. "A Study in Language and Cognition." *Journal of Abnormal and Social Psychology* 49 (1954): 454–462.

Carroll, J. B. "Introduction." In *Language, Thought and Reality: Selected Writings of Benjamin Lee Whorf*, edited by J. B. Carroll, 1–34. Cambridge, MA: MIT Press, 1956.

Carroll, J. B., and J. B. Casagrande. "The Function of Language Classification on Behavior." In *Readings in Social Psychology*, 3d ed., edited by E. E. Maccoby, T. M. Newcomb, and E. L. Hartley, 18–31. New York: Henry Holt, 1958.

Casson, R. W., ed. *Language, Culture, and Cognition: Anthropological Perspectives*. New York: Macmillan, 1981.

Chatterjee, R. "Reading Whorf Through Wittgenstein: A Solution to the Linguistic Relativity Problem." *Lingua* 67 (1985): 37–63.

Chomsky, N. *Aspects of the Theory of Syntax*. Cambridge, MA: MIT Press, 1965.

Chomsky, N. *American Power and the New Mandarins*. New York: Pantheon Books, 1969.

Davidson, S., J. S. Schindler, and R. L. Weil. *Accounting: The Language of Business*. New York: Thomas Horton and Daughters, 1974.

Dickhaut, J. "Alternative Information Structures and Probability Revisions." *Accounting Review* (January 1973): 61–79.

Dopuch, N., and J. Ronen. "The Effects of Alternative Inventory Valuation Methods—An Experimental Study." *Empirical Research in Accounting: Selected Studies* (1972): 215–240.

Dyckman, T. R. "The Effects of Alternative Accounting Techniques on Certain Management Decisions." *Journal of Accounting Research* (Spring 1964): 91–107.

Elias, N. "The Effects of Human Asset Statements on the Investment Decision: An Experiment." *Empirical Research in Accounting: Selected Studies* (1972): 215–240.

Ervin-Tripp, S. "Sociolinguistics." In *Advances in Experimental Social Psychology*, edited by L. Berkowitz, 91–165. New York: Academic Press, 1969.

Fishman, J. A. "A Systematization of the Whorfian Hypothesis." *Behavioral Science* (1960): 323–339.

Fishman, J. A. *The Sociology of Language*. Rowley, MA: Newbury House Publishers, 1972.

Fodor, J. A. "How to Learn to Talk: Some Simple Ways." In *The Genesis of Language: A Psycholinguistic Approach*, edited by F. Smith and G. Miller. Cambridge, MA: MIT Press, 1966.

Fryder, N. H., and J. P. Van der Ger. "Codability and Recognition: An Experiment with Facial Expressions." *Acta Psychologica* 18 (1961): 360–367.

Fusi, V. "Action and Possession in Maori Language and Culture: A Whorfian Approach." *L'Homme* 94 (1985): 117–145.

Glanzer, R., and W. H. Clark. "Accuracy of Perceptual Recall: An Analysis of Organization." *Journal of Verbal Learning and Learning Behavior* 1 (1962): 225–242.

Glanzer, R., and W. H. Clark. "The Verbal Loop Hypothesis: Binary Numbers." *Journal of Verbal Learning and Learning Behavior* 3 (1963): 301–305.

Goodenough, W. "Cultural Anthropology and Linguistics." In *Language in Culture and Society: A Reader in Linguistics and Anthropology*, edited by D. H. Hymes, 36–39. New York: Harper & Row, 1964.

Green, P. E., and A. Maheshwari. "Common Stock Perception and Preference: An Application of Multidimensional Scaling." *Journal of Business* (October 1969): 439–457.

Haried, A. A. "The Semantic Dimension of Financial Statements." *Journal of Accounting Research* (Autumn 1972): 376–391.

Haried, A. A. "Measurement of Meaning in Financial Reports." *Journal of Accounting Research* (Spring 1973): 117–145.

Harvey, D. *Explanation in Geography*. London: E. Arnold, 1969.

Haugen, E. "Linguistic Relativity: Myths and Methods." In *Language and Thought: Anthropological Issues*, edited by W. McCormack and S. Wurm, 11–28. The Hague: Mouton, 1977.

Hawes, L. C. *Pragmatics of Analoguing*. Reading, MA: Addison-Wesley, 1975.

Heider, E. R. "Universals in Color Naming and Memory." *Journal of Experimental Psychology* 93 (1972): 10–20.

Hofstedt, T. R. "A State-of-the-Art Analysis of Behavioral Accounting Research." *Journal of Contemporary Business* (Autumn 1975): 27–49.

Hoijer, H. "Cultural Implications of the Navaho Linguistic Categories." *Language* (1951): 111–120.

Hoijer, H. "The Relation of Language to Culture." In *Anthropology Today*, edited by A. L. Kroeber, 554–573. Chicago: University of Chicago Press, 1953.

Hoijer, H. "The Sapir-Whorf Hypothesis." In *Language in Culture* (Comparative Studies of Cultures and Civilizations, no. 3; Memoirs of the American Anthropological Association, no. 79), edited by H. Hoijer, 92–105. Chicago: University of Chicago Press, 1954.

Holland, D., and N. Quinn, eds. *Cultural Models in Language and Thought*. Cambridge: Cambridge University Press, 1987.

Horngren, C. T. *Accounting for Management Control*. Englewood Cliffs, NJ: Prentice-Hall, 1974.

Hymes, D. H. "Linguistic Aspects of Cross-cultural Personality Study." In *Studying Personality Cross-culturally*, edited by B. Kaplan, 313–359. New York: Harper & Row, 1961.

Ijiri, Y. "Theory of Accounting Measurement." In *Studies in Accounting Research No. 10*. Sarasota, FL: American Accounting Association, 1975.

Jain, T. N. "Alternative Methods of Accounting and Decision Making: A Psycholinguistic Analysis." *Accounting Review* (January 1973): 95–104.

Jensen, R. "An Experimental Design for the Study of Effects of Accounting Variations in Decision Making." *Journal of Accounting Research* (Autumn 1966): 16–32.

Kay, P., and W. Kempton. "What Is the Sapir-Whorf Hypothesis?" *American Anthropologist* 86 (1984): 65–79.

Kay, P., and C. K. McDaniel. "The Linguistic Significance of the Meanings of Basic Color Terms." *Language* 54 (1978): 610–646.

Kosch. E. "Linguistic Relativity." In *Human Communication: Theoretical Explorations*, edited by A. Silverstein, 107–108. Hillsdale, NJ: Lawrence Erlbaum, 1974.

Lantz, D., and V. Stefflre. "Language and Cognition Revisited." *Journal of Abnormal and Social Psychology* 69 (1964): 472–481.

Lee, D. "Conceptual Implications of an Indian Language." *Philosophy of Science* (1938): 89–102.

Lenneberg, E. H. "Cognition in Ethnolinguistics." *Language* 29 (1953): 463–471.

Lenneberg, E. H. *Biological Foundations of Language*. New York: Wiley, 1967.

Liu, L. "Reasoning Counterfactually in Chinese: Are There Any Obstacles?" *Cognition* 21 (1985): 239–270.

Lucy, J. A. "The Historical Relativity of the Linguistic Relativity Hypothesis." *Quarterly Newsletter of the Laboratory of Comparative Human Cognition* (1985): 103–108.

Lucy, J. A. "Whorf's View of the Linguistic Mediation of Thought." In *Semiotic Mediation: Sociocultural and Psychological Perspectives*, edited by E. Mertz and R. Parmentier, 73–97. Orlando, FL: Academic Press, 1985.

Lucy, J. A. *Grammatical Categories and Cognition: A Case Study of the Linguistic Relativity Hypothesis*. Cambridge: Cambridge University Press, 1992.

Lucy, J. A. *Language, Diversity and Thought: A Reformulation of the Linguistic Relativity Hypothesis*. Cambridge: Cambridge University Press, 1992.

Lucy, J. A., and, R. A. Shweder. "Whorf and His Critics: Linguistic and Nonlinguistic Influences on Color Memory." *American Anthropologist* 81 (1979): 581–615.

Lucy, J. A., and, J. V. Wertsch. "Vygotsky and Whorf: A Comparative Analysis." In *Social and Functional Approaches to Language and Thought*, edited by M. Hickman, 67–86. Cambridge: Cambridge University Press, 1987.

Lusk, E. J. "Cognitive Aspects of Annual Reports: Field, Independence/Dependence." *Empirical Research in Accounting: Selected Studies* (1973): 191–202.

Maclay, H. "An Experimental Study of Language and Non-linguistic Behavior." *Southwestern Journal of Anthropology* 14 (1958): 220–229.

Mandelbaum, D. G., ed. *The Selected Writings of Edward Sapir in Language, Culture, and Personality*. Berkeley: University of California Press, 1949.

Mathiot, M. "Noun Classes and Folk Taxonomy in Papago." In *Language in Culture and Society: A Reader in Linguistics and Anthropology*, edited by D. H. Hymes, 154–161. New York: Harper & Row, 1964.

Mathiot, M. "The Cognitive Significance of the Category of Nominal Numbers in Papago." In *Studies in Southwestern Ethnolinguistics*, edited by D. H. Hymes and W. Bittle, 201. The Hague: Mouton, 1967.

McDonald, D. *Comparative Accounting Theory*. Reading, MA: Addison-Wesley, 1972.

Oliver, B. L. "The Semantic Differential: A Device for Measuring the Interprofessional Communication of Selected Accounting Concepts." *Journal of Accounting Research* (Autumn 1974): 299–316.

Penn, J. "Linguistic Relativity Versus Innate Ideas: The Origins of the Sapir-Whorf Hypothesis in German Thought." *Janua Linguarum, series minor* 120 (1972): 32–44.

Rosch, E. "Linguistic Relativity." *ETC: A Review of General Semantics [et cetera]* 44 (1987): 254–279.

Sapir, E. *Language: An Introduction to the Study of Speech*. New York: Harcourt Press, 1921.

Sapir, E. "The Relation of American Indian Linguistics to General Linguistics." *Southwestern Journal of Anthropology* 3 (1947): 1–4.

Sapir, E. "Language." In *The Selected Writings of Edward Sapir in Language, Culture, and Personality*, edited by D. G. Mandelbaum, 7–32. Berkeley: University of California Press, 1949.

Sapir, E. "The Status of Linguistics as a Science." In *The Selected Writings of Edward Sapir in Language, Culture, and Personality*, edited by D. G. Mandelbaum, 162. Berkeley: University of California Press, 1949.

Sapir, E. "Culture." In *Language and Personality: Selected Essays*, edited by D. G. Mandelbaum. Berkeley: University of California Press, 1956.

Sapir, E. "Conceptual Categories in Primitive Languages." In *Language in Culture and Society: A Reader in Linguistics and Anthropology*, edited by D. H. Hymes, 128. New York: Harper and Row, 1964.

Schlesinger, I. M. "The Wax and Ware of Whorfian Views." In *The Influence of Language on Culture and Thought*, 8. Berlin: Mouton de Gruyter, 1991.

Silverstein, M. "Cognitive Implications of Referential Hierarchy." In *Social and Functional Approaches to Language and Thought*, edited by M. Hickman. Cambridge: Cambridge University Press, 1987.

Stam, J. H. "An Historical Perspective on 'Linguistic Relativity.' " In *Psychology of Language and Thought: Essays on the Theory and History of Psycholinguistics*, edited by R. W. Reiber, 239–262. New York: Plenum, 1980.

Stefflre, V., V. Castillo, and L. Morley. "Language and Cognition in Yucatan: A Cross-cultural Replication." *Journal of Personality and Social Psychology* 4 (1966): 112–115.

Voegelin, C. F. "Linguistics Without Meaning and Culture Without Words." *Words* 5 (1949): 36–42.

Vorster, J., and G. Schuring. "Language and Thought: Developmental Perspectives on Counterfactual Conditionals." *South African Journal of Psychology* 19 (1989): 34–38.

Weinreich, U. *Languages in Contact*. The Hague: Mouton, 1968.

Whorf, B. L. "The Relation of Habitual Thought and Behavior to Language." In *Language, Culture and Personality*, edited by L. Spier, 75–93. Menasha: University of Wisconsin, 1941.

Whorf, B. L. "The Hopi Language, Toreva Dialect." In *Linguistic Structures of Native America*, edited by H. Hoijer, 158–183. New York: Viking Fund, 1946.

Whorf, B. L. *Language, Thought, and Reality: Selected Writings of Benjamin Lee Whorf*. Edited by J. B. Carroll. Cambridge, MA: MIT Press, 1956.

Witkowski, S. R., and, C. H. Brown. "Whorf and Universals of Color Nomenclature." *Journal of Anthropological Research* 38 (1982): 411–420.

Zaltman, G., C. R. A. Pison, and R. Angelman. *Metatheory and Consumer Research*. New York: Holt, Rinehart & Winston, 1973.

Appendix: The Impact of Socio-economic Accounting Statements on the Investment Decision: An Empirical Study

AHMED BELKAOUI

Graduate School of Business, University of Chicago

Abstract

In this experiment, alternative disclosures of socio-economic accounting information, namely the abatement costs of pollution, were investigated as accounting techniques which may influence the investment decision of potential users. The theoretical rationale stemming from the linguistic relativity paradigm in accounting was that in general the accounting techniques may tend to facilitate or render more difficult various (nonlinguistic) managerial behaviors on the part of the users, and that in this particular context the investment decision effects from different professional groups using alternative socio-economic information will be different. The findings attest to the general relevance of socio-economic accounting information for the bankers under any investment strategy, and for the accountants only under an investment strategy focusing on capital gains.

Conventional accounting data may be considered to be biased in favor of not putting ecology improvement programs into effect (AAA, 1973, p. 249). A major consequence, summed up by the Beams–Fertig thesis (1971), is that the corporations that report the least activity in avoiding social cost will appear more successful to investors and will be favored by the market. While empirical evidence on the above thesis is still inconclusive (Belkaoui, 1976; Bragdon *et al.*, 1971; Spicer, 1978), there is wide evidence that most external parties are increasingly demanding information on the environmental effects of organizational behavior (AAA, 1973, p. 79; Simon *et al.*, 1972; Longstreth & Rosenbloom, 1973).

In response to this new situation the Study Group on Objectives of Financial Statements (1973, pp. 53–55 and 66) proposed as an objective of financial statements the reporting of those activities which are important to the role of the enterprise in its social environment. In fact most accounting associations have expressed a strong interest in the related issue of socio-economic accounting (AAA, 1971, 1972, 1973, 1974, 1975, 1976; NAA, 1974). The resulting socio-economic accounting statements will differ from the conventional ones mainly through the internalization and disclosure of the social costs and benefits arising from production (Estes, 1972; Belkaoui, 1973, 1975; Beams & Fertig, 1971). Strong

evidence suggests that the socio-economic accounting type of information in the annual reports is significant and increasing (Beresford, 1973; Ackerman, 1973). Given this situation the scholarly socio-economic accounting inquiry should focus on the development and validation of appropriate ways of measuring and disclosing social costs and benefits. Secondly, to assess the relevance of this new information to users it should also focus on evaluating the behavioral impact of such disclosure.

Accordingly, the purpose of this paper is to report on a field experiment undertaken to determine whether the investment decision by an external user would be made differently with the addition of socio-economic accounting information. More specifically, the following questions will be investigated:

(1) Will the socio-economic accounting information cause the investment decision to be different from the conventional accounting information?

(2) Assuming that investors are members of different professional groups, will the investment decision differ among those groups?

(3) Assuming that the investment strategies of the investors are different, will it have any effect on the investment decision?

(4) Finally, what are the demographic and perceptual variables most associated with these

differential investment decisions when socio-economic accounting information is reported?

Similar questions have been the subject of studies investigating the decision effects resulting from using alternative accounting procedures. Most of the experiments used for those studies lack a theoretical framework to justify or motivate the reporting effects on individual decision making (Dyckman *et al.*, 1978). The research questions in this study, however, are theoretically supported by the linguistic relativity paradigm in accounting (Belkaoui, 1978, 1980; Jain, 1973).

The remainder of this paper is divided into six sections. The next section relates this study to previous research on similar issues and questions. The second section introduces the linguistic relativity paradigm to motivate the research questions of interest in this study. The third section describes the experiment. The fourth section presents the results. The fifth section provides a discussion of the statistical results. The final subdivisions of the paper contain a brief summary and final conclusions.

RELATED RESEARCH

The interest in this paper lies in the behavior of users of accounting information for decision making. It adds more evidence to those studies which support the contention that alternative reporting procedures can influence decision making. These studies, which are mostly experiments, examined the decision effects resulting from using various alternative accounting procedures, namely:

(a) using alternative inventory techniques (Bruns, 1965; Dyckman, 1964, 1966; Jensen, 1966; Dopuch & Ronen, 1973);

(b) using alternative methods of reporting income from intercorporate investments (Barrett, 1971);

(c) including segmented data in financial statements of diversified firms (Ortman, 1975);

(d) including additional information provided by a human resource accounting system (Hendricks, 1976; Elias, 1972);

(e) including nonaccounting data (Belkaoui & Cousineau, 1977; Hofstedt, 1972); and

(f) using alternative tax allocation techniques (Livingstone, 1967).

From these studies it appears that the influence of alternative techniques on decision making has not always been conclusive. The degree of influence was found to depend on the nature of the particular decision defined by the experimental task, the nature and the characteristics of the decision makers used as subjects, and the content and format of the alternative accounting techniques presented in the experiment.

THEORY

The general idea advanced by Jain (1973) and Belkaoui (1978) is that accounting is a language and according to the Sapir-Whorf hypothesis its lexical characteristics and grammatical rules will affect the linguistic and nonlinguistic behavior of users. On that basis Belkaoui (1978) introduced four propositions derived from the linguistic relativity paradigm to conceptually integrate research findings on the impact of accounting rules and nonlinguistic behavior. Of particular interest to this study is the fourth hypothesis on the relationships between the accounting rules and nonlinguistic behavior. It was expressed as follows:

> . . . The accounting techniques may tend to facilitate or render more difficult various (nonlinguistic) managerial behaviors on the part of the users (Belkaoui, 1978, p. 102).

In the context of the present study this proposition implies that in general the investment decision effects of investors from different professional groups using alternative forms of social and accounting information will be different.

Hypothesis 1

In connection with Question (1), Hypothesis 1 was formulated:

> Socio-economic accounting information will induce different stock investment decision behavior than will conventional accounting information.

Since there is evidence to suggest some degree of association between a firm's investment in social programs and its profitability (Spicer, 1978; Bragdon & Marlin, 1973), it may be expected that investors will invest different amounts of funds in a firm whose financial statements show an increase in "social awareness expenditures" as opposed to a firm showing a decrease or zero of these expenditures. More importantly, on the basis of the proposition from the linguistic relativity paradigm it may also be stated that the investment decision as a nonlinguistic or managerial behavior will be facilitated or rendered more difficult and consequently be different by the addition of socio-economic accounting information.

Determining how easy or difficult the investment decision is, with the addition of socio-economic accounting information may be difficult. One school of thought, mentioned earlier as the Beams-Fertig thesis, suggests that the investors will favor firms showing a decrease in or zero "social awareness" expenditures. Another school of thought believes that "ethical investors" form a clientele that responds to demonstrations of corporate social concern (Simon *et al.*, 1972), or that corporate expenditures for social improvement may benefit the corporation over the long run in many ways (Bowman, 1973).

Hypothesis 2

In connection with Question (2), Hypothesis 2 was formulated:

> Given a reporting of either socio-economic or conventional accounting information the investment decision will differ between different occupational groups.

While the main proposition from the linguistic relativity paradigm and the first hypothesis suggest that the investment decision will differ with the addition of socio-economic accounting information, it may be expected that this difference will be more evident for investors from different professional groups. The assumption is that occupational groups in the field of management differ in the extent of their exposure and orientation to accounting which may lead their respective members to have a different understanding of, and pay differing levels of attention to, the socio-economic accounting information. In other words, for the accounting techniques to facilitate or render more difficult nonlinguistic or managerial behavior depends on the mastery of the difference between accounting techniques by the users and their membership to a given occupational group.[1]

Hypothesis 3

In connection with Question (3), Hypothesis 3 was formulated:

> Given a reporting of either socio-economic or conventional accounting information, the investment decision will differ according to the type of investment strategy adopted.

Since there is evidence to suggest the existence of differences in investment style and strategy (Lewellen *et al.*, 1977), it may be assumed that they may lead eventually to different investment decisions. Combined with the linguistic relativity paradigm it may be suggested that the type of investment strategy adopted leads to a different understanding and attention paid to accounting information which will affect the investment decision. More detailed questions arising from the interaction effects are: (i) will the difference in the investment behavior caused by the differences in the investment strategy be greater with the socio-economic than with the conventional accounting information? (ii) will the same difference in the investment behavior be a function of the occupational grouping?

Hypothesis 4

In connection with Question (4), Hypothesis 4 was formulated:

> Given either a reporting of socio-economic or conventional accounting information the investment decision will be associated with perceptual and background variables.

Evidence from surveys (Lewellen *et al.*, 1977) and from laboratory experiments (Belkaoui & Cousineau, 1977; Elias, 1972; Hendricks, 1976) seems to indicate that investment behavior is a function of personal circumstances as expressed by demographic and perceptual variables. Again combined with the linguistic relativity paradigm it may be suggested that the managerial behavior induced by the accounting techniques is associated with perceptual and background variables. More explicitly, the ecological concern and cognitive "make-up" of an individual may predispose him to

---

[1] While this study investigated the differences in the perceptions of accounting techniques, prior studies have focused on the differences in meaning of selected accounting concepts to various professional groups (Haried, 1972, 1973; Oliver, 1974; Flamholtz & Cook, 1978; and Belkaoui, 1980). Of interest to this study is the introduction by Belkaoui (1980) of a *sociolinguistic* construct to explain the different accounting linguistic behavior between various professional groups in accounting. The affiliation of users with different professional organizations or communities with their distinct interaction networks was found to create different accounting language repertoires.

understand and appreciate the socio-economic accounting disclosure and invest in socially responsible firms (Simon et al., 1972).

METHOD

The experiment was designed as $3 \times 3 \times 2 \times N$ with the investment decision between two hypothetical firms as the only dependent variable. Two hundred and twenty-five subjects participated in the experiment.

The experimental factors

Three independent variables were used: membership in professional groups, accounting information and investment strategy.

Membership in professional groups. The subjects chosen belonged to three different occupational groups. They were (1) fourth year undergraduate students majoring in accounting and finance, and first and second year MBA students from the School of Commerce at Syracuse University, (2) senior officers from four Syracuse commercial banks, and (3) accountants, members of the National Association of Accountants, Syracuse chapter. In the choice of the three groups the main concern was to deal with the two caveats of behavioral field experiments, namely the response ratio and validity. Following advice given by Barrett (1971) the response ratio was improved by employing the "captive audiences" of the local chapter of the NAA and the trust officers of local banks and the validity problem was reduced by having the experiment run under the auspices of management at the subject's place of employment. The selection procedure consisted of first contacting the banks' upper management, and second, the NAA local chapter official and asked for cooperation. Seventy-five senior bank officers accepted participation in the experiment. Informed of the number of senior bank officers the NAA chapter secured the participation of 75 of their members. Finally 75 students were asked to participate in the experiment during class time. It is unlikely that the first 75 individuals contacted in the banking and accounting groups accepted participation in the experiment although the impression given was that the maximum number of senior officers had been secured in the banking group.

A liaison man for each bank and the NAA local chapter official were handed the number of questionnaires required, given appropriate instructions and given the responsibility of conducting the experiment. A subject description summary is exhibited in Table 1.

TABLE 1. Subject Descriptions

	Mean	Minimum	Maximum
Age	25	20	55
Number of college level courses taken in accounting and finance	4	1	8
Number of years engaged in financial analysis	5	0	16

The accounting information factor. This centered on the dichotomy between conventional and socio-economic accounting information. A problem arose in a proper definition of the socio-economic accounting information. Because of the variety of information susceptible to connote social responsibility (Estes, 1975) a choice was made for the disclosure of pollution abatement cost. The rationale for this choice is based upon (1) the general public belief that pollution abatement is a major indicator of a socially responsible firm (McGraw-Hill, 1970) and (2) the relative materiality of these expenditures. For some large firms they may reach up to 4% of sales and 100% of capital investment (AAA, 1973, p. 88). They are also reported to be as high as 75% of capital investment in the steel industry (Bylinski, 1971, p. 130). Three accounting treatments were investigated: (1) the conventional treatment, not including any information on abatement costs, (2) a footnote treatment, including abating cost information in the footnotes and (3) a total treatment, including the abatement cost information in both the profit and loss statement and the footnotes. The differentiation between the footnote treatment and the total treatment was based on the general stipulation that detailed information may be more useful than aggregated data (Abdel-Khalik, 1973).

The investment strategy. This variable was operationalized by choosing two categories of investment style: (1) investment for dividend income and (2) investment for capital gains. The choice was limited to these two strategies thought to represent the extremes on a continuum of investment strategies. For example Lewellen *et al.* (1977, p. 305) identified four objectives, namely, short term capital gains, intermediate term capital gains, long term capital gains and dividend income. Omitting the temporal distinction for capital gains the categories may be reduced to the two levels of the investment strategy factor chosen for this study.

The experimental treatments and the criterion variable

In the experiment, the participants were asked to compare two firms, Abel Chemical Inc. and Jabel Chemical Inc., and then allocate a given amount of money as equity investment between the two firms. The 1971 annual report of an actual chemical company was chosen as a basis for the construction of financial statements in conformity with the three treatments of socio-economic accounting information. It is a chemical company which manufactures and markets organic and inorganic chemicals for textile, pulp and paper agricultural markets, aerosol insecticides, chemical products and mechanical components used in the air conditioning and refrigeration industries. The two companies presented as Abel Chemical Inc. and Jabel Chemical Inc. were established through a modification of the financial characteristics of the chemical company initially selected. As a result

the two firms are of comparable size but differ in terms of profitability. The manipulation of the experimental treatments resulted in three packets as follows:

(1) The first packet includes the financial statements of both companies prepared according to conventional accounting treatments, i.e., ignoring possible socio-economic information. Abel was made less profitable than Jabel. The first packet is referred to as *the conventional treatment*.

(2) The second packet includes the same statements, with in addition footnotes pertaining to the abatement costs of pollution by the two firms. Abel was made again less profitable than Jabel. However, the difference in profitability was due to different pollution control policy. Abel was shown with a higher amount on pollution abatement resulting in the difference in profitability. The second packet is referred to as the *footnote treatment*.

(3) The third packet includes again the same statements, with in addition information on the pollution abatement costs disclosed in both the profit and loss statements and the footnotes. This treatment is referred to as *the total treatment*.

Each packet includes the financial statements and a questionnaire. Tables 2, 3 and 4 show respectively a copy of the financial statements of Abel and Jabel under the conventional, footnote and total treatments.

TABLE 2. (a) Jabel Chemical Inc. (*Conventional treatment*)

CONSOLIDATED BALANCE SHEET as of December 31	1970	1969
ASSETS		
Current Assets		
Cash	$ 579,000	658,000
Certificates of deposit	392,000	–
Marketable securities, at cost,		
which approximates market	899,000	–
Receivables	3,500,000	2,950,000
Inventories, at lower of average		
cost of market	3,400,000	3,300,000
Prepayments	246,000	150,000
Total current assets	9,016,000	7,058,000
Plant and Equipment, at cost		
Land	350,000	194,000
Buildings and equipment	14,550,000	13,482,000
Returnable containers	620,000	455,000
	15,520,000	14,131,000
Less – Accumulated depreciation	7,520,000	6,580,000
Patents, Trademarks and Goodwill,		
in process of amortization	186,000	196,000
	17,202,000	14,805,000

LIABILITIES
Current Liabilities

Accounts payable	2,074,000	1,495,000
Dividends payable	130,000	120,000
Accrued liabilities	598,000	480,000
Accrued Federal income taxes	520,000	190,000
Customers' deposits on returnable containers	450,000	380,000
Total current liabilities	3,772,000	2,665,000
Deferred Income Taxes	1,005,000	821,000
Deferred Investment Credit, being amortized over life of related equipment	320,000	331,000
	5,097,000	3,817,000

Stockholders' Investment

5% non-cumulative preferred stock, $100 par value – authorized 6500 shares; outstanding 5491 shares in 1970 and 5642 in 1969	549,000	564,000
Common stock, $2 par value, authorized 1,000,000 shares; outstanding 647,620 in 1970 and 1969	1,295,000	1,295,000
Paid in surplus	42,000	39,000
Retained Earnings	10,219,000	9,090,000
Total stockholders' investment	12,105,000	10,988,000
	17,202,000	14,805,000

	1970	1969
Net Sales	29,100,000	23,400,000
Costs and Expenses		
Cost of goods sold	19,900,000	16,300,000
Selling, general and administrative	3,600,000	2,300,000
Research, development and technical service	780,000	700,000
Depreciation	955,000	860,000
Provision for income taxes	1,858,000	1,294,000
	27,093,000	21,454,000
Net Income	2,007,000	1,946,000
Dividends on Preferred Stock ($5 per share)	28,000	28,000
Net Income on Common Stock	1,979,000	1,918,000
Retained Earnings, Beginning of Year	9,620,000	8,100,000
Dividends on Common Stock (68-1/2¢ per share and 61-1/2¢ per share)	444,000	398,000
Retained Earnings, End of Year	11,155,000	9,620,000
Net Income per Common Share	3.09	2.9

Four Year Summary

	1970	1969	1968	1967
Net Sales	29,100,000	23,400,000	23,404,000	18,700,000
Net Income	2,007,000	1,946,000	1,500,000	1,009,000
Total Assets	17,202,000	14,805,000	13,486,000	11,659,000
Per Share of Common Stock				
Net Income	3.09	2.9	2.28	1.51
Dividends declared	0.68-1/2	0.61-1/2	0.48	0.38
Price Range Com. (OTC Bid)	42-23	29-20	24-16	20-14

TABLE 2. (b) Abel Chemical Inc. (*Conventional treatment*)

CONSOLIDATED BALANCE SHEET, as of December 31

	1970	1969
ASSETS		
Current Assets		
Cash	579,000	658,000
Certificates of deposit	392,000	–
Marketable securities, at cost,		
which approximates market	899,000	–
Receivables	3,393,000	2,938,000
Inventories, at lower of average		
cost of market	3,327,000	3,411,000
Prepayments	246,000	149,000
Total current assets	8,836,000	7,156,000
Plant and Equipment at cost		
Land	334,000	194,000
Buildings and equipment	14,151,000	13,482,000
Returnable containers	587,000	455,000
	15,072,000	14,131,000
Less – Accumulated depreciation	7,424,000	6,580,000
	7,648,000	7,551,000
Patents, Trademarks and Goodwill,		
in process of amortization	172,000	196,000
	16,656,000	14,903,000
LIABILITIES		
Current Liabilities		
Accounts payable	1,566,000	1,609,000
Dividends payable	130,000	114,000
Accrued liabilities	598,000	480,000
Accrued federal income taxes	508,000	185,000
Customers' deposits on returnable containers	424,000	375,000
Total current liabilities	3,226,000	2,763,000
Deferred Income Taxes	1,005,000	821,000
Deferred Investment Credit, being amortized		
over life of related equipment	320,000	331,000
	4,551,000	3,915,000
Stockholders' Investment		
5% non-cumulative preferred stock, $100 par		
value – authorized 6500 shares; outstanding		
5491 in 1970 and 5642 in 1969	549,000	564,000
Common stock, $2 par value – authorized		
1,000,000 shares; outstanding 647,620 in		
1970 and 1969	1,295,000	1,295,000
Paid-in surplus	42,000	39,000
Retained earnings	10,219,000	9,090,000
Total stockholders' investment	12,105,000	10,988,000
	16,656,000	14,903,000
	1970	1969
Net Sales	28,169,000	22,969,000
Costs and Expenses		
Cost of goods sold	18,921,000	16,389,000
Selling, general and administrative	3,000,000	1,300,000
Research, development and technical		
service	1,834,000	1,730,000
Depreciation	955,000	856,000
Provision for income taxes	1,858,000	1,294,000
	26,568,000	21,569,000

Net Income			1,601,000	1,400,000
Dividends on Preferred Stock ($5 per share)			28,000	28,000
Net Income on Common Stock			1,573,000	1,372,000
Retained Earnings, Beginning of Year			9,090,000	8,116,000
Dividends on Common Stock				
(68-1/2 per share and 61-1/2¢ per share)			444,000	398,000
Retained Earnings, End of Year			10,219,000	9,090,000
Net Income Per Common Share			2.43	2.12

Four Year Summary

Net Sales	28,169,000	22,969,000	22,402,000	18,649,000
Net Income	1,601,000	1,400,000	1,499,000	1,007,000
Total Assets	16,656,000	14,903,000	13,286,000	11,659,000
Per Share of				
Common Stock:				
Net Income	2.43	2.12	2.27	1.51
Dividends Declared	0.68-1/2	0.61-1/2	0.48	0.38
Price Range:				
Com. (OTC bid)	42-23	29-20	24-16	20-14
	1970	1969	1968	1967

In conducting the experiment for each of the subject groups, it was specifically requested that the three packets be distributed randomly so that each member of a group received one and only one of the packet. The criterion variable was obtained by asking the participants to allocate a certain amount of money between the two companies, Abel and Jabel, under two investment strategies. The main instructions read as follows:

> ... We are providing you with information packets concerning JABEL CHEMICAL INC. and ABEL CHEMICAL INC. These are two fictional chemical companies. On the basis of the information available to you, you have been asked to help Mr. John Smith make a portfolio decision between these two companies.
> Mr. Smith, who has been investing in non-chemical companies, has $30,000 in cash which he would like to invest in common stock of chemical companies. Following analysis of the information provided on the two investment alternatives, what proportion of each common stock would you advise Mr. Smith to buy if:
> Case A – Mr. Smith wishes to invest for income reasons?
> Case B – Mr. Smith wishes to invest for capital growth?

The main instructions were followed by the financial statements of Abel and Jabel and the following question:

> ... Now that you had a chance to evaluate both ABEL CHEMICAL INC. and JABEL CHEMICAL INC. What proportion of the $30,000 would you advise Mr. Smith to invest in each firm respectively if:
> a) Mr. Smith wishes to invest for income reasons?
> b) Mr. Smith wishes to invest for capital growth?

The participants were also explained the differences in the two investment strategies to insure uniformity of interpretation.

The perceptual and background variables

To investigate the fourth hypothesis pertaining to the possible association between the investment decisions and perceptual and background variables, the following variables are selected:

(1) the age of the subject;
(2) the number of college level courses in accounting and finance;
(3) the extent to which portfolio selection is an important part of his job;
(4) the degree of acceptance of the disclosure of the abatement costs of pollution to improve the investment decisions;
(5) the number of years in which the participant was engaged in evaluating financial statements;
(6) the perception of the importance of the issue of "ecological crisis";
(7) the trade-off between pollution control and profitability.

These variables were included in a questionnaire to be answered after the completion of the main experimental portfolio decision task. Because the subjects may be sensitized to the experimental variables if they glanced through the complete questionnaire before responding to the individual questions, especially for subjects receiving statements with abatement costs in either the footnote or the total treatments, they were warned and reminded explicitly in the questionnaire as a basic condition to the validity of the experiment to respond to the experimental task before continuing with the questionnaire. Besides, it was insured that a reinforcement of this warning was made by the administrators of the experiment for the three groups.

TABLE 3. (a) Jabel Chemical Inc. (*Footnote treatment*)

CONSOLIDATED BALANCE SHEET, AS OF DECEMBER 31

	1970	1969
ASSETS		
Current Assets		
Cash	$ 579,000	658,000
Certificates of deposit	392,000	—
Marketable securities at cost, which approximates market	899,000	2,950,000
Receivables	3,500,000	
Inventories, at lower of average cost or market	3,400,000	3,300,000
Prepayments	246,000	150,000
Total current assets	9,016,000	7,058,000
Plant and Equipment, at cost (Note 1)		
Land	350,000	194,000
Buildings and equipment	14,550,000	13,482,000
Returnable containers	620,000	455,000
	15,520,000	14,131,000
Less – Accumulated depreciation	7,520,000	6,580,000
	8,000,000	7,551,000
LIABILITIES		
Current Liabilities		
Accounts payable	2,074,000	1,495,000
Dividends payable	130,000	120,000
Accrued liabilities	598,000	480,000
Accrued federal income taxes	520,000	190,000
Customers' deposits on returnable containers	450,000	380,000
Total current liabilities	3,772,000	2,665,000
Deferred Income Taxes	1,005,000	821,000
Deferred Investment Credit, being amortized over life of related equipment	320,000	331,000
	5,097,000	3,817,000
Stockholders' Investment		
5% non-cumulative preferred stock, $100 par value – authorized 6500 shares; outstanding 5491 shares in 1970 and 5642 in 1969	594,000	564,000
Common stock, $2 par value – authorized 1,000,000 shares, outstanding 647,620 in 1970 and 1969	1,295,000	1,295,000
Paid in surplus	42,000	39,000
Retained Earnings	10,219,000	9,090,000
Stockholders' investment	12,105,000	10,988,000
	17,202,000	14,805,000

	1970	1969
Net Sales	29,100,000	23,400,000
Costs and Expenses		
Cost of goods sold	19,900,000	16,300,000
Selling, general and administrative	3,600,000	2,300,000
Research, development and technical service (Note 2)	780,000	700,000
Depreciation	955,000	860,000
Provision for income taxes	1,858,000	1,294,000
	27,093,000	21,454,000
Net Income	2,007,000	1,946,000
Dividends on Preferred Stock ($5 per share)	28,000	28,000
Net Income on Common Stock	1,979,000	1,918,000
Retained Earnings, Beginning of Year	9,620,000	8,100,000
Dividends on Common Stock (68-1/2¢ per share and 61-1/2¢ per share)	444,000	398,000
Retained Earnings, End of Year	11,155,000	9,620,000
Net Income per Common Share	3.09	2.9

The accompanying notes are an integral part of this consolidated statement.

Note 1: Plant and equipment includes $500,000 a year gross capital expenditures for equipment necessary to accommodate less pollutant raw materials and to reduce the emission of contaminants resulting from chemical production.

Note 2: This includes $700,000 a year as utility expenditures for air pollution control as follows:
a) operating costs related to the characteristics of high quality raw materials and to the use of control equipment $350,000 a year
b) R. and D expenditures to improve the air pollution control program $350,000 a year.

Four Year Summary

	1970	1969	1968	1969
Net Sales	29,100,000	23,400,000	23,404,000	18,700,000
Net Income	2,007,000	1,946,000	1,500,000	1,009,000
Total Assets	17,202,000	14,805,000	13,486,000	11,659,000
Per share of common stock:				
Net income	3.09	2.9	2.28	1.51
Dividends declared	0.68-1/2	0.61-1/2	0.48	0.38
Price range Com. (OTC bid)	42-23	29-20	24-16	20-14
Per share of common stock before pollution expenditures				
Net Income	4.1	3.0		

TABLE 3. (b) Abel Chemical Inc. (*Footnote treatment*)

CONSOLIDATED BALANCE SHEET, AS OF DECEMBER 31

	1970	1969
ASSETS		
Current Assets		
Cash	579,000	658,000
Certificates of deposit	392,000	–
Marketable securities, at cost, which approximates market	899,000	–
Receivables	3,393,000	2,938,000
Inventories, at lower of average cost or market	3,327,000	3,411,000
Prepayments	246,000	149,000
Total current assets	8,836,000	7,156,000
Plant and Equipment, at cost (Note 1)		
Land	334,000	194,000
Buildings and equipment	14,151,000	13,482,000
Returnable containers	587,000	455,000
	15,072,000	14,131,000
Less – Accumulated depreciation	7,424,000	6,580,000
	7,648,000	7,551,000
Patents, Trademarks and Goodwill, in process of amortization	172,000	196,000
	16,656,000	14,903,000
LIABILITIES		
Current Liabilities		
Accounts payable	1,566,000	1,609,000
Dividends payable	130,000	114,000
Accrued liabilities	598,000	480,000
Accrued federal income taxes	508,000	185,000
Customers' deposits on returnable containers	424,000	375,000
Total current liabilities	3,226,000	2,763,000
Deferred Income Taxes	1,005,000	821,000
Deferred Investment Credit, being amortized over life of related equipment	320,000	331,000
	4,551,000	3,915,000

Net Sales	28,169,000	22,969,000
Costs and Expenses		
Cost of goods sold	18,921,000	16,389,000
Selling, general and administrative	3,000,000	1,300,000
Research, development and technical service (Note 2)	1,834,000	1,730,000
Depreciation	955,000	856,000
Provision for income taxes	1,858,000	1,294,000
	26,568,000	21,569,000
Net Income	1,601,000	1,400,000
Dividends on Preferred Stock ($5 per share)	28,000	28,000
Net Income on Common Stock	1,573,000	1,372,000
Retained Earnings, Beginning of Year	9,090,000	8,116,000
Dividends on Common Stock	444,000	398,000
(68-1/2¢ per share and 61-1/2¢ per share)		
Retained Earnings, End of Year	10,219,000	9,090,000
Net Income per Common Share	2.43	2.12

The accompanying notes are an integral part of this consolidated statement.

Note 1: Plant and equipment includes $650,000 a year capital expenditures for equipment necessary to accommodate less pollutant inputs and to reduce the emission of contaminants resulting from chemical production.

Note 2: This includes $1,730,000 a year as utility expenditures for air pollution control as follows:

a) operating costs related to the characteristics of high quality raw materials and to the use of control equipment $1,020,000 a year.

b) R and D expenditures to improve the air pollution control program $710,000 a year.

Stockholders' Investment

	1970	1969
5% non-cumulative preferred stock, $100 par value – authorized 6500 shares; outstanding 5491 in 1970 and 5642 in 1969	549,000	564,000
Common stock, $2 par value – authorized 1,000,000 shares; outstanding 647,620 in 1970 and 1969	1,295,000	1,295,000
Paid-in surplus	42,000	39,000
Retained earnings	10,219,000	9,090,000
Total stockholders' investment	12,105,000	10,988,000
	16,656,000	14,903,000

Four Year Summary

Net Sales	28,169,000	22,969,000	22,402,000	18,649,000
Net Income	1,601,000	1,400,000	1,499,000	1,007,000
Total Assets	16,656,000	14,903,000	13,286,000	11,659,000
Per Share of Common Stock:				
Net Income	2.43	2.12	2.27	1.51
Dividends Declared	0.68-1/2	0.61-1/2	0.48	0.38
Price Range:				
Com. (OTC bid)	42-23	29-20	24-16	20-14
Per share of Common stock Before pollution Expenditures				
Net income	5.1	4.8	–	–

TABLE 4. (a) Jabel Chemical Inc. (*Total treatment*)

	1970	1969
Net Sales	29,100,000	23,400,000
Costs and Expenses		
Costs of goods sold	19,900,000	16,300,000
Selling, general and administrative	3,680,000	2,300,000
Abatement costs of pollution (Note 2)	700,000	700,000
Depreciation	955,000	860,000
Provision for income taxes	1,858,000	1,294,000
	27,093,000	21,454,000
Net Income	2,007,000	1,946,000
Dividends on Preferred Stock ($5 per share)	28,000	28,000
Net Income on Common Stock	1,979,000	1,918,000
Retained Earnings, Beginning of Year	9,620,000	8,100,000
Dividends on Common Stock (68-1/2¢ per share and 61-1/2¢ per share)	444,000	398,000
Retained Earnings, End of Year	11,155,000	9,620,000
Net Income per Common Share	3.09	2.9

CONSOLIDATED BALANCE SHEET, as of December 31

	1970	1969
ASSETS		
Current Assets		
Cash	579,000	658,000
Certificates of deposit	392,000	–
Marketable securities, at cost, which approximates market	899,000	
Receivables	3,500,000	2,950,000
Inventories at lower of average cost or market	3,400,000	3,300,000
Prepayments	246,000	150,000
Total current assets	9,016,000	7,058,000
Plant and Equipment (Note 1)		
Land	350,000	194,000
Buildings and equipment	14,550,000	13,482,000
Returnable containers	620,000	455,000
	15,520,000	14,131,000
Less – Accumulated depreciation	7,520,000	6,580,000
	8,000,000	7,551,000
Patents, Trademarks and Goodwill, in process of amortization	186,000	196,000
	17,202,000	14,805,000

The accompanying notes are an integral part of this consolidated statement.

Note 1: Plant and equipment includes $500,000 a year gross capital expenditures for equipment necessary to accommodate less pollutant raw materials and to reduce the emission of contaminants resulting from chemical production.

Note 2: This includes $700,000 a year as utility expenditures for air pollution controls as follows:

a) operating costs related to the characteristics of high quality raw materials and to the use of control equipment – $350,000 a year.

b) R and D expenditures to improve the air pollution control program $350,000 a year.

Four Year Summary

	1970	1969	1968	1967
Net Sales	29,100,000	23,400,000	23,404,000	18,700,000
Net Income	2,007,000	1,946,000	1,500,000	1,009,000
Total Assets	17,202,000	14,805,000	13,486,000	11,659,000
Per Share of Common Stocks Net Income	3.09	2.9	2.28	1.51
Dividends Declared	0.68-1/2	0.61-1/2	0.48	0.38
Price Range Per Share of Com (OTC bid)	42–23	29–20	24–16	20–14
Per Share of Common Stock Before Pollution Expenditures	4.1	3.0	–	–

LIABILITIES

Current Liabilities	1970	1969
Accounts payable	2,074,000	1,495,000
Dividends payable	130,000	120,000
Accrued liabilities	598,000	480,000
Accrued federal income taxes	520,000	190,000
Customers' deposits on returnable containers	450,000	380,000
Total current liabilities	3,772,000	2,665,000
Deferred Income Taxes	1,005,000	821,000
Deferred Investment Credit, being amortized over life of related equipment	320,000	331,000
Stockholders' Investment		
5% non-cumulative preferred stock, $100 par value – authorized 6500 shares; outstanding 5491 shares in 1970 and 5642 in 1969	5,097,000	3,817,000
Common stock, $2 par value – authorized 1,000,000 shares, outstanding 647,620 in 1970 and 1969	594,000	564,000
Paid in surplus	1,295,000	1,295,000
	42,000	39,000
Retained earnings	10,219,000	9,090,000
Total stockholders' investment	12,105,000	10,988,000
	17,202,000	14,805,000

TABLE 4. (b) Abel Chemical Inc. (*Total treatment*)

	1970	1969
Net Sales	28,169,000	22,969,000
Costs and Expenses		
Cost of goods sold	18,921,000	16,389,000
Selling, general and administrative	2,104,000	1,300,000
Abatement costs of pollution (Note 2)	1,730,000	1,730,000
Depreciation	955,000	856,000
Provision for income taxes	1,858,000	1,294,000
	26,568,000	21,569,000

CONSOLIDATED BALANCE SHEET, as of December 31

ASSETS	1970	1969
Current Assets		
Cash	579,000	658,000
Certificates of deposit	392,000	–
Marketable securities, at cost, which approximates market	899,000	–
Receivables	3,393,000	2,938,000
Inventories, at lower of average cost or market	3,327,000	3,411,000
Prepayments	246,000	149,000
Total current assets	8,836,000	7,156,000

Net Income	1,601,000	1,400,000
Dividends on Preferred Stock ($5 per share)	28,000	28,000
Net Income on Common Stock	1,573,000	1,372,000
Retained Earnings, Beginning of Year	9,090,000	8,116,000
Dividends on Common Stock (68–1/2¢ per share and 61–1/2¢ per share)	444,000	398,000
Retained Earnings, End of Year	10,219,000	9,090,000
Net Income per Common Share	2.43	2.12

The accompanying notes are an integral part of this consolidated statement.

Note 1: Plant and equipment includes $650,000 a year capital expenditures for equipment necessary to accommodate less pollutant inputs to reduce the emission of contaminants resulting from chemical production.

Note 2: This includes $1,730,000 a year as utility expenditures for air pollution control as follows:

a) operating costs related to the characteristics of high quality raw materials and to the use of control equipment – $1,020,000 a year.

b) R and D expenditures to the art of air pollution control program, $710,000 a year.

Four Year Summary

	1970	1969	1968	1967
Net Sales	28,169,000	22,969,000	22,402,000	18,649,000
Net Income	1,601,000	1,400,000	1,499,000	1,007,000
Total Assets	16,656,000	14,903,000	13,286,000	11,659,000
Per Share of Common Stock:				
Net Income	2.43	2.12	2.27	1.51
Dividends Declared	0.68–1/2	0.61–1/2	0.48	0.38
Price Range:				
Com. (OTC bid)	42–23	29–20	24–16	20–14
Per Share of Common Stock Before Pollution Expenditures				
Net Income	5.1	4.8	–	–

Plant and equipment at cost (Note 1)		
Land	334,000	194,000
Buildings and equipment	14,151,000	13,482,000
Returnable containers	587,000	455,000
	15,072,000	14,131,000
Less – Accumulated depreciation	7,424,000	6,580,000
	7,648,000	7,551,000
Patents, Trademarks and Goodwill, in process of amortization	172,000	196,000
LIABILITIES		
Current Liabilities		
Accounts payable	1,566,000	1,609,000
Dividends payable	130,000	114,000
Accrued liabilities	598,000	480,000
Accrued federal income taxes	508,000	185,000
Customers' deposits on returnable containers	424,000	375,000
Total current liabilities	3,226,000	2,763,000
Deferred Income Taxes	1,005,000	821,000
Deferred Investment Credit, being amortized over life of related equipment	320,000	331,000
	4,551,000	3,915,000
Stockholders' Investment		
5% non-cumulative preferred stock, $100 par value – authorized 6500 shares: outstanding 5491 in 1971 and 5642 in 1969	549,000	564,000
Common Stock, $2 par value – authorized 1,000,000 shares; outstanding 647,620 in 1970 and 1969	1,295,000	1,295,000
Paid in surplus	42,000	39,000
Retained earnings	10,219,000	9,090,000
	12,105,000	10,988,000
Total stockholders' investment	16,656,000	14,903,000

The experimental design

A split-plot design is used in this study. It includes three factors: two between variables each one at three levels, and one within variables at two levels. They were (1) the membership to occupational group as the first between variable (Factor A) with level a_1 for accountants, level a_2 for bankers and level a_3 for students, (2) the accounting treatment as the second between variable (Factor B) with b_1 as the conventional treatment, b_2 as the footnote treatment and b_3 as the total treatment, and (3) the investment policy as the within variable (Factor C) with C_1 as the investment for dividend income and C_2 as the investment for capital gains. It is a design where there are repeated measures on only one of the three factors, namely the investment strategy, resulting in 18 cells. The design is shown in Table 5.

Each of the groups was observed under both levels of C, i.e., investment policies. *But each group was only assigned to one combination of Factors A and B.* The notation S_{ij} denotes the groups of participants assigned to the treatment combination ab_{ij} with the participant effect nested under A and B.

The structural model on which the analysis is based has the following form.

$$X_{ijkm} = + \alpha_i + \beta_j + \alpha\beta_{ij} + \pi_n(ij) + \gamma_k + \alpha\gamma_{ik} + \beta\gamma_{jk}$$

$$+ \alpha\beta\gamma_{ijk} + \gamma\pi_{km(ij)} + 0(ijkm)$$

where

X_{ijkm} = percentage invested in Jabel Chemical Inc. after an arcsine transformation

α_i = effect of treatment A, which is constant for all subjects within treatment population i

β_j = effect of treatment B, which is a constant for all subjects within treatment population j

$\alpha\beta_{ij}$ = effect that represents nonadditivity of effects and B_j

$\Pi_n(ij)$ = effect of subject n, which is nested under level ab_{ij}

γ_k = effect of treatment C, which is a constant for all subjects within treatment population k

$\alpha\gamma_{ik}$ = effect that represents nonadditivity of effects α_i and γ_k

$\beta\gamma_{jk}$ = effect that represents nonadditivity of effects α_i, β_j and γ_k

$\gamma\Pi km(ij)$ = effect that represents nonadditivity of effects γ_k and $\Pi_m(ij)$

0 = experimental error

To meet the assumption implicit in the use of analysis of variance, a change in the scale of measurement of the criterion was deemed appropriate (Tukey, 1949). Because our observations were proportions, they were transformed on the basis of an arcsine transformation (Winer, 1971, p. 399).

RESULTS

The impact of the experimental factors

Tables 6 and 7 portray, respectively, the results of the analysis of variance and the table of means

TABLE 5. $3 \times 3 \times 2 \times N$ Split-plot design

Factor A – Occupational Group	Factor B – Accounting Treatments	Factor C – Investment Strategy	
		C_1 (Income)	C_2 (Capital Gains)
a_1 – accountants	b_1 – conventional	S_{11}	S_{11}
	b_2 – footnote	S_{12}	S_{12}
	b_3 – total	S_{13}	S_{13}
a_2 – bankers	b_1 – conventional	S_{14}	S_{14}
	b_2 – footnote	S_{22}	S_{22}
	b_3 – total	S_{23}	S_{23}
a_3 – students	b_1 – conventional	S_{31}	S_{31}
	b_2 – footnote	S_{32}	S_{32}
	b_3 – total	S_{33}	S_{33}

TABLE 6. Analysis of Variance

	Source	df	SS	MS	F	Significant level
		Analysis of variance (2 Between, 1 Within)				
Subjects		224	199.730			
A.	Occupational group	2	5.303	2.651	3.200	*
B.	Accounting treatments	2	6.196	3.098	3.739	*
AB.		4	9.245	9.311	2.789	*
E(AB).		216	178.986	0.879		
C.	Investment strategy	1	17.036	17.036	33.468	*
AC.		2	7.539	3.769	7.405	*
BC.		2	5.492	2.746	5.395	*
ABC.		4	5.318	1.379	2.612	*
E(ABC).		216	109.947	0.509		
W.		225	145.311			
Total		450	1056.326			

*Significant at $a = 0.05$.

TABLE 7. Table of means

$A\ B\ C$

Summary Table

		C1	C2
B_1	B_1	1.561	1.499
A_1	B_2	1.849	0.930
	B_3	1.912	0.631
	B_1	2.210	1.959
A_2	B_2	1.486	1.355
	B_3	1.630	1.334
	B_1	1.496	1.465
A_3	B_2	1.609	1.474
	B_3	1.788	1.394

testing the implicit null hypothesis of "no effect" for the three experimental factors and their interactions. All main effects and interactions effects were significant at a 0.05 level leading to the acceptance of this study's first hypothesis namely:

(1) The accounting treatment of pollution control expenditures (conventional, footnote, or total treatment) had a significant impact on the subject's investment decision ($F=3.200$, $p=0.05$).

(2) The three subject types, belonging to three different occupational groups, did differ significantly in terms of their investment decision ($F=3.739$, $p=0.05$).

(3) The investment strategy of the subject (investing for dividend income or investing for capital gains) was a significant determinant of the subject's investment decision ($F=33.468$, $p=0.05$).

In fact, when interactions are significant, additional insight into the effects of factor treatment can be achieved by analyzing simple main effects. Results of these simple main effects are illustrated in Table 8. In what follows, the most salient relationships are discussed:

(1) The accounting treatment for pollution control had a significant impact on the subject's investment decision when the bankers were investing for income ($F=3.487$, $p=0.05$) and when the accountants and bankers were investing for capital gains ($F=8.837$, $p=0.05$; $F=3.202$, $p=0.05$).

(2) The three subject types differed in their investment decisions when given the conventional treatment and investing for income ($F=7.299$, $p=0.05$) and when given any accounting treatment and investing for capital gains ($F=3.546$, $p=0.05$; $F=3.438$, $p=0.05$; $F=6.491$, $p=0.05$).

(3) The subject's investment strategy had a significant impact on his or her investment decision in all cases.

The impact of the background and perceptual variables

For better interpretation the fourth hypothesis was divided as follows:

4_a = Under the conventional treatment, the

subject's investment decision is not associated with each of the background and perceptual variables.

4_b = Under the footnote and total treatment for pollution control information, the subject's investment decision is not associated with each of the background and perceptual variables.

TABLE 8. Summary of simple main effects*

Effects	df	SS	MS	F	Significance
AB at c_1	4	9.467	2.367	3.658	†
B at $a_1 c_1$	2	1.980	0.990	1.941	
B at $a_2 c_1$	2	6.525	3.262	3.487	†
B at $a_3 c_1$	2	0.569	0.284	0.551	
A at $b_1 c_1$	2	8.677	4.339	7.299	†
A at $b_2 c_1$	2	1.672	0.836	1.692	
A at $b_3 c_1$	2	0.995	0.497	0.562	
AB at c_2	4	5.095	1.274	1.844	
B at $a_1 c_2$	2	8.793	4.396	8.837	†
B at $a_2 c_2$	2	5.523	2.761	3.202	†
B at $a_3 c_2$	2	0.144	0.072	0.098	
A at $b_1 c_2$	2	5.155	2.578	3.546	†
A at $b_2 c_2$	2	4.552	2.276	3.438	†
A at $b_3 c_2$	2	9.168	4.584	6.491	†
BC at a_1	2	9.758	4.879	10.893	†
B at $a_1 c_1$	2	1.980	0.990	1.941	
B at $a_1 c_2$	2	8.793	4.396	8.837	†
C at $a_1 b_1$	1	56.250	56.250	62.27	†
C at $a_1 b_2$	1	52.250	52.250	55.70	†
C at $a_1 b_3$	1	54.500	54.500	60.50	†
BC at a_2	2	0.181	0.090	0.164	
B at a_2	2	13.477	6.732	5.283	†
C at a_2	1	1.917	1.917	3.480	†
BC at a_3	2	0.873	0.436	0.826	
B at a_3	2	0.304	0.152	0.243	
C at a_3	1	1.308	1.308	2.477	
AC at b_1	2	0.352	0.176	0.464	†
A at b_1	2	11.267	5.634	6.100	
C at b_1	2	0.501	0.501	1.320	†
AC at b_2	2	5.272	2.636	5.103	
A at $b_2 c_1$	2	1.672	0.836	1.692	†
A at $b_2 c_2$	2	4.552	2.276	3.438	†
C at $a_1 b_2$	1	52.250	52.250	55.70	†
C at $a_2 b_2$	1	42.25	42.25	46.60	†
C at $a_3 b_2$	1	51.25	51.25	54.60	†
AC at b_3	2	7.587	3.793	5.823	†
A at $c_1 b_3$	2	0.995	0.497	0.562	
A at $c_2 b_3$	2	9.168	4.584	6.491	†
C at $a_1 b_3$	1	54.500	54.500	60.50	†
C at $a_2 b_3$	1	64.100	64.100	71.100	†
C at $a_3 b_3$	1	58.100	58.100	64.050	†

*A = Professional group
B = Accounting treatment
C = Investment strategy
a_1 = Bankers
a_2 = Accountants
a_3 = Students

b_1 = Conventional treatment
b_2 = Footnote treatment
b_3 = Total treatment
c_1 = Investment for income
c_2 = Investment for capital gains

† Significant at = 0.05.

The problem put by these two hypotheses is to determine the degree of association between two sets of attributes. The first attribute is the investment decision as measured by the choice made by the subject between Jabel and Abel in terms of the higher percentage invested in both firms. In other words if the subject elected to invest a higher percentage of the funds in a given company that company was considered his investment choice. The second attribute is the level of the background variable or the extent of agreement with a perceptual variable. The degree of association between these two sets of attributes is measured by the contingency coefficient C (Siegel, 1956, p. 197). In what follows the most salient relationships are discussed:

(1) With one exception, no significant relationships were found between the investment decision and the different levels of each of the background variables under the conventional accounting treatment. The only exception involves the association between the number of college level courses in accounting and finance and the conventional accounting treatment. (C=0.3164, p=0.05)

(2) However, with two exceptions, significant relationships were found between the investment decision and the different levels of each of the background variables under both the footnote and the total treatment. The investment decisions under the footnote treatment and the total treatment were significantly associated with the age of the participant (C=0.1540, p=0.05; C=0.3028, p=0.05), the degree of acceptance of the disclosure of abatement costs of pollution to improve the investment decisions (C=0.3510, p=0.05; C=0.2006, p=0.05), the number of years engaged in evaluating financial statements (C=0.3244, p=0.05; C=0.2305, p=0.05), the importance of the issue of the ecological crisis (C=0.3384, p=0.05, C=0.2561, p=0.05), the trade-off between pollution control and profitability (C=0.1911, p=0.05; C=0.4910, p=0.001). The two exceptions involve the absence of association between on one part the number of college level courses taken in accounting and finance and the degree to which portfolio selection is an important part of the subject's job and the two accounting treatments.

More explicitly the older the participant, and the higher the number of years evaluating financial statements, the higher the degree of acceptance of the disclosure of pollution abatement expendi-

tures, the greater the awareness of the "ecological crisis", the higher the acceptance of a trade-off between pollution control and profitability and the greater the awareness of the impact of the disclosure of pollution expenditures on the reports.

DISCUSSION

In this experiment, the forms of the disclosure of socio-economic accounting information, namely the abatement costs of pollution, were investigated as accounting techniques which may influence the investment decisions of potential users. The theoretical rationale stemming from the linguistic relativity paradigm in accounting was that in general the accounting techniques may tend to facilitate or render more difficult various (non-linguistic) managerial behaviors on the part of the users, and that in this particular context the investment decision effects from different professional groups using alternative socio-economic accounting information will be different.

The results show that in general the various accounting treatments for pollution control information had an effect on the investment decision. Their effect was mostly significant with the bankers under any investment policy. The accountants reacted to the information only when investing for capital gains, while the students did not perceive the importance of the abatement cost information at all. The bankers seemed to be more aware of the importance of accounting information and specific information. The students and the accountants do not yet seem to perceive the full importance of the abatement costs information on the reports. This result may be due to:

(a) the fact that the bankers are held responsible for any resource allocation and this shows their tendency to adopt a more socially oriented investment attitude;

(b) the difference in the degree of expertise in investment analysis between the bankers on one side and the accountants and the students on the other side.

In fact, membership in a professional group had an effect on the investment decision. In particular, it had an effect when the investors were presented with conventional treatments under any investment policy. When presented with any form of disclosure of abatement costs information, the effect was dependent on the investment policy of the investor. The effect was only significant when the participants were investing for capital gains. It appears that the investors from any professional group become more aware of the importance of abatement costs information only when investing for capital gains.

In general the investment policy of the participant had an effect on the investment decision of all the participants from any of the professional groups represented. However, the investment policy did have a strong effect only when the reports disclosed in any form the abatement costs information. It appears that the investment policies of the investors lead to different investment decisions with additional disclosure on the abatement costs of pollution.

Besides the membership in a professional group, the type of accounting treatment for pollution control presented and the investment policy, the investors' behavior was associated with other demographic and perceptual variables.

Abatement cost information ought to be disclosed completely in the financial statements. Its impact on the investors' behavior has been significant in this experiment, especially for bankers. The additional disclosure of pollution cost information has been used to improve the investment decision, especially for investment for capital gains by most of the participants in this behavioral field experiment.

A field experiment such as the one above is subject to numerous methodological and environmental limitations. The relative accuracy of any of the information in this study cannot be discussed without realization of these limitations.

First, the sample taken was limited to the officers of the Syracuse commercial banks, the members of the NAA Chapter of Syracuse, and the accounting and finance students of Syracuse University. A more representative sample could be taken from the membership list of the Financial Analysts Federation where participants would only include individuals engaged in stock evaluation work.

Second, the results obtained from this experiment are presented as additional evidence that the addition of pollution control information constitutes an improvement of accounting disclosure.

SUMMARY AND CONCLUSIONS

This study was motivated by the general interest for the disclosure of socio-economic accounting information. The purpose of the paper was to report the results of a field experiment testing the effects and interactions of three factors: subject type; accounting treatment of socio-economic accounting information; and investment strategy. The rationale from the linguistic relativity paradigm is that the accounting treatments of socio-economic accounting affect individual investment decisions in a way which depend on the professional group of the user and the investment strategy adopted.

The findings attest to the general relevance of socio-economic accounting information for the bankers under any investment strategy, and for the accountants only under an investment strategy focusing on capital gains. The significant interaction effects between the three examined factors provide a warning about any generalizations to be derived from a similar field experiment. In other words, the informational content of any new information, e.g., socio-economic accounting information, is to be ascertained in terms of its relations to relevant environmental variables. In this study, investment for capital gains and membership to the banking profession appeared most associated with the use of the socio-economic accounting information.

BIBLIOGRAPHY

Abdel-khalik, A. R., The Effect of Aggregating Accounting Reports on the Quality of the Lending Decision: An Empirical Investigation, *Empirical Research in Accounting: Selected Studies* (1973), pp. 104–138.

Ackerman, R., How Companies Respond to Social Demands, *Harvard Business Review* (July–August, 1973), pp. 88–98.

American Accounting Association, Committee on Accounting for Social Performance, Report of the Committee on Accounting for Social Performance, *The Accounting Review*, Supplement to Vol. LI (1976).

American Accounting Association, Committee on Environmental Effects of Organizational Behavior, Report of the Committee on Environmental Effects of Organizational Behavior, *The Accounting Review*, Supplement to Vol. XLIII (1973), pp. 73–119.

American Accounting Association, Committee on Measurement of Social Costs, Report of the Committee on Measurement on Social Costs, *The Accounting Review*, Supplement to Vol. XLIX (1974), pp. 98–113.

American Accounting Association, Committee on Measures of Effectiveness for Social Programs, Report of the Committee on Measures of Effectiveness for Social Programs, *The Accounting Review*, Supplement to Vol. XLVII (1972), pp. 336–396.

American Accounting Association, Committee on Nonfinancial Measures of Effectiveness, Report of the Committee on Nonfinancial Measures of Effectiveness, *The Accounting Review*, Supplement to Vol. XLVI (1971), pp. 164–211.

American Accounting Association, Committee on Social Costs, Report of the Committee on Social Costs, *The Accounting Review*, Supplement to Vol. XLX (1975), pp. 50–89.

American Institute of Certified Public Accountants, Report of the Study Group on the Objectives of Financial Statements, *Objectives of Financial Statements* (American Institute of Certified Public Accountants, 1973).

Barrett, M. E., Accounting for Intercorporate Investments: A Behavioral Field Study, *Empirical Research in Accounting: Selected Studies 1971*, Supplement to Volume 9 of the *Journal of Accounting Research*, pp. 50–92.

Beams, F. A. & Fertig, Paul E., Pollution Control Through Social Cost Conversion, *The Journal of Accounting* (November, 1971), pp. 37–42.

Belkaoui, A. & Cousineau, Alain, Accounting Information, Nonaccounting Information, and Common Stock Perception, *The Journal of Business* (July, 1977), pp. 334–342.

Belkaoui, A., The Accounting Treatments of Pollution Costs, *The Certified General Accountant* (August, 1973), pp. 19–21.

Belkaoui, A., The Impact of the Disclosure of the Environmental Effects of Organizational Behavior on the Market, *Financial Management* (Winter, 1976), pp. 26–31.

Belkaoui, A., The Whys and Wherefores of Measuring Externalities, *The Certified General Accountant* (January, 1975), pp. 29–32.

Belkaoui, A., Linguistic Relativity in Accounting, *Accounting, Organizations and Society* (Vol. 3, No. 2, 1978), pp. 97–104.

Belkaoui, A., The Interprofessional Linguistic Communication of Accounting Concepts: An Experiment in Sociolinguistics, *Journal of Accounting Research* (Fall, 1980), Forthcoming.

Beresford, D., *Compilation of Social Measurement Disclosure in Fortune 500 Annual Reports* (Ernst & Ernst, 1973).

Bowman, Edward H., Corporate Social Responsibility and the Investor, *Journal of Contemporary Business* (Winter, 1973).

Bragdon, Joseph H., Jr. & Marlin, John, Is Pollution Profitable?, *Risk Management* (April, 1972).

Bruns, W. Jr., Inventory Valuation and Management Decisions, *The Accounting Review* (April, 1965), pp. 345–357.

Bylinski, G., The Mounting Bill for Pollution Control, *Fortune* (July, 1971), p. 130.

Dopuch, N. & Ronen, J., The Effects of Alternative Inventory Valuation Methods – An Experimental Study, *Journal of Accounting Research* (Autumn, 1973), pp. 191–211.

Dyckman, T. R., Gibbins, M. & Swieringa, R. J., The Impact of Experimental and Survey Research, in Abdel-khalik, A. R. and Keller, T. F. (eds.), *The Impact of Accounting Research on Practice and Disclosure* (Duke University Press, 1978).

Dyckman, T. R., The Effects of Alternative Accounting Techniques on Certain Management Decisions, *Journal of Accounting Research* (Spring, 1964), pp. 91–107.

Dyckman, T. R., On the Effects of Earnings – Trend, Size and Inventory Valuation Procedures in Evaluating a Business Firm, in Jaedicke, R., Ijiri, Y. and Nielson, O. (eds.), *Research in Accounting Measurement* (American Accounting Association, 1966), pp. 175–185.

Flias, N., The Effects of Human Asset Statements on the Investment Decision: An Experiment, *Empirical Research in Accounting: Selected Studies* (1972), pp. 241–266.

Estes, Ralph W., Socio-Economic Accounting and External Diseconomies, *The Accounting Review* (April, 1972).

Flamholtz, E. & Cook, E., Connotative Meaning and its Role in Accounting Change: A Field Study, *Accounting, Organizations and Society* (October, 1978), pp. 115–139.

Haried, A., The Semantic Dimensions of Financial Statements, *Journal of Accounting Research* (Autumn, 1973).

Haried, A., Measurement of Meaning in Financial Reports, *Journal of Accounting Research* (Spring, 1972).

Hendricks, J., The Impact of Human Resource Accounting Information on Stock Investment Decisions: An Empirical Study, *The Accounting Review* (April, 1976), pp. 292–305.

Hofstedt, T. R., Some Behavioral Parameters of Financial Analysis, *The Accounting Review* (October, 1972), pp. 679–692.

Jain, Tribhowan N., Alternative Methods of Accounting and Decision Making: A Psycholinguistic Analysis, *The Accounting Review* (January, 1973), pp. 95–104.

Jensen, R., An Experimental Design for the Study of Effects of Accounting Variations in Decision Making, *Journal of Accounting Research* (Autumn, 1966), pp. 224–238.

Lewellen, W. G., Lease, R. C. & Schlarbaum, G. C., Patterns of Investment Strategy and Behavior among Individual Investors, *The Journal of Business* (July, 1977), pp. 296–333.

Livingstone, J. L., A Behavioral Study of Tax Allocation in Electric Utility Regulations, *The Accounting Review* (July, 1967), pp. 544–552.

Longstreth, B. & Rosenbloom, H. David, *Social Responsibility and the Institutional Investor* (Praeger, 1973).

McGraw-Hill Publication Co., *Annual McGraw-Hill Survey of Pollution Control Expenditures* (New York, N.Y.: McGraw-Hill, 1970).

National Association of Accountants, Report of the Committee on Accounting for Corporate Social Performance, *Management Accounting* (February, 1974).

Oliver, B., The Semantic Differential: A Device for Measuring the Interprofessional Communications of Selected Accounting Concepts, *Journal of Accounting Research* (Autumn, 1974).

Ortman, R. F., The Effects on Investment Analysis of Alternative Reporting Procedure for Diversified Firms, *The Accounting Review* (April, 1975), pp. 298–304.

Report of the Study Group on *Objectives of Financial Statements* (American Institute of Certified Public Accountants, October, 1973).

Siegel, S., *Nonparametric Statistics for the Behavioral Sciences* (New York, N.Y.: McGraw-Hill, 1956).

Simon, J. G., Pavers, C. W. & Gunnemann, J. P., *The Ethical Investor* (New Haven, CT: Yale University Press, 1972).

Spicer, Barry H., Investors, Corporate Social Performance and Information Disclosure: An Empirical Study, *The Accounting Review* (January, 1978), pp. 34–111.

Tukey, J. W., One Degree of Freedom for Nonadditivity, *Biometrics*, 5 (1949), pp. 232–242.

Winer, B. J., *Statistical Principles in Experimental Design* (New York, N.Y.: McGraw-Hill, 1971), 2nd Edition.

APPENDIX   QUESTIONNAIRE

1.   Occupation
         Trust Officer   _____
         Loan Officer   _____
         Investment Officer   _____
         Senior Accountant   _____
         Junior Accountant   _____
         Broker   _____
         Other (please specify)   _____

2.   Professional Background
         Chartered Financial Analyst   _____
         Certified Public Accountant   _____
         Lawyer   _____
         M.B.A., M.S., or M.A.   _____
         Ph.D. (please specify field)   _____
         Other (please specify)   _____

3.   Age   _____

4.   The approximate number of college level courses in accounting and finance
         none   _____
         1–2   _____
         3–4   _____
         5–6   _____
         over 6   _____

5.   Would you say that portfolio selection for investors is an important part of your job?
         very important   _____
         moderately important   _____
         not important at all   _____
         don't know   _____

6.   The abatement costs of pollution should be disclosed in published financial statements in order
      to improve investment decisions.
         strongly agree   _____
         mildly agree   _____
         neutral   _____
         mildly disagree   _____
         strongly disagree   _____

7.   Approximate number of years you have been engaged in evaluating financial statements
      _____

8.   How important to you is the issue of "ecological crisis"?
         very important   _____
         moderately important   _____
         not important at all   _____
         don't know   _____

9.   A company should spend money on pollution if it can afford it in the sense of NOT reducing
      its profitability.
         strongly agree   _____
         mildly agree   _____
         neutral   _____
         mildly disagree   _____
         strongly disagree   _____

3

SOCIOLINGUISTIC THESIS
AND ACCOUNTING

INTRODUCTION

The study of language as a communication form is important for an understanding of human behavior. In general, the study of language has focused on four areas: structural linguistics, developmental psycholinguistics, linguistic relativity, and sociolinguistics. *Structural linguistics* is devoted to the process of acquisition of language and the identification of formal structural properties.

Developmental psycholinguistics deals with formulating language acquisition and use as a special instance of a more general cognitive functioning. The main objective is to acquire a better understanding of the human thought process by an examination of grammatical organization and transformation.

Linguistic relativity deals with the role of language in our conception of the world. In brief, our worldview, as speakers of a given language, forces us to interpret the world through the unique grammatical forms and categories that the language supplies.[1]

Sociolinguistics, or the sociology of language, is concerned with the existence of different linguistic repertoires in a single language associated with different social strata and corresponding to different social behaviors. This is the study of the characteristics of language varieties, the characteristics of the functions, and the characteristics of their speakers as these three constantly interact and change one another within a speech community. Sociolinguistics is the subject of this chapter.

Accordingly, this chapter explores the nature of sociolinguistics in general and the deficit hypothesis in particular and shows its application to accounting in terms of explaining the existence of various accounting repertoires used by different professional groups, the schism in accounting, and the different performance of experts and novices on experimental tasks.

NATURE OF SOCIOLINGUISTICS

The role of language in defining communities and social relationships is the realm of sociolinguistics. Sociolinguistics assumes that the socialization of individual consciousness and the social molding of personality are largely determined by language. Different languages as well as different dialects contribute acceptable linguistic systems to be judged as useful to their own speakers and to the needs of these speakers. As stated by Trudgill:

It follows that value judgments concerning the correctness and purity of linguistic varieties are *social* rather than linguistic. There is nothing at all inherent in non-standard varieties which makes them inferior. Any apparent inferiority is due only to their association with speakers from under-privileged, low-status groups.[2]

Sociolinguistics examines the interrelationships between these languages and society, looking at language as a social and cultural phenomenon. It is interested in explaining why people speak differently in different social contexts and in identifying the social functions of language and the way it is used to convey social meaning.[3] The discipline deals with the interaction between two aspects of human behavior—the use of language and the social organization of behavior. The focus is on the generally accepted social organization of language usage within speech communities. Known as the *descriptive sociology of language*, this focus seeks to discover who speaks or writes what linguistic codes, to whom, when, and why. A second focus, the *dynamic sociology of language*, is concerned with the discovery of the determinants explaining changes in the social organization of language use and behavior. As stated by Fishman:

Regardless of the nature of language varieties involved in the verbal repertoire of a speech community (occupational, social class, regional, etc.) and regardless of the interaction between them (for initially regional dialects may come to represent social varieties as well, and vice versa) descriptive sociology of language seeks to disclose their linguistic and functional characteristics and to determine how much of the entire speech community's verbal repertoire is available to various smaller interaction networks within that community, since the entire verbal repertoire may be more extensive than the verbal repertoire controlled by subgroups within that community. Dynamic sociology of language on the other hand seeks to determine how changes in the fortunes and interactions of net-works of speakers alter the ranges (complexity) of their verbal repertoire.[4]

What both foci imply is the existence in any speech community of verbal varieties of languages, or "verbal repertoires." Thus, the sociology of language attempts to explain the underlying causes of the verbal rep-ertoire in any speech community. The implication of the above statement is that within each language there are linguistic codes that play an im-portant role as a mediator of the perceptual cognitive processes in defin-ing the social environment. The focus may be on the individual in small, informal intergroup interactions, such as in microsociolinguistics, or on interaction at the large intergroup level, such as in macrosociolinguistics. In both cases, the goal of the sociolinguist is "to show the systematic covariance of linguistic and social structure—and perhaps even to show a causal relationship in one direction or the other."[5] Social structure is seen as determining language use.

DIMENSIONS OF SOCIOLINGUISTICS

Sociolinguistics aims to determine the causes behind language varia-tions. The most salient causes have been associated with ethnicity, gen-der, social class, and regions.

Ethnicity has been used in sociolinguistics to explain the existence of different linguistic repertoires or speech communities. Basically, various ethnic groups use a distinctive language associated with their ethnic identity. They resort to the use of their own linguistic repertoire to signal their ethnicity. Black English in the United States is a good example of the existence of a distinct linguistic repertoire used by some Afro-Americans as a distinct way of differentiating themselves from the ma-jority group. Wardhaugh presents an interesting assessment:

The particular combination of linguistic differences between blacks and whites and the social changes which are occurring in the race relationships in society are likely to lead to linguistic change. The setting seems almost ideal. The one factor that makes the situation less ideal is the pervasiveness of the black-white color issue; if linguistic variation and change are closely related to social variation and change, any barrier to the latter must also affect the former in some way.[6]

Gender has also been used in sociolinguistics to explain the existence of different speech communities. Basically, men and women report to different linguistic repertoires because different social attributes and be-haviors are expected from men and women. As stated by Trudgill:

Sex varieties, then, are the result of different social attitudes towards the behaviors of men and women, and of the attitudes men and women themselves consequently have to language as a social symbol.[7]

The sex difference in language may be, of course, reflecting social status or power differences in those cases of hierarchical communities when men in each of the levels of hierarchy are more powerful than women. Their sex differences in language are also very much evident in corporate America, which leave women at a disadvantage, because women are less likely than men to have learned to blow their own horns.[8]

Social class has also been used in sociolinguistics to explain the existence of different speech communities. Basically, there are social class differences in the use of standard language. A good example is the existence of social-class differences in phonological usage despite common norms of correctness[9] and the frequent presence of stigmatized features in lower-class speech.[10] As stated by Weener, "Children from lower class homes or minority ethnic groups usually speak a distinctive dialect form, and display retarded development on measures of language skills and general cognitive functioning."[11]

Sometimes these social-class differences translate into *regional* differences. As stated by Edwards: "Regional dialects come to be associated with 'low' levels of occupation and education, and so to elicit stereotypes of their users."[12]

THE DEFICIT HYPOTHESIS

Early references to social-class differences in the use of language include Fries's study of "American English" and the analysis of its "standard" and "vulgar" forms.[13] He concludes:

Over and over again . . . it appeared that the differences between the language of the educated and those with little education did not lie primarily in the fact that the former used one set of forms and the latter an entirely different set . . . the actual deviation of the language of the uneducated from Standard English seemed much less than is usually assumed. . . . The most striking difference lies in the fact that Vulgar English seems essentially poverty-stricken. It uses less of the resources of the language, and a few forms are used frequently.[14]

Another reference is a study by Schatzman and Strauss[15] on the use of narratives by ten "upper-class" and ten "lower-class" people whom they questioned after a disaster caused by a tornado. The results showed the verbal inadequacy of the lower class, because their narratives were relatively unorganized. These studies had a particular influence on the deficit hypothesis. Basil Bernstein played a major role in the formulation of the deficit hypothesis. He started with the general principle that the speech habits of lower-class groups with little social influence differ from those of middle-class groups who at the same time have assured, powerful, and influential positions in addition to their material and intellectual privileges.[16] Basically, the deficit hypothesis arises from the different linguistic repertoires of lower-class and middle-class groups that limit the achievement of adequate social success by lower-class groups. The linguistic repertoires of lower-class groups do not allow them to achieve the same social and material privileges of middle-class groups. While the linguistic relativity implies a dependency relationship between language and thought, on one hand, the deficit hypothesis implies a dependency relationship between language and social structure. The essential argument of Bernstein is that the form of a social relationship acts selectively on the linguistic code used.[17] It led him in his early writing to distinguish between a "public" language of the lower class and a "formal" language of the middle class.[18]

The distinction evolved with the characterization of the public language as the restricted speech code and the formal language as the elaborated speech code.[19] An elaborated code allows the speaker to put his message in a verbally explicit form that requires a high level of verbal planning. A restricted code arises whenever speech is refracted through a common cultural identity. Pure forms of a restricted code involve ritualistic codes of communication such as relationships regulated by protocol, types of religious services, cocktail party routines, some storytelling techniques.[20] A speaker is led by different social relationships to adapt his or her planning procedures and to select one of the linguistic codes. The codes are planning procedures leading to linguistic choices. They exist only in the mind, at the psychological level. As stated by Bernstein:

In the case of an elaborated code. the speaker will select from a wide range of syntactic alternatives and so it will not be easy to make an accurate assessment of the organizing elements he uses at any one time. However, with a restricted code, the range of alternatives, syntactic alternatives, is considerably reduced and so it is much more likely that prediction is possible. In the case of a restricted code, the vocabulary is drawn from a narrow range; this in itself is no indication that the code is a restricted one.

If a speaker is oriented towards using an elaborated code, then the code through its planning procedures, will facilitate the speaker in his attempt to put into words his purposes, his discrete intent, his unique experience in a verbally explicit form. If a speaker is moving towards a restricted code, then this code, through its planning procedures, will *not* facilitate the verbal expansion of the individual's discrete intent.[21]

The choice of the different speeches is argued first to be determined by membership in a particular social class. It is also argued to be determined by the range of alternatives that a role system makes available to individuals for the verbal realization of different meanings.[22] A role system that reduces this range of alternatives is a closed type, while a role system that permits a range of alternatives is an open one. Elaborated codes are more compatible with open role systems, while restricted codes are more compatible with closed systems. As explained by Bernstein:

In the area where the role system is open, novel meanings are likely to be encouraged and a complex conceptual order explored. In the area where the role system is closed, novel meanings are likely to be discouraged and the conceptual order limited. Where the role system is of the closed type, verbal meanings are likely to be assigned; the individual (or child) steps into the meaning system and leaves it relatively undisturbed. Where the role system is of the open type, the individual is more likely to achieve meaning on his own terms, and here there is the potential of disturbing or changing the pattern of received meanings. We can begin to see that in the area where the role system is open, there is an induced motivation to explore, to actively seek out, and to extend meanings. By contrast, where the role is closed there is little induced motivation to explore and create novel meanings.[23]

THE SOCIOLINGUISTIC THESIS IN ACCOUNTING

Language, Trust, and the Public Accounting Profession

Accounting institutions have a privilege status in society due to their appropriation of their self-regulatory power[24, 25] and to the existence of incentives to maintain a good reputation.[26] As a result, society trusts the public accounting profession.[27] The trust works differently for informed and uninformed users. Because they may have been trained in accounting or a related discipline, informed users, including management and insiders, understand the language used by accounting professionals. Uninformed users, however, may not be trained in the language of accounting, forcing the auditor profession to rely on various impression management techniques to create a schema of the trustworthy auditor.[28] As stated by Neu:

In other words, this schema should convince uninformed users that auditors can be trusted to behave in a manner that is, (1) moral (or just), (2) neutral with respect to distributional issues, (3) involves the exercise of significant expertise, and (4) help solve the nation's problems.[29]

Basically, the accounting profession faces two separate situations: one involving informed users, using similar linguistic repertoires and thereby capable of detecting any breach of trust, and one involving uninformed users, not versed in the same accounting linguistic repertoire used by accountants. As a result, three outcomes are possible:

1. Auditors are more likely to breach the trust of uninformed users than the trust of informed users when conflicts arise,
2. Uninformed users are unlikely to find out about these breaches,
3. Uninformed users have no choice but to trust the public accounting profession.[30]

The whole issue of trust and the accounting profession may be viewed using the sociolinguistic thesis whereby both the accountants and the informed users exercise a knowledge of the same accounting language and the uninformed users do not. The sharing of the same linguistic repertoire by the informed users and the accounting professionals makes it difficult for the accountant to breach the trust of the informed. In the case of the uninformed user, the accounting profession uses language and other symbolic actions to enact and sanction behavior that shows their knowledge and to secure the trust of the "powerless" uninformed user. They do this by creating schemata emphasizing their ethical and trustworthy nature. As stated by Luscombe:

Look behind the negative, green-eye shaded stereotype—uncreative, introverted, pedantic, obsessed with accuracy to the last penny—and you have the positive image of a professional with the utmost integrity who never makes a statement, particularly one for third-party use, without having taken the greatest care to ensure that the statement is objective and appropriate. That's the image that has given our clients a deep-rooted trust in the credibility and reliability of our services.[31]

The schemata also emphasize the reliance on a specialized, sophisticated linguistic repertoire that conveys their understanding of a specific technology, problems, and solutions.

Linguistic Codes for Accounting Professional Groups

The application of the sociolinguistics thesis to accounting suggests the existence of several varieties of accounting language, or "repertoires." The implication of the above statement is that within accounting there are linguistic codes that play an important role as a mediator of the perceptual cognitive processes used in defining the social environment. Basically, the affiliation of users and preparers with different professional organization communities with their distinct interaction networks may create different accounting language repertoires. Accounting from different professional groups may use different linguistic codes because of different organizational constraints and objectives. At worst, a confounding lack of communication may emerge. Based on this theoretical analysis, Belkaoui assumed that various professional affiliations in accounting create different linguistic repertoires or codes for intragroup communications and/or intergroup communications; those, in turn, lead to a differential understanding of accounting and social relationships.[32] This led to the following hypothesis to be tested:

The perceptions of accounting concepts as measured by the individual weights assigned by the participants to the dimensions of the common perceptual space are a function of the professional accounting group affiliation.[33]

A selected set of accounting concepts was subjected to analysis using multidimensional scaling techniques to evaluate the intergroup differences between three groups of users. A sociolinguistic construct was used to justify the possible lack of consensus on the meaning of accounting concepts. There were intergroup perceptual differences of accounting concepts on both the conjunctive and disjunctive dimensions and no difference on the relational dimension. The result implies that the meanings of accounting concepts do vary in the manner with which they can be recognized, grasped, or understood by the users. This result allowed the verification of the existence of different linguistic codes in accounting used by members of different accounting professional groups. The whole study is reprinted in the Appendix to Chapter 3.

Linguistic Codes and Experts vs. Novices

With the increasing focus on capturing experts' knowledge structures, various studies have examined expert-novice differences in judgment/ decision making.[34, 35, 36] The expert versus novice knowledge structures research in other domains than accounting yielded the following results on experts:

1. They recall large chunks of information,

2. They recall more information,

3. They possess superior categorization of information,

4. They produce good abstract representation of information,

5. They produce more cohesive representation of information,

6. They show better clusters of presented information, and

7. They show superior inferential capability.[37]

The research on expert versus novice in accounting yielded the following results on experts:

1. They rely on hypotheses, rules of thumb, structured checklists, or standard lists of questions to guide information search,
2. They build an overall picture, or develop a "feeling" for the task based on prior knowledge,
3. They search for contradictory evidence and consistently focus on potential contradictions,
4. They integrate both supporting and contradicting evidence to zero in on underlying problems,
5. They organize the wide-ranging incoming information into large chunks of information,
6. They respond to the deeper features of information as a result of well-developed schemas,
7. They recall more information,
8. They cluster the wide-ranging incoming information into proper categories,
9. They verbalize more words in processing information,
10. They engage in less information processing time,
11. They exhibit mixed evidence of interactive cue processing,
12. They show different frequency distributions of decisions from novices,
13. They show higher levels of confidence in predictions/decisions,
14. Their decisions are not affected by verbalization,
15. Their judgments are more likely to suffer from conjunction fallacy, and
16. Their judgments differ significantly from novices in unstructured and semi-structured tasks.[38]

While not specifically investigated, a sociolinguistic thesis could have explained most of these results. More specifically, experts used a different linguistic code from novices because of their higher familiarity with the tasks and their linguistic requirements. As a result of the use of different linguistic repertoires, the experts' performance on all the tasks will be different from those of the novices.

Linguistic Codes and the Schism in Accounting

The situation in accounting research has drastically improved over the years. Witness the following description of the situation made on December 20, 1923, in an address to the American Association of University Instructors in Accounting, made by Henry Rand Hatfield:

I am sure that all of our colleagues look upon accounting as an intruder, a Saul among the prophets, a pariah whose very presence detracts somewhat from the sanctity of the academic walls. It is true that we ourselves speak of the science of accounts, or the art of accounting, even of the philosophy of accounts. But accounting is, alas, only a pseudo-science unrecognized by J. McKeen Cattel; its products are displayed neither in the salon, nor in the national academy; we find it discussed by neither realist, idealist, or phenomenalist. The humanists look down on us as being who dabble in the sordid figures of dollars and cents instead of toying with infinities and searching for the illusive soul of things; the scientists and technologists despise us as able only to record rather than perform deeds.[39]

Needless to say, the situation has changed in favor of a dynamic research agenda, as evidenced by the transformation of accounting into a full-fledged "normal science" with competing paradigms striving for dominance. Accounting research is grounded in a common set of assumptions about social science and society and has generated a healthy debate about how to enrich and extend our understanding of accounting in practice.

The intellectual boundaries of accounting research are constantly expanding, with different approaches used to uncover different aspects of accounting problems. The end result has been a "renaissance" of accounting research. As stated by Antle:

Accounting institutions raise a stunning variety of questions and issues that defy traditional intellectual boundaries. Our problems have psychological, sociological, economic and political dimensions. If you scan our scholarly journals, you will see this reflected in our work. We have articles on the psychology of expert information processing, the sociology of the auditing profession, the theoretical and empirical economic effects of accounting choices, and the politics of accounting regulation. The breadth of knowledge required to be a true accounting scholar is breathtaking, humbling and frustrating.[40]

While the situation is very favorable to all those involved in research and the creation of knowledge, it does not seem to be beneficial to those involved in the real world of accounting practice. It has in fact resulted in a schism between accounting practitioners and academics.[41] A good characterization of the schism follows:

Too many academic researchers seem to have relatively little interest in policy issues and seem content with their interest in modeling and number-crunching on a grand scale. For the last quarter century academics have pursued research activities that practitioners have found generally irrelevant to their needs.

Some assert that on the one hand academic researchers are more comfortable manipulating computerized data banks and that on the other hand practitioners have great reluctance in permitting academics access to data necessary to research practice issues. These are probably valid observations, but they need not persist. Accounting firms, in particular, have been generous in their support of academics, both with endowed chairs and unrestricted research funds. Yet, they sit on a virtual gold mine of data that many in academia believe are inaccessible to them.[42]

One of the consequences of the schism in accounting is (1) a decline of the number of practitioners joining academic associations like the American Accounting Association and (2) a reluctance to participate in academic ventures. As stated by Simmons:

The cultural trend among the firms, especially at the individual office level, seems to be counter to the idea of increased participation. The increased focus seems to be on revenue producing activities. A reluctance to donate human capital back to activities that purport to advance the cause of the overall profession is uncharacteristic of the traditions of accounting firms.[43]

The dilemma of academics lies in the fact that research has not reached its potential:

Many practitioners as well as academics have complained for years that academic research in accounting has added little to the practice of accounting (read the solution of current problems). Academics, it is maintained, typically do not study the right issue (a statistical type III error). When they do study the right issue the research is seldom well executed (although the researcher perhaps should be). When the research is well done, it is often not timely (a statistical type IV error). And in the minuscule number of cases where things have been done well to this point, the researcher cleverly hides the results under bales of academic jargon designed to secure publication in an erudite academic journal rather than readership.[44]

The research failures are, therefore, disguised by the recourse to a specific linguistic code that is practically uncomprehensible to other accounting professional groups.

The failure of research efforts to contribute to practice may therefore be easily traceable to communication problems arising from the specific and difficult linguistic code used by academics. As stated by Skinner:

First, there is the problem of communication. Research and practice are almost two solitudes, each self-sufficient and self-contained. The average practitioner does not read the research literature and would not understand most of it if he did. This is not surprising since it was not written for him. . . . Various explanations are given for this state of affairs. The use of jargon and mathematical expression allows the development of ideas economically; full explanation of methodology permits reader assessment of the strength of the research findings; and, in a less kindly vein, articles written in such a fashion impress one's peers in other academic disciplines, and, increasingly as a factor in promotion and tenure decisions. Whatever the explanation, the fact is clear enough: most research findings simply do not get through to the world of practice.[45]

The solution lies in the academics trying to adapt their linguistic code to the situation to better communicate their findings to practitioners. Such a proposal was made by Abdel-Khalik as follows:

To the extent that the markets of research producers and of research users are segmented, it is not feasible to expect all research to communicate effectively to all potential users. Rather, it should be expected that academically oriented research communicate well to academicians, while other research, which may also be conducted by academicians and which deal with problems of current interest to practitioners or standard setters, should be written in such a way that interested practitioners, standard setters, and academicians can understand, critique, and appreciate it.[46]

The Rhetoric of Research

The linguistic code attributed earlier to academics and presented as a major explanation for the schism in accounting is in fact the result of the use of rhetoric in accounting research. Accounting researchers belong to specific communities sharing some values and known as "invisible colleges."[47] By belonging to invisible colleges, they share common characteristics:

Research communities can be identified in different ways: substantively (perspective taken on the accounting phenomenon); linguistically (the languages and methods in which researchers write and speak); institutionally (e.g., a particular school, a special interest section of professional organizations, specific conferences, or a particular journal in which a community publishes).[48]

The most salient characteristic is the sharing of a linguistic code. It is through this specific language that academics convey knowledge to targeted audiences that speak the same language. Accounting knowledge becomes first a specific use of a linguistic code. As stated by Arrington and Schweiker:

The indeterminacy of the "facts" of accounting relates to rhetoric through recognition of the *linguistic* character of knowledge. Accounting, as a phenomenon *in* the world, refers to a broad array of actions, institutions, histories, and consequences that are economic, political, social and moral. But accounting knowledge can only be a linguistic product, made up of words, sentences, paragraphs, symbols, numbers, equations, and statistics that organize themselves into theories, hypotheses, narratives and research papers. Language, not "facts," is thus the empirical stuff of knowledge.[49]

It is this linguistic code, the base of the rhetoric of accounting, that is used to convince other members of the invisible college to accept the results of researching legitimate knowledge. Language, or preferably rhetoric, is used to persuade and please the other members of the invisible college, editors, reviewers, and colleagues. As a result, academics find themselves adopting (1) a specific discourse to please the specific audience of peers and justify the knowledge they produced, (2) a style of writing, and (3) even a persona.[50] Accounting knowledge, as any other type of knowledge, can only be linguistic. As argued by Rorty:

Truth [or knowledge] cannot be out there—cannot exist independently of the human mind—because sentences cannot so exist, or be out there. The world is out there, but descriptions of the world are not. Only descriptions of the world can be true or false. The world on its own—unaided by the describing activities of human beings—cannot.[51]

SUMMARY AND CONCLUSIONS

Sociolinguistics recognizes the existence of different linguistic repertoires in a single language associated with different social strata, ethnic status, gender, and/or region and resulting in different linguistic behavior. This thesis is shown to be applicable to accounting by identifying specific accounting linguistic codes associated with different speech communities or professional and academic groups in accounting. The existence of different linguistic codes in accounting is responsible for (1) the existence of the schism in accounting, (2) the recourse to rhetoric in the selling of accounting research to targeted audiences of the same invisible colleges, (3) different perception of accounting concepts by members of different accounting professional groups, and (4) the different human information processing, cognitive, and task performance of novices versus experts.

NOTES

1. N. Chomsky, *Aspects of the Theory of Syntax* (Cambridge, MA: MIT Press, 1965).
2. P. Trudgill, *Sociolinguistics: An Introduction to Language and Society* (New York: Penguin Books, 1983), 20.
3. J. Holmes, *An Introduction to Sociolinguistics* (Harlow Essex, United Kingdom: Longman Group UK Limited, 1992), 1.
4. J. A. Fishman, *The Sociology of Language* (Rowley, MA: Newbury House, 1972), 5–6.
5. W. Bright, ed., *Sociolinguistics* (The Hague: Mouton, 1966), 11.
6. R. Wardhaugh, *The Contents of Language* (Rowley, MA: Newbury House, 1952), 131.
7. P. Trudgill, *Sociolinguistics: An Introduction to Language and Society*, 94.
8. Holmes, *An Introduction to Sociolinguistics*, 166.
9. W. Labov, "Phonological Correlates of Social Stratification," *American Anthropology* 66 (1964): 164–176.
10. R. Shuy, "The Sociolinguistics and Urban Language Problems," in *Lan-*

guage and Poverty: Perspectives on a Theme, ed. F. Williams (New York: Markhan, 1971), 15–26.

11. S. Weener, "Some Dialect Differences in the Recall of Verbal Messages," *Journal of Educational Psychology* 60 (1969): 194.

12. A. D. Edwards, *Language in Culture and Class* (London: Heinemann, 1976), 51.

13. C. Fries, *American English Grammar* (New York: Appleton-Century, 1940), 287.

14. Ibid.

15. L. Schatzman, and A. Strauss, "Social Class and Modes of Communication," *American Journal of Sociology* 60 (1955): 329–338.

16. B. Bernstein, "Social Structure, Language and Learning," *Educational Research* 3 (1961): 163–176.

17. Ibid.

18. B. Bernstein, "Some Sociological Determinants of Perception," *British Journal of Sociology* 9 (1958): 159–174.

19. B. Bernstein, "Elaborated and Restricted Codes: Their Origins and Some Consequences," in *Directions in Sociolinguistics: The Ethnography of Communication*, ed. J. J. Gumperz and D. Hymes (New York: Holt, Rinehart and Winston, 1972), 55–68.

20. B. Bernstein, "Elaborated and Restricted Codes: An Outline," in *Explorations in Sociolinguistics*, ed. S. Lieberson, in *International Journal of American Linguistics* 33, no. 2 (1967): 255.

21. Bernstein, "Elaborated and Restricted Codes: Their Social Origins and Some Consequences," 57.

22. B. Bernstein, "A Sociolinguistic Approach to Socialization: With Some Reference to Educability," in *Language and Poverty: Perspectives on a Theme*, ed. F. Williams (Chicago: Parkham Books, 1972), 34.

23. Ibid.

24. A. Duff, "Up to the Task," *CA Magazine* 2 (1988): 32.

25. J. McDonald, "An Incredible Experience," *CA Magazine* 2 (1988): 3.

26. D. Simunic, and M. Stein, *Product Differentiation in Auditing: Auditor Choice in the Market for Unseasoned New Issues* (Vancouver: CGA Research Foundation, 1987).

27. D. New, "Trust, Impression Management and the Public Accounting Profession," *Critical Perspectives in Accounting* 2 (1991): 295–313.

28. Ibid., 299.

29. Ibid.

30. Ibid., 306.

31. N. Luscombe, "Caring with Caution," *CA Magazine* 2 (1985): 3.

32. A. Belkaoui, "The Interprofessional Linguistic Communication of Accounting Concepts: An Experiment in Sociolinguistics," *Journal of Accounting Research* 18, no. 2 (Autumn 1980): 362–374.

33. Ibid., 364.

34. J. S. Davis, and I. Solomon, "Experience, Expertise, and Expert-Performance Research in Public Accounting," *Journal of Accounting Literature* 8 (1989): 150–164.

35. J. L. Colbert, "The Effect of Experience on Auditors' Judgments," *Journal of Accounting Literature* 8 (1989): 137–149.

36. F. Choo, "Expert-Novice Differences in Judgment/Decision Making Research," *Journal of Accounting Literature* 8 (1989): 106–136.

37. Ibid., 123–124.

38. Ibid., 115–116.

39. H. R. Hatfield, "A Historical Defense of Bookkeeping," *Journal of Accounting* (April 1924): 241.

40. R. Antle, "Intellectual Boundaries in Accounting Research," *Accounting Horizons* (June 1989): 103.

41. R. Bloom, H. G. Heymann, J. Flugleister, and M. Collins, *The Schism in Accounting* (Westport, CT: Quorum Books, 1994).

42. A. Wyatt, "Presidential Address to American Accounting Association," *Accounting Horizons* (December 1991): 103–104.

43. J. K. Simmons, "AAA Presidential Address," *Accounting Horizons* (December 1989): 88.

44. T. R. Dyckman, "Commentary on Practice to Research—'What Have You Done for Me Lately?' " *Accounting Horizons* (March 1989): 115.

45. R. M. Skinner, "The Impact of Financial Accounting Research on Policy and Practice," in *The Impact of Accounting Research on Policy and Practice*, ed. J. W. Buckley, (Reston, VA: Council of Arthur Young Professors, 1981), 29.

46. A. R. Abdel-Khalik, "How Academic Research Should Be Restructured for Impact," in Ibid., 179–180.

47. D. Grave, *Invisible Colleges* (Chicago, IL: University of Chicago Press, 1972).

48. C. E. Arrington and W. Schweiker, "The Rhetoric and Rationality of Accounting Research," *Accounting Organizations and Society* 17, no. 6 (1992): 515.

49. Ibid., 516.

50. Ibid., 515.

51. R. Rorty, *Contingency, Irony, and Solidarity* (Cambridge: Cambridge University Press, 1989), 5.

REFERENCES

Antle, R. "Intellectual Boundaries in Accounting Research." *Accounting Horizons* (June 1989): 103.

Arrington, C. E., and A. Ruxty. "Accounting, Interests, and Rationality: A Communicative Relation." *Critical Perspectives in Accounting* 2 (1991): 31–58.

Arrington, C. E., and W. Schweiker. "The Rhetoric and Rationality of Accounting Research." *Accounting Organizations and Society* 17, no. 6 (1992): 511–533.

Belkaoui, A. "The Interprofessional Linguistic Communication of Accounting Concepts: An Experiment in Sociolinguistics." *Journal of Accounting Research* 18, no. 2 (Autumn 1980): 362–374.

Bernstein, B. B. "Language and Social Class." *British Journal of Sociology* 11 (September 1960): 271.

Bernstein, B. "Social Structure, Language and Learning." *Educational Research* 3 (1961): 163–176.

Bernstein, B. B. "Linguistic Codes, Hesitation Phenomena and Intelligence." *Language and Speech* 5 (January-March 1962): 31–46.

Bernstein, B. B. "Social Class, Linguistic Codes and Grammatical Elements." *Language and Speech* 5 (October-December 1962): 221–240.

Bloom, R., H. G. Heymann, J. Flugleister, and M. Collins. *The Schism in Accounting.* Westport, CT: Quorum Books, 1994.

Bright, W. ed. *Sociolinguistics.* The Hague: Mouton, 1966.

Brown, R. *Words and Things.* New York: Free Press of Glencoe, 1958.

Chomsky, N. *Aspects of the Theory of Syntax.* Cambridge, MA: MIT Press, 1965.

Choo, F. "Expert-Novice Differences in Judgment/Decision Making Research." *Journal of Accounting Literature* 8 (1989): 106–136.

Cohen, M. *Pour une sociologie de langage.* Paris: Albin-Michel, 1956.

Colbert, J. L. "The Effect of Experience on Auditors' Judgments." *Journal of Accounting Literature* 8 (1989): 137–149.

Davis, J. S., and I. Solomon. "Experience, Expertise, and Expert-Performance Research in Public Accounting." *Journal of Accounting Literature* 8 (1989): 150–164.

Duff, A. "Up to the Task." *CA Magazine* 2 (1988): 32.

Edwards, A. D. *Language in Culture and Class.* London: Heinemann, 1976.

Fishman, J. A. *The Sociology of Language.* Rowley, MA: Newbury House, 1972.

Fries, C. *American English Grammar.* New York: Appleton-Century, 1940.

Hatfield, H. R. "A Historical Defense of Bookkeeping." *Journal of Accounting.* (April 1924): 241.

Hertzler, J. O. "Towards a Sociology of Language." *Social Forces* 32 (December 1953): 109–119.

Holmes, J. *An Introduction to Sociolinguistics.* Harlow, Essex, United Kingdom: Longman Group UK Limited, 1992.

Kohn, M. L. "Social Class and Parental Values." *American Journal of Sociology* 64 (January 1959): 337–351.

Kohn, M. L. "Social Class and the Exercise of Parental Authority." *American Sociological Review* 24 (January 1959): 352–366.

Labov, W. "Phonological Correlates of Social Stratification." *American Anthropology* 66 (1964): 164–176.

Luscombe, N. "Caring with Caution." *CA Magazine* 2 (1985): 3.

McDonald, J. "An Incredible Experience." *CA Magazine* 2 (1988): 3.

New, D. "Trust, Impression Management and the Public Accounting Profession." *Critical Perspectives in Accounting* 2 (1991): 295–313.

Pride, J. B. *The Social Meaning of Language.* London: Oxford University Press, 1971.

Schatzman, L., and A. Strauss. "Social Class and Modes of Communication." *American Journal of Sociology* 60 (1955): 329–338.

Shuy, R. "The Sociolinguistics and Urban Language Problems." In *Language and Poverty: Perspectives on a Theme,* edited by F. Williams, 15–26. New York: Markhan, 1971.

Simmons, J. K. "AAA Presidential Address." *Accounting Horizons* (December 1989): 88.

Simunic, D., and M. Stein. *Product Differentiation in Auditing: Auditor Choice in the Market for Unseasoned New Issues.* Vancouver: CGA Research Foundation, 1987.

Tanner, D. *Talking? from 9 to 5.* New York: William Morrow, 1994.

Trudgill, P. *Sociolinguistics: An Introduction to Language and Society*. New York: Penguin Books, 1983.

Wardhaugh, R. *The Contents of Language*. Rowley, MA: Newbury House, 1952.

Appendix: The Interprofessional Linguistic Communication of Accounting Concepts: An Experiment in Sociolinguistics

AHMED BELKAOUI*

Introduction

Accounting can be viewed as a language, which embodies both lexical and grammatical characteristics (Belkaoui [1978]). Within the linguistic relativity school, the role of language is emphasized as a mediator and shaper of the environment; this would imply that accounting language may predispose "users" to a given mode of perception and behavior. This explanation is congruent with the "Sapir-Whorf Hypothesis" (Belkaoui [1978], Jain [1973]). Furthermore, the affiliation of users with different professional organizations or communities with their distinct interaction networks may create different accounting language repertoires. Accountants from different professional groups may use different linguistic codes because of different organizational constraints and objectives. At worst, a confounding lack of communication may emerge. The objective of this paper is to explore the application of sociolinguistics, the sociology of language, to accounting. Specifically, three professional groups of users and producers of accounting information were selected in order to determine if there were any differences in the linguistic behavior of users and producers of accounting concepts.

The subject of this paper is not unique in accounting. Several previous

* Associate Professor, University of Ottawa. I wish to thank Professors Janice M. Belkaoui, Nicholas Dopuch, Stylianos Perrakis, and especially an anonymous reviewer for their helpful suggestions. I am also indebted to the late Professor Zbigniew A. Jordan for his insightful instructions in the philosophy of science in general and the sociology of language in particular. [Accepted for publication June 1979.]

Source: A. Belkaoui, "The Interprofessional Linguistic Communication of Accounting Concepts: An Experiment in Sociolinguistics." Journal of Accounting Research, volume 18, no. 2 (Autumn 1980): 362–374. ©, Institute of Professional Accounting 1980. Reprinted with permission.

empirical and conceptual studies have examined the semantic problems of external accounting communications (Haried [1972; 1973], Oliver [1974], Flamholtz and Cook [1978], Libby [1979], Belkaoui [1978], and Jain [1973]). The research described in this paper differs, however, in that it introduces a sociolinguistic construct to explain the different accounting linguistic behavior of the participants.

Theoretical Justification and Hypotheses

SOCIOLOGY OF LANGUAGE

Accounting can be viewed as a language because it possesses both lexical and grammatical characteristics. That is, accounting may be defined as a set of lexical or symbolic representations, such as debit, credit, etc., assigned a meaning through translation rules known as accounting terminologies and used as parameters for a set of grammatical or manipulative rules known as accounting techniques. Hence, the accounting terms are accounting vocabulary, and the accounting rules are its syntax.

Sociolinguistics assumes that the socialization of individual consciousness and the social molding of personality are largely determined by language (Luckmann [1975, p. 7]). The discipline deals with the interaction between two aspects of human behavior—the use of language and the social organization of behavior. One focus is on the generally accepted social organization of language usage within speech communities. This focus is known as the descriptive sociology of language and seeks to discover who speaks or writes what linguistic codes, to whom, when, and why. A second focus is concerned with the discovery of the determinants explaining changes in the social organization of language use and behavior. It is known as the dynamic sociology of language. What both foci imply is the existence in any speech community of several varieties of language or "verbal repertoires." Thus, the sociology of language attempts to explain the underlying causes of the verbal repertoires of a given speech community (Fishman [1970, p. 4]). The implication of the above statement is that within each language there are linguistic codes which play an important role as a mediator of the perceptual cognitive processes employed in defining the social environment (Bernstein [1958], Schatzman and Strauss [1955], Cowan [1969], Erwin-Tripp [1969], and Whiteman and Deutsch [1968]).

ACCOUNTING CONCEPTS AND INTERLINGUISTIC BEHAVIOR

Relating this to accounting, we may assume that various professional affiliations in accounting create different linguistic repertoires or codes for intragroup communications and/or intergroup communications; these, in turn, lead to a differential understanding of accounting and social relationships. This leads to the following hypothesis to be tested:

The perceptions of accounting concepts, as measured by the individual weights assigned by the participants to the dimensions of the common perceptual space, are a function of the professional accounting group affiliation.

Multidimensional techniques will be used to evaluate the differences in accounting concept perceptions by participants from different professional accounting groups. The presumed differences may be a function of certain psychological, perceptual, and background variables. The examined variables are: (1) the subject's age, (2) the number of accounting courses taken, (3) his familiarity with financial statements, and (4) his familiarity with accounting concepts.[1]

Methodology

RESEARCH DESIGN

Participants from three professional groups were presented with a questionnaire (see Appendix A) and asked to assign similarity judgments to all pairs of twelve selected accounting concepts. The similarity judgments are usually interpreted as "psychological distances" to be scaled by multidimensional scaling techniques. They are assumed to represent a type of "mental map" used by the respondent to view pairs of concepts that are near to each other as similar and pairs of concepts that are far from each other as dissimilar. If the respondent is able to provide numerical measures as similarity judgments, then multidimensional scaling techniques may be used to construct a "physical" multidimensional map whose interpoint distances most closely relate to the input data (Green and Carmone [1969]).

Two multidimensional scaling techniques, the *TORSCA* and the *INDS-CAL* models were applied to individual similarity judgments to estimate the dimensions of the common perceptual space and each individual participant's saliences. Then, regression was used to assess the relationship between saliences and the selected background variables.

ACCOUNTING CONCEPTS, PROFESSIONAL GROUPS, AND EXPERIMENTAL DECISIONS

Accounting concepts used in this study were chosen to reflect two categories of concepts related to accounting theory construction. Going concern, entity, stable monetary unit, and periodicity were chosen to represent underlying assumptions, and cost, revenue, matching, objectivity, consistency, full disclosure, materiality, and conservatism were chosen to represent generally accepted accounting principles.

---

[1] These four variables represent neither an exhaustive list nor an ideal choice of variables. For example, the grades a person received in accounting courses as opposed to the mere quantity of courses taken would be more indicative of his fluency in accounting. Future research should consider replicating this study using these and other variables.

Participants in the experiment were selected from three different groups with different levels of experience and education: accounting professors, chartered accountants, and accounting students.[2] The accounting professors were randomly chosen from the list of Canadian professors who were members of the American Accounting Association in 1975. The chartered accountants were randomly chosen from the *1975 Directory of Canadian Chartered Accountants*. The student group consisted of forty-nine students enrolled in an undergraduate accounting theory course at the University of Quebec, an institution with which the author was not associated in order to reduce the possibility of respondent-experimenter bias. One hundred questionnaires each were sent to the Canadian accounting professors and to the Canadian chartered accountants. A second mailing followed which included a cover letter emphasizing the urgency and the importance of the research project. The final sample response rates were forty-four for the Canadian professors and forty-five for the Canadian chartered accountants.

Each of the participants was asked to do the following: (1) provide information on certain background variables; (2) for each of seventeen accounting concepts and three financial statements, assign a familiarity rating according to a seven-point scale ranging from "not familiar" to "extremely familiar"; (3) for each of the pair of twelve concepts used as stimuli, assign an integer rating on a seven-point scale ranging from "very dissimilar" to "very similar"; (4) list the criteria used for assigning the similarities.

MULTIDIMENSIONAL SCALING TECHNIQUES

Two multidimensional scaling techniques were used in this study. One is the *TORSCA* nonmetric scaling routine (Young [1968]). Given $n(n-1)/2$ similarity/dissimilarity measures, the *TORSCA* program first yields a set of orthogonal coordinates for the final configuration and then estimates the dimensionality of the data. The second algorithm used is the Caroll and Chang [1970] *INDSCAL* model. In contrast to the *TORSCA* solution, the stimulus configuration obtained from the *INDSCAL* algorithm is uniquely oriented. The *INDSCAL* model assumes that all individuals share a common perceptual space, but assigns differential weights or saliences to the different dimensions of the group stimulus space. Those individual saliences provide an ideal data base or operational measure to evaluate possible inter- and intragroup perceptual differences of accounting concepts.

---

[2] The list of users is certainly not exhaustive. Other professional user groups, such as financial accountants employed in industry, management accountants, financial executives, financial analysts, etc., might be tested in future studies.

Analysis and Results

PRELIMINARY FINDINGS

The input to *TORSCA* is a single rank-order similarity matrix computed by averaging the cell ranks obtained across all the participants. The resulting average stress indices are .235, .935, and .075 for two, three, and four dimensions, respectively. Based on these results, a "goodness of fit" is provided by three dimensions (stress $\leq$ .05). The input to the *INDSCAL* model is the $138 \times 12 \times 12$ matrix of similarities judgments for all participants. The "Variance Accounted For" (a measure of goodness of fit in *INDSCAL*) is .7530, .7321, and .6230. Goodness of fit improved for three dimensions but tapered off for number 4. Dimension 4 explained no more variance than could be accounted for in random data. On the basis of both the "Stress" and "Variance Accounted For" measures, the three dimensional solution will be used in this study. Accordingly, the graphical portrayal of the three-dimensional solution is presented in figure 1.

IDENTIFICATION OF PERCEPTUAL DIMENSIONS

As mentioned earlier in the description of the experimental decisions, the participants were asked to state, in order of importance, the criteria used in making their similarity judgments. Although the answers were expressed in different ways, there seemed to be a consensus toward assigning similarity judgments on the basis of the existence or absence of common perceptual qualities between each pair of accounting concepts. An examination of the answers showed evidence of a process of concept formation used by the participants. This process consists of either the recognition of shared or linked characteristics in the accounting concepts (stimulus generalization) or the recognition of shared differences (stimulus discrimination). In either case, the process of concept formation results in the grouping of experiences into conceptual classes on the basis of similarities in their characteristics (McDavid and Harari [1974, pp. 78–79]). In fact, Hunt and Hovland [1960] classified the concepts as being either conjunctive, relational, or disjunctive. Conjunctive concepts are perceived as those sharing common perceptual characteristics. Relational concepts are those concepts linked by some fixed relationship. Finally, disjunctive concepts are those concepts which differ on the basis of one or more characteristics. The above classification is used to label the three dimensions obtained in the *INDSCAL* model solution listed in table 1 and portrayed in figure 1.

Looking at the stimulus configuration of figure 1, the matching and period concepts and the revenue and the cost principles are on opposite equal sides of dimension II; similarly, the matching and period concepts and the revenue and the objectivity principles are on the same equal side of dimension I. Finally, the materiality and the cost principles and the

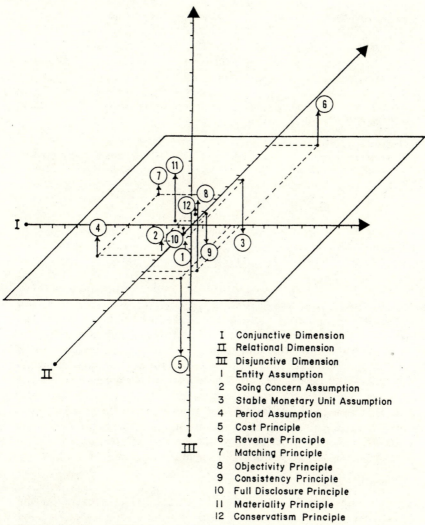

I   Conjunctive Dimension
II   Relational Dimension
III Disjunctive Dimension
1   Entity Assumption
2   Going Concern Assumption
3   Stable Monetary Unit Assumption
4   Period Assumption
5   Cost Principle
6   Revenue Principle
7   Matching Principle
8   Objectivity Principle
9   Consistency Principle
10   Full Disclosure Principle
11   Materiality Principle
12   Conservatism Principle

FIG. 1.—Stimulus configuration.

stable monetary unit and objectivity principles are on opposite sides of dimension III. On the basis of the above findings, dimension I may be labeled as the conjunctive dimension, dimension II as the relational dimension, and dimension III as the disjunctive dimension.

INTERGROUP PERCEPTUAL DIFFERENCES

The *INDSCAL* model computes the weights or saliences that each participant assigned to each of the three dimensions. A one-way analysis of variance for the three groups of participants is used to determine if they have different saliences on each of the three dimensions. The results

TABLE 1

Accounting Concepts' Saliences on a Three-Dimensional Solution

Accounting Concepts	Saliences		
	Conjunctive Dimension	Relational Dimension	Disjunctive Dimension
1. The entity assumption	0.10958	−0.11081	0.01988
2. The going concern assumption	−0.09451	−0.13328	0.05632
3. The stable monetary unit assumption	0.07746	0.37684	−0.38394
4. The period assumption	−0.54777	−0.27065	0.13442
5. The cost principle	0.29858	−0.42546	−0.61864
6. The revenue principle	0.40617	0.60794	0.24200
7. The matching principle	−0.50195	0.21318	0.00479
8. The objectivity principle	0.38284	−0.38137	0.47760
9. The consistency principle	0.04580	0.08842	−0.23043
10. The full disclosure principle	−0.01356	−0.03209	−0.03597
11. The materiality principle	−0.13058	0.00143	0.32729
12. The conservatism principle	−0.03206	0.06586	0.00668

of the analysis of variance are portrayed in table 2. The first hypothesis of no intergroup perceptual differences is rejected for both the conjunctive and disjunctive dimensions but accepted for the relational dimension. This suggests that when accounting concepts share common perceptual characteristics (conjunctive dimension), or differ on the basis of one or more characteristics (disjunctive dimension), the three groups of participants assigned different weights. There is, however, a consensus on the meaning of relational concepts (i.e., concepts linked by some fixed relationship). These results at least partially corroborate the sociolinguistic thesis that various professional affiliations in accounting create different linguistic repertoires, which, in turn, may lead to different approaches to the understanding of accounting and social relationships.

INTRAGROUP PERCEPTUAL DIFFERENCES

To determine whether these differences held, after allowing for the subject's background, the saliences for each dimension were regressed against the following variables: (1) the subject's age, (2) the number of accounting courses taken, (3) his familiarity with financial statements, and (4) his familiarity with accounting concepts. The results of the regression analysis are shown in table 3. The four independent variables have no effect on the three dimensions' saliences. Thus, the accounting concept perception and the resulting saliences could be considered as independent of these variables.

DISCUSSION OF RESULTS

There are intergroup perceptual differences of accounting concepts on both the conjunctive and disjunctive dimensions and no differences on the relational dimension. This result is in agreement with other experi-

TABLE 2

Results of the Analysis of Variances on the Three Dimensions' Saliences

| | Dimensions | | | | | | | | | | | |
| | Conjunctive | | | | Relational | | | | Disjunctive | | | |
	Sum of Squares	Degrees of Freedom	Mean Squares	F	Sum of Squares	Degrees of Freedom	Mean Squares	F	Sum of Squares	Degrees of Freedom	Mean Squares	F
Between groups	0.0626	2	0.0313	4.3630*	0.0002	2	0.0001	0.0241	0.0502	2	0.0251	3.265*
Within groups	0.3944	135	0.0072		0.2625	135	0.0048		0.4261	135	0.0077	
Total	0.5469	137			0.2627	137			0.4375	137		

* Significant at the 0.05 level.

TABLE 3

Regression Results on the Three Dimensions' Saliences

| Source of Variation | Dimensions | | | | | | | | | | | |
| | Conjunctive | | | | Relational | | | | Disjunctive | | | |
	Sum of Squares	Degrees of Freedom	Mean Squares	F	Sum of Squares	Degrees of Freedom	Mean Squares	F	Sum of Squares	Degrees of Freedom	Mean Squares	F
Regression	0.05041	4	0.01260	1.6429	0.02727	4	0.00682	1.5346	0.02137	4	0.00519	0.7409
Error Between groups	0.40655	133	0.00767		0.23547	133	0.00444		0.41437	133	0.00782	
Total	0.45696	137			0.26275	137			0.43754	137		
R^2	0.3321				0.3222				0.2301			

mental studies which have shown that disjunctive concepts are somewhat more difficult to recognize than conjunctive or relational ones (Hunt and Hovland [1960]) and other studies which have shown that simple relational concepts embracing similar concrete objects are more easily recognized (Heidbreder, Bensley and Ivy [1948]; Grant [1951]). Furthermore, this result also implies that the meanings of accounting concepts do vary in the manner with which they can be recognized, grasped, or understood by the users. Intergroup perceptual differences of accounting concepts on both the conjunctive and disjunctive dimensions agree with the sociolinguistic thesis that various professional affiliations in accounting create different linguistic repertoires or codes, which, in turn, lead to a different understanding of accounting and social relationships. An appropriate task may be to investigate the determinants of the linguistic repertoires in accounting using the following arguments.

(a) One may argue that each of the professional groups included in this study belong to accounting institutions whose communicative networks are determined, among other factors, by the functional requirements of the institution. Given the basic differences in their "motives," each of these institutions develops its own "institutional language" (Luckmann [1975, p. 34]). Accordingly, what the results of this study have established is that in the field of accounting there is a relationship between occupational structures and linguistic repertoires.[3]

(b) Following Bernstein's [1958] results on the modes of linguistic usage of the British middle class and working class, I am suggesting that there are two profession-linked linguistic codes in accounting. The academicians in our study use a formal language, the professional accountants a public language, and the students a mix of both, which explains the intergroup perceptual differences of accounting concepts. We may define a formal accounting language as one that involves complex syntactical properties used to clarify, expand, and make meaning more explicit. In comparison, a public accounting language is one that involves highly limited and restricted syntactical properties which reduce the possibilities for clarification and expansion.

The above points are presented as arguments for the sociolinguistic explanation of the linguistic perceptual differences found in this study among accounting professional groups. These are also specific issues in need of more investigation and whose solutions may provide better communication between the academicians and the nonacademicians on the meaning and scope of accounting.

Summary and Recommendations

A selected set of accounting concepts was subjected to analysis using multidimensional scaling techniques to evaluate the intergroup percep-

---

[3] A vast amount of literature exists on the relationship of language with other factors, such as kinship systems, political institutions, religious roles, and economic role systems. A good survey is provided by Luckmann [1975, pp. 34–38].

tual differences between three groups of users. A sociolinguistic construct was used to justify the possible lack of consensus on the meaning of the accounting concepts. The *INDSCAL* model applied to the matrix of similarity judgments enabled the identification of three dimensions and subject's saliences. The dimensions were labeled as conjunctive, relational, and disjunctive by analogy to the process of concept formation. An analysis of variance applied to the individual saliences on each dimension allowed the verification of the sociolinguistic thesis for both the conjunctive and disjunctive concepts. There was, however, a consensus between the three groups only on the meaning of the relational concepts. Finally, the saliences on each dimension were found to be independent of the subject's age, number of accounting courses taken, and his familiarity with financial statements and accounting concepts.

Needless to say, these preliminary results point to the need for more conceptual and empirical research on the determinants of the interprofessional linguistic communication of accounting concepts. Specific issues identified which need further research include: (*a*) the presence and the nature of the "institutional language" within each accounting professional group; (*b*) the presence of a profession-linked linguistic code in the accounting field composed of a "formal language" and a "public language"; and (*c*) testing whether the public language is understood by users of public data (e.g., financial analysis) and whether the formal language is understood by users of formal data (e.g., students).

APPENDIX A

Questionnaire

1. Name: _____
2. Age: _____
3. Area of Undergraduate Studies: _____
4. Number of Accounting Courses Taken: _____
5.

Based on your background and experience, indicate the degree of importance you would assign to each of the following information when comparing the financial performance of two firms.

Circle the number corresponding to your evaluation.

	NOT IMPORTANT						EXTREMELY IMPORTANT
Balance Sheet	1	2	3	4	5	6	7
Profit and Loss Statement	1	2	3	4	5	6	7
Funds Flow Statement	1	2	3	4	5	6	7

Indicate the degree of familiarity with the following accounting concepts.

Circle the number corresponding to your evaluation.

	Not Familiar						Extremely Familiar
Conservatism	1	2	3	4	5	6	7
Materiality	1	2	3	4	5	6	7
Full Disclosure	1	2	3	4	5	6	7
Consistency	1	2	3	4	5	6	7
Objectivity	1	2	3	4	5	6	7
Matching	1	2	3	4	5	6	7
Revenue Principle	1	2	3	4	5	6	7
Cost Principle	1	2	3	4	5	6	7
Period Concept	1	2	3	4	5	6	7
Stable Monetary Unit	1	2	3	4	5	6	7
Going Concern	1	2	3	4	5	6	7
Entity Concept	1	2	3	4	5	6	7
Entity Theory	1	2	3	4	5	6	7
Proprietary Theory	1	2	3	4	5	6	7
Fund Theory	1	2	3	4	5	6	7
Accrual Accounting	1	2	3	4	5	6	7
Cash Accounting	1	2	3	4	5	6	7

7. *Consider the Following Accounting Hypotheses*

Hypothesis No. 1 Entity Assumption
　　　　　 No. 2 Going Concern Assumption
　　　　　 No. 3 Stable Monetary Unit Assumption
　　　　　 No. 4 Period Assumption
　　　　　 No. 5 Cost Principle
　　　　　 No. 6 Revenue Principle
　　　　　 No. 7 Matching Principle
　　　　　 No. 8 Objectivity Principle
　　　　　 No. 9 Consistency Principle
　　　　　 No. 10 Full Disclosure Principle
　　　　　 No. 11 Materiality Principle
　　　　　 No. 12 Conservatism Principle

Assuming you are familiar with these accounting hypotheses, indicate the degree of similarity of each pair of concepts. The criteria to be used are left to your discretion—be consistent in your evaluation.

Example:　If you think that hypotheses 1 and 2 are very dissimilar accounting concepts, *circle* 1.

Hypothesis 1 & Hypothesis 2

Very Dissimilar		1	2	3	4	5	6	7	Very Similar

Hypothesis 1 & Hypothesis 3

Very Dissimilar	1	2	3	4	5	6	7	Very Similar

Hypothesis 1 & Hypothesis 4

Very Dissimilar	1	2	3	4	5	6	7	Very Similar

Hypothesis 10 & Hypothesis 11

Very Dissimilar	1	2	3	4	5	6	7	Very Similar

↓

Hypothesis 10 & Hypothesis 12

Very Dissimilar	1	2	3	4	5	6	7	Very Similar

Hypothesis 11 & Hypothesis 1

Very Dissimilar	1	2	3	4	5	6	7	Very Similar

↓

Hypothesis 11 & Hypothesis 12

Very Dissimilar	1	2	3	4	5	6	7	Very Similar

8. List the criteria used for assigning similarities in question no. 7.

REFERENCES

BELKAOUI, A. "Linguistic Relativity in Accounting." *Accounting Organizations and Society* (October 1978): 97–100.

BERNSTEIN, B. "Some Sociological Determinants of Perception: An Inquiry in Sub-Cultural Differences." *British Journal of Sociology* (1958): 159–74.

CAROLL, J. D., AND J.-J. CHANG. "Analysis of Individual Differences in Multidimensional Scaling via N-Way Generalization of 'Eckart-Young' Decomposition." *Psychometrika* 35 (1970): 238–319.

COWAN, P. "The Link Between Cognitive Structure and Social Structure in Two-Child Verbal Interaction." Symposium presented at the Society for Research on Child Development. Reported in *Advances in Experimental Social Psychology*, vol. 4, edited by L. Berkowitz. New York: Academic Press, 1969.

ERWIN-TRIPP, S. "Sociolinguistics." In *Advances in Experimental Social Psychology*, vol. 4, edited by L. Berkowitz. New York: Academic Press, 1969.

FISHMAN, J. A. *Sociolinguistics: A Brief Introduction.* Rowley, Mass.: Newbury House Publishers, 1970.

FLAMHOLTZ, E., AND E. COOK. "Connotative Meaning and Its Role in Accounting Change: A Field Study." *Accounting, Organizations and Society* (October 1978): 115–40.

GRANT, D. A. "Perceptual versus Analytical Responses to the Number Concept of a Weigel-Type Card Sorting Test." *Journal of Experimental Psychology* (1951): 23–29.

GREEN, P. E., AND F. J. CARMONE. "Multidimensional Scaling: An Introduction and Comparison of Nonmetric Unfolding Techniques." *Journal of Marketing Research* (August 1969): 330–41.

HARIED, A. A. "The Semantic Dimensions of Financial Statements." *Journal of Accounting Research* (Autumn 1972): 376–91.

———. "Measurement of Meaning in Financial Reports." *Journal of Accounting Research* (Spring 1973): 117–45.

HEIDBREDER, E., M. BENSLEY, AND M. IVY. "The Attainment of Concepts: IV. Regularities and Levels." *Journal of Psychology* (1948): 299–329.

HUNT, D. E., AND C. I. HOVLAND. "Order of Consideration of Different Types of Concepts." *Journal of Experimental Psychology* (1960): 220–25.

JAIN, T. N. "Alternative Methods of Accounting and Decision Making: A Psycholinguistic Analysis." *The Accounting Review* (January 1973): 95–104.

LIBBY, R. "Bankers' and Auditors' Perceptions of the Message Communicated by the Audit Report." *Journal of Accounting Research* (Spring 1979): 99–122.

LUCKMANN, T. *The Sociology of Language.* Indianapolis: Bobbs-Merrill Co., 1975.

McDAVID, J. W., AND H. HARARI. *Psychology and Social Behavior.* New York: Harper & Row, 1974.

OLIVER, B. L. "The Semantic Differential: A Device for Measuring the Interprofessional Communication of Selected Accounting Concepts." *Journal of Accounting Research* (Autumn 1974): 299–316.

SCHATZMAN, L., AND A. STRAUSS. "Social Class and Modes of Communication." *American Journal of Sociology* (1955): 329–38.

WHITEMAN, M., AND M. DEUTSCH. "Social Disadvantage as Related to Intellective and Language Development." In *Social Class, Race, and Psychological Development,* edited by M. Deutsch, I. Katz, and A. R. Jensen. New York: Holt, Rinehart & Winston, 1968.

YOUNG, F. W. "TORSCA-9: An IBM 360/75 FORTRAN IV Program for Nonmetric Multidimensional Scaling." *Journal of Marketing Research* (1968): 319–20.

4

BILINGUAL THESIS IN ACCOUNTING

INTRODUCTION

The global economy is best characterized by a new economic and corporate world in which national boundaries are losing their importance. An emerging characteristic of this global economy includes the forming of partnerships between firms, accounting or nonaccounting firms, of different nationalities, willing to forget their rivalries, in order to share in the profit opportunities of a world market, to share the material and labor costs and risks associated with the development of products, to reduce the impact of fluctuating currencies around the world, and to avoid protectionism and government-imposed obstacles such as tariffs, import limits, and regulations. One consequence of this situation is the need to be proficient in more than one language to allow easy communication between the different nationalities involved. One question of interest for this book is, What is the impact of this bilingual requirement on the practice of accounting? This chapter explores this question after defining and introducing the known benefits of bilingualism.

NATURE OF BILINGUALISM

Bilingualism is an important feature and requirement of the global economy. It has also existed for a longer time in all the parts of the world characterized by different cultures and ethnics. Various definitions of *bilingualism* have been offered in the literature. Bloomfield offered the following definition:

In cases where . . . perfect foreign language learning is not accompanied by loss of the native language, it results in bilingualism, native-like control of two languages. After each childhood few people have enough muscular and nervous freedom or enough opportunity and leisure to reach perfection in a foreign language, yet bilingualism of this kind is commoner than one might suppose, both in cases like that of our immigrants and as a result of travel, foreign study, or similar association. Of course one cannot define a degree of perfection at which a good foreign speaker becomes bilingual: the distinction is relative.[1]

The definition implies that bilingualism occurs with equal proficiency in both the native language and the new foreign language. The mastery of more than one language is also emphasized: "The practice of alternately using two languages will be called bilingualism, and the person involved, bilingual."[2]

An incorporation of both the alternative use of two languages and the degree of proficiency will provide a more complete definition of bilingualism. That is exactly what is provided by Mackey:

It seems obvious that if we are to study the phenomena of bilingualism we are forced to consider it as something entirely relative. We must moreover include the use not only of two languages, but of any number of languages. We shall therefore consider bilingualism as the alternate use of two or more languages by the same individual.[3]

There are also various types of bilingualism:

1. A distinction is made between "incipient bilingualism"[4] or "ascendant bilingualism,"[5] indicating an increase in the proficiency in two languages, and "recessive bilingualism," indicating a decrease.[6]

2. A distinction is made between *horizontal bilingualism*, a situation where two distinct languages have an equivalent status; *vertical bilingualism*, a situation where a language and a dialect coexist within the same speaker; and *diagonal bilingualism*, a situation where individuals use both a dialect and an "unrelated" standard language.[7]

3. An equal competence in more than one language is referred to as *ambilingualism, equilingualism,* or *balanced bilingualism*.[8]

4. A distinction is made between *primary bilingualism*, a situation where two languages have been learned naturally, and *secondary bilingualism*, a situation where two languages have been formally learned, through instruction.[9]

5. A distinction is made between *semilingualism*, where a bilingual is suffering linguistic deficiency in both languages,[10] and *receptive bilingualism*, where the individual understands and reads a second language without speaking or writing in that second language.[11]

6. The use and function of an individual's use of two languages are

emphasized in *functional bilingualism*. Here, there is a concern with when, where, and with whom people use their two languages.[12]

7. A distinction is made between *additive bilingualism*, where the addition of a second language and culture are unlikely to replace the first language and culture, and *subtractive bilingualism*, where they will.[13]

8. A distinction is made between *simultaneous bilingualism*, where the addition of a second language occurs early in life, like by the age of three,[14] and *sequential bilingualism*, where the addition of a second language occurs later in life.

9. An important distinction is generally made between bilingualism that is the use of more than one different language and diglossia, which is the use of separate codes within a single community for internal (intrasociety) communication.[15] This separation of codes within diglossia was characterized as follows:

This separation was most often along the lines of a H(igh) language, on the one hand, utilized in conjunction with religion, education and other aspects of high culture, and a L(ow) language, on the other hand, utilized in conjunction with everyday pursuits of health, home and work. Ferguson spoke of H and L as superposed languages.[16]

On this basis, Fishman identified the existence of four separate linguistic situations:

1. Speech communities characterized by both diglossia and bilingualism,
2. Diglossia without bilingualism,
3. Bilingualism with diglossia,
4. Neither diglossia nor bilingualism.[17]

10. Francescato suggested a list of traits applying to bilingualism on the basis of binary features:

1. spontaneous vs. guided bilingualism. Bilingualism is spontaneous when children learn their second language by direct experience; guided when they do so by the help of teachers and pre-programmed experience.
2. simultaneous vs. successive. Bilingualism is simultaneous if subjects learn both languages in the home, successive if they learn their second language starting later, when they have acquired already a relatively advanced competence in their first language.
3. collective vs. isolated. Bilingualism is collective when it is a feature characterizing the community (nation, minority group, etc.); isolated is when the children are not members of a bilingual community, but on the contrary they are forced to learn a second language (different from the one used in the family) outside their family.[18]

DIMENSIONS OF BILINGUALISM

Bilingualism and Cognitive Development

The earlier years were hard on bilingualism. Well-intentioned people thought the cognitive impact would be negative. Laurie portrays this deficit viewpoint:

If it were possible for a child to live in two languages at once equally well, so much the worse. His intellectual and spiritual growth would not thereby be doubled, but halved. Unity of mind and character would have great difficulty in asserting itself in such circumstances.[19]

Later, views changed in favor of bilingualism. The research on the issue can be grouped into three overlapping periods that Baker[20] terms

1. The period of detrimental effects in the nineteenth and early twentieth centuries where philosophers, educators, and philologists thought that bilingualism had an adverse effect on the cognitive development of the child.
2. The period of neutral effects, reporting no difference between bilinguals and monolinguals on intelligence,[21] and
3. The period of additive effects, spurred by the Canadian research of Peal and Lambert,[22] showing clear cognitive advantages with bilingualism.

The results on additive effects are best reviewed in terms of the impact on cognitive flexibility, linguistic and metalinguistic abilities, concept formation, divergent thinking skills and creativity, and cognitive style.[23]

The research on *cognitive flexibility* shows in general the bilinguals to be more cognitively flexible than unilinguals. For example, studies showed that bilingualism provided (1) greater mental flexibility in their performance on tests of general reasoning[24] or perceptual and "set changing" tasks[25] and (2) a greater attention to structure and details.[26] Ben-Zeev summarized her results as follows:

Two strategies characterized the thinking patterns of the bilingualism relation to verbal material: readiness to impute structure and readiness to reorganize. The patterns they seek are primarily linguistic, but this process also operates with visual patterns, as in their aptness at isolating the dimensions of a matrix. With visual material the spatial reorganizational skill did not appear, however.[27]

Research focused on the impact of bilingualism on *metalinguistic awareness,* or the ability to think about and reflect upon the nature and function of language. A good definition of metalinguistic awareness follows:

As a first approximation, metalinguistic awareness may be defined as the ability to reflect upon and manipulate the structural features of spoken language, treating language itself as an object of thought, as opposed to simply using the language system to comprehend and produce sentences. To be metalinguistically aware is to begin to appreciate that the stream of speech, beginning with the acoustic signal and ending with the speaker's intended meaning, can be looked at with the mind's eye and taken apart.[28]

The results of research show that fully fluent bilinguals have increased metalinguistic abilities. Bilinguals were found to be superior to monolinguals on measures of cognitive control of linguistic processes and in the processing of words and the development of the concept of a word;[29] the processing of test items was also found to vary depending on the level of bilingualism, with a better performance achieved by bilinguals. As stated by Galambos and Hakuta:

The information-processing approach successfully accounts for our findings that bilingualism by and large enhances the metalinguistic abilities to note errors and correct errors. . . . The bilingual experience requires that the form of the two languages being learned be attended to on a routine basis. Experience at attending to form would be predicted to facilitate any task that required the child to focus on form upon demand.[30]

Results from Bain's[31] and Liedtke and Nelson's[32] studies show that balanced bilinguals seem to enjoy some advantages over monolinguals in *concept formation abilities*, especially a greater grasp of linear measurement concepts, and a greater faculty in discovering additive rules in a string of numbers.

Some research examined the relationship between bilingualism and *divergent thinking* or creative thinking. The hypothesis may be stated as follows:

The underlying hypothesis concerning creative thinking and bilingualism is that the ownership of two or more languages may increase fluency, flexibility, originality and elaboration in thinking. Bilinguals will have two or more words for a single object or idea. For example, in Welsh, the word ysgol not only means a school but also a ladder. Thus having the word "ysgol" in Welsh and "school" in English provides the bilingual with an added dimension—the idea of the school as a ladder. In the same way, having two or more words for folk dancing or square dancing in different languages may give a wider variety of associations than having a single word in one language.[33]

Most of research results point to the superiority of bilinguals to monolinguals on divergent thinking. Cummins, however, warns that the differences can be explained by a threshold:

There may be a threshold level of cognitive competence which a bilingual child must attain both in order to avoid cognitive deficits and to allow the potentially beneficial aspects of becoming bilingual to influence his cognitive growth.[34]

Research on bilingualism and *cognitive style* is limited. Cognitive style is generally linked to individual variations in modes of perceiving, remembering, and thinking, or to distinctive ways of apprehending, storing, remembering, transforming, and utilizing information. Speaking two languages may lead to bicognitivity in the sense that "in the same way that the bilingual child switches language codes in response to the demand characteristics of the socio-linguistic situation, so the bicognitive child switches cognitive styles as demanded."[35] In fact, in their experiment, Duncan and DeAvila found that proficient bilinguals outperformed monolinguals on field dependence/independence tests, with bilinguals showing more advanced skills as perceptually disembedding and producing the more articulate or "field-independent" drawings."[36]

An excellent explanation of the superior cognitive ability of bilinguals, based on Sternberg's triarchic model of intelligence,[37, 38] has been provided by Reynolds.[39] It is summarized in Exhibit 4.1.

Bilingualism and Code Switching

Code switching is a common phenomenon experienced by bilinguals. It involves generally the use of two or more languages in the same conversation or utterance.[40] It can manifest itself in situational switching, metaphorical switching, code mixing, or style shifting. It is deliberate sometimes for social, political, and economic reasons, constituting a marked choice of language.[41] Three factors have been chosen as determinants of code switching, namely: normative, motivated, and socio-structural factors.[42]

Normative factors include those proposed by traditional sociolinguistics and those proposed by interactional sociolinguistics. Traditional sociolinguistics attributed code switching to the topic of communication, the social setting in which it occurs, the purpose of the communication, and the characteristics of the interlocutors.[43] Interactional sociolinguistics—Myers-Scotton, in particular—argued "that the linguistic code choices which participants make, interpreted according to the negotiation maxims, generate conversational implications regarding the rights and obligations between speaker and addressee for the current talk exchange."[44] This negotiation of identities approach was systematized in terms of the following six metamaxims determining code choice:

The unmarked choice maxim where the code choice is used to affirm established roles;

Exhibit 4.1
Why Bilinguals Might Be More "Intelligent"—Using Sternberg's Model

Contextual Subtheory Adaptation, selection, and shaping of environments	*Bilingual Possibility* Bilinguals, having experience in separate linguistic (and social) environments, may be more adept at adaptation (e.g., code-switching), selection (e.g., interacting with alternate cultures), and shaping (e.g., language legislation)
Experiential Subtheory Efficacious adaptation to novelty allows automatization to occur earlier in one's experience with new tasks or situations Automatization allows resources to be allocated to processing novelty in the environment	*Bilingual Possibility* Adaptation to novelty of language switching and dual linguistic codes early in life allows easier automatization in dealing with linguistic tasks Automatization of language processing (necessary in translation, code-switching, etc.) frees resources for novel linguistic tasks
Componential Subtheory Metacomponents Performance components Knowledge-acquisition components	*Bilingual Possibility* Necessity of controlling and monitoring two language systems (lexicons, social referents, etc.) improves efficiency of metacomponential system Having command of two languages leads to greater use of verbal mediation and increased use of language as a cognitive regulatory tool. Having two interlocking performance systems for linguistic codes gives double the resources for executing verbal tasks (or tasks with verbal substrates) as well as nonverbal tasks (e.g., spatial tasks) that can be recoded into verbal tasks. Also, there is greater use of learning strategies when learning two languages Having two interlocking verbal systems allows for ease in encoding new information and combining with one or the other lexicon or verbal semantic memory

Note: From *Bilingualism, Multiculturalism, and Second Language Learning* (p. 167) by A.G. Reynolds, 1991, Hillsdale, NJ: Lawrence Erlbaum Associates, Inc. Copyright © 1991 by A.G. Reynolds. Reprinted by permission.

The deference maxim where the code choice shows deference to those from whom something is desired;

The virtuosity maxim where the code choice is triggered by a lack of linguistic ability;

The exploratory choice maxim where the code choice is a candidate for an unmarked choice in a noncoventionalized exchange;

The multiple-identities maxim where different choices are made to express multiple identities; and

Floating the maxim where the choices are made to disidentify with established rights and obligations.[45]

Motivational factors focus on factors inducing speech convergence, the tendency for interlocutors to use the same languages, and speech convergence, the tendency for interlocutors to accentuate language differences. Most of the motivational factors are included in a model of code switching known as *speech accommodation theory*. It identifies the following antecedents for convergence and divergence:

1. People will attempt to converge toward the speech and nonverbal patterns believed to be characteristic of their message recipients, be the latter defined in individual, relational, or group terms when speakers:
    (a) desire recipients' social approval (and the perceived costs of acting in an approval-seeking manner are proportionally lower than the perceived rewards);
    (b) desire a high level of communicalation efficiency;
    (c) desire a self-, couple-, or group-presentation shared by recipients;
    (d) desire appropriate situational or identity definitions; when recipients'
    (e) actual speech in the situation matches the belief that the speakers have about recipients' speech style;
    (f) speech is positively valued, that is, nonstigmatized;
    (g) speech style is appropriate for the speakers as well as for recipients.
2. The magnitude of such convergence will be a function of
    (a) the extent of speakers' repertoires, and
    (b) individual, relational, social, and contextual factors that may increase the needs for social comparison, social appraloval, and or high communicational efficiency.
3. Speakers will attempt to maintain their communication patterns, or even diverge away from their message recipients' speech and nonverbal behaviors when they
    (a) desire to communication a contrastive self-image;
    (b) desire to dissociate personally from the recipients or the recipients' definition of the situation;
    (c) define the encounter in intergroup or relational terms with communication style being a valued dimension of their situationally salient ingroup or relational identities;
    (d) desire to change recipients' speech behavior, for example, moving it to a more acceptable level;
    (e) exhibit a stigmatized form, that is, a style that deviates from a valued norm, which is
    (f) consistent with speakers' expectations regarding recipient performance.

4. The magnitude of such divergence will be a function of

   (a) the extent of the speakers' repertoires, and

   (b) individual, relational, social, and contextual factors increasing the salience of the cognitive and affective functions in (3) above.[46]

Sociostructural factors include mainly the language vitality. This language vitality has been modeled in terms of status and demographic and institutional support factors.[47] Perceptions of high vitality motivate speakers to use the particular language or to switch to it. Research shows more positive attitudes about the use of language results from the perception of a high vitality.[48, 49]

Bilingualism, Brain Lateralization, and Mental Representation

As a result of the differences observed in cognitive thinking and code switching, one may ask whether there are differences in brain functions between bilinguals and monolinguals. Most of the findings in the field of neuropsychology indicate that for right-handed adults, and to a lesser extent left-handers, the left hemisphere of the brain is dominant for language functioning. Given this finding on brain lateralization, two important questions emerge:

1. Whether there are differences in cerebral lateralization between bilinguals and monolinguals; and

2. Whether there are differences in cerebral lateralization among bilinguals in either or both of their languages.[50]

A review of the literature on this topic yielded the following five propositions:[51]

1. Proficient bilinguals will use the right hemisphere more than monolinguals for both first- and second-language processing.[52]

2. The right hemisphere involvement is greater in the acquisition of second language than of the first language.[53]

3. The stage hypothesis claims that the right hemisphere involvement will decrease as proficiency in a second language grows, while the left hemisphere involvement will increase.[54] The right hemisphere is thought to better meet the processing requirements of the beginning language learner,[55] while the left hemisphere to better process phonetic and syntactic analysis.[56] Hence, the core aspects of language processing reside in the left hemisphere.

4. The manner hypothesis claims that informal language acquisition leads to greater right hemisphere participation,[57] while formal language acquisition leads to greater left hemisphere participation.[58]

5. The age hypothesis claims that there is a predominance of a left hemisphere "semantic-type" strategy in early bilinguals, a right hemisphere "acoustic-type" in late bilinguals.[59] A metaanalysis review of research found the left hemisphere to strongly dominate language processing for both unilinguals and bilinguals, with differences between unilinguals and bilinguals the exception rather than the rule, casting some doubts on the results of the five hypotheses.[60] As stated by Vaid and Hall: "The large negative findings from the meta-analysis must be taken seriously as reflecting a general lack of support for the five hypotheses as they have been addressed in the literature to date."[61]

The inconclusive result on brain lateralization raises the issue of mental representation. Three hypotheses emerge: A first hypothesis argued for an independent processing of the second language through a separate storage and retrieval system, with translation as the link between both systems.[62] A second hypothesis argued for a shared storage system with two different input and output systems.[63] A third hypothesis argued for an integrated model:[64]

The model specifies the functional relations between the verbal symbolic systems that underlie the bilingual's two languages and a third (image) system specialized for processing information about nonverbal objects and events. The three systems are assumed to be capable of functioning independently. At the same time, they can interact because of interconnections that permit one system to initiate activity in another. The image system, representing knowledge of the world, is connected to both verbal systems. The verbal systems are interconnected via representations corresponding to translation equivalents thereby approximating one-to-one relations as compared to the one-to-many relations that characterize the associative networks within each language system.[65]

BILINGUAL THESIS IN ACCOUNTING

Concept Perception

As a language, accounting includes both lexical and grammatical characteristics. The lexical characteristics include mainly accounting terms and concepts proper to accounting. Of relevance to the construction of an accounting theory, there are two types of professional concepts. The terms *going concern, entity, stable monetary unit,* and *periodicity* represent underlying assumptions of accounting theory, while the terms *cost, revenue, matching, objectivity, consistency, full disclosure, materiality,* and *conservatism* represent generally accepted accounting principles within the profession.[66] Given the result that speakers of different languages acquire and maintain separate worldviews, and given the result that bilingual individuals possess a different worldview from unilinguals,[67] there is then the possibility that bilingualism in the accounting profession may also lead to different perceptions of the accounting concepts. Based on these considerations, Monti-Belkaoui and Belkaoui tested for (1) differences in the perception of professional accounting concepts by unilingual accounting subjects from two different languages, (2) differences in perceptions of professional accounting concepts between bilingual and unilingual accounting students, and (3) whether switching from one language to another leads to better perception.[68] Subjects were unilingual and bilingual French and English Canadian students of accounting. They were asked to assign to each of the paired accounting concepts an integer rating, on a seven-point scale ranging from "very dissimilar" to "very similar," and list the criteria they used for assigning similarity ratings. Multidimensional scaling techniques applied to the matrix of subjects' similarity judgments on pairs of concepts enabled the identification of three dimensions. The dimensions were labeled as conjunctive, relational, and disjunctive. The findings support the contention that unilingual speakers of separate languages differ from each other and from bilingual speakers in their perception of professional concepts. Some of the findings also provide support for the contention that language switching may enhance understanding. The evidence suggests that fluency in two languages aids in the uniform acquisition and comprehension of accounting concepts.

Cognitive Development

The cognitive revolution in social psychology has created strong interest in the knowledge structure in memory in general and how people learn in particular. This research paradigm also affects accounting and auditing. Given that the difference between declarative knowledge and procedural knowledge is equivalent to the difference between content knowledge and the use of that knowledge or between "knowing what" and "knowing how," Waller and Felix used the concepts to propose a model of how an ordinary person learns from experience:[69]

Its thesis is that learning from experience involves the formation and the development of generalized cognitive structures that organize experience-based declarative and procedural knowledge in long term memory. Declarative knowledge is organized by categories, which depend on similarity of class membership relations, and schemata, which depend on spatial and/or temporal relations. Procedural knowledge is organized into production systems, i.e., hierarchies of condition-action pairs.[70]

What the model implies is that schemata are developed through a gradual process of abstracting domain-specific knowledge on the basis of experience. The difference between the expert's and the novice's knowledge structure is through the result of difference in experience.

The notion of schematas (knowledge structures or templates) was also used by Gibbins to make general propositions, corollaries, and hypotheses about the psychological operations of professional judgment in the "natural," everyday settings experienced by public accountants.[71] Professional judgment in public accounting was described as a five-component process:

• Schematas or knowledge structures accumulated through learning or experience,

• A triggering event or stimulus,

• A judgment environment,

• A judgment process, and

• A decision/action.

Basically, the auditor judgment is viewed as a responsive, continuous, unconscious, instrumental process of sequentially matching cues to knowledge structures to generate preferences and responses based on experience.[72]

Finally, Belkaoui proposed a model of the judgment/decision process in accounting as an exercise in social perception and cognition, requiring both formal and implicit judgment.[73] The primary input to this process is an accounting problem that needs to be solved and requires a judgment preceding either a preference or decision. The model consists of the following steps:

1. Observation of the accounting phenomenon by the decision maker,

2. Schema formation or building of the accounting phenomenon,

3. Schema organization or storage,

4. Attention and recognition process triggered by a stimulus,

5. Retrieval of stored information needed for the judgment decision,

6. Reconsideration and integration of retrieval information with new information,

7. Judgment process, and

8. Decision/action response.

All these models point to cognitive processes and knowledge as determinants of accounting expertise. Various accounting and auditing research examined the implications of this model. A review of this research is presented by Bonner and Pennington.[74] The review classified the research in categories of cognitive processes described by Hayes-Roth et al.[75] as: retrieval of knowledge from memory, external information search, comprehension, hypothesis generation, hypothesis evaluation, design, estimation, and choice. The end result of this is that accounting relies on cognitive processes and knowledge as determinants of task performance and behavior. This research is, however, based on the assumption that the accountants are unilinguals. In a global economy, there is a greater likelihood of accountants functioning in different cultures requiring uses of more than one language. This required bilingualism in the accounting context may lead to greater use of verbal mediation and increased use of language as a cognitively regulatory tool. Having more than one linguistic code gives higher resources for executing verbal tasks as well as nonverbal tasks that can be recoded in verbal tasks. The existence of more than one language system may allow for greater ease in encoding accounting information and combining with one or the other verbal semantic memory. The main thesis in this discussion is that bilingualism in accounting may lead to an improvement in the cognitive development and functioning required by a complex accounting environment.

Cognitive Style

Kogan's taxonomy is generally used as a theoretical framework to separate decision makers' cognitive characteristics into three primary components: cognitive style, cognitive abilities, and cognitive strategies.[76] Cognitive style is defined in terms of distinctive ways of acquiring, storing, retrieving, and transforming information. Cognitive ability is related to the level of skills in performing the tasks identified in the definition of cognitive style. Finally, cognitive strategy is related to the ongoing, multidirectional interactions between cognitive styles and abilities and the environment. Cognitive style as measured by the Myers-Briggs-type indicator enables the classification of individuals as "thinking" individuals or as "sensing" individuals.[77] Cognitive ability, as measured by the embedded figures test,[78] enables the classification of individuals as high analytics or low analytics. Cognitive strategy has been measured, for example, by the intolerance of ambiguity test or the California Psychological Inventory Test.[79] A review of accounting research on cognitive styles, cognitive abilities, and cognitive characteristics has been provided by Ho and Rogers.[80] The results are mixed, indicating a positive impact of cognitive characteristics in certain cases and neutral impact in other cases.

One general limitation of all these studies is the failure to distinguish between monolingual and bilingual students. This differentiation is important given the potential that (1) bilingualism may lead to bicognitivity and (2) bilinguals may switch linguistic codes as well as cognitive styles and the finding that bilinguals have shown more advanced skills at perceptually disembedding and producing the most articulate or "field-independent" drawings in an experiment. Interesting research questions include the investigation of the impact of bilingualism as a moderating variable in accounting research on cognitive styles. More specifically, it is important to determine whether bilingual accountants may be tempted to switch cognitive styles as they switch linguistic codes in the performance of accounting tasks and in the processing of accounting information. Specific task environments and situations may call for code switching for better communication, followed by switching of cognitive styles. More specifically, what are the normative, motivational, and sociostructural factors that may induce a bilingual accountant to switch codes while performing an accounting task and also to switch cognitive styles?

Cognitive Flexibility and Divergent Thinking

Can the results of the impact of bilingualism on cognitive flexibility and divergent thinking be extrapolated to bilingual accountants and managers performing various accounting tasks?

First, we have stated earlier in the chapter that bilinguals showed a greater neutral flexibility in their performance on tests of general reasoning and a greater attention to structure and details. Does it mean that bilingual accountants will outperform unilingual accountants because of their higher cognitive flexibility? The answer to this research question can have profound consequences on accountants and managers practicing in multinational firms.

Second, there is an ongoing interest in the benefits of convergent versus divergent thinking. A good differentiation between both concepts follows:

Divergent thinking is not a matter of having any one idea. Rather it is the *progression* of ideas in your mind when you are going from the specific to the general, from the narrow to the broad, and from the concrete to the conceptual. When you're generating options rather than choosing among them, that's divergent thinking. Think of divergent thoughts as "split-apart" thinking, spreading and expanding outwardly. Convergent thinking operates in just the reverse way. It narrows down the problem to a smaller, more manageable size and perspective. It casts out various options in favor of a preferred few. It zeroes in on selected key factors, magnifies them, analyzes them, and evaluates the options to prepare the way to make the choices. Convergent thinking is reductive; it settles on a smaller and more detailed picture to prepare us for action.[81]

Most of the accountant's work seems to require convergent thinking, looking for specific solutions to specific problems. There seems to be a correct answer to each accounting-specific question, leading to convergent thinking. When would an accountant exercise the alternative style of divergent thinking? The research reviewed earlier argued for a positive impact of bilingualism on divergent thinking. Bilingualism seems to increase fluency, flexibility, originality, and elaboration in thinking. Can that also be the case for accounting in the sense that bilingual accountants or managers will be more predisposed to adopt a divergent thinking style?

CONCLUSIONS

Bilingualism presents clear advantages. Proficiency in more than one language is shown to lead to greater mental flexibility and cognitive flexibility, increased metalinguistic ability, some advantages in concept formation abilities, a predisposition to divergent thinking, and advanced skills in cognitive style. All these advantages can be assumed to be present in all the situations where accountants who are bilinguals are functioning in contexts requiring the use of more than one language. With the importance of the global economy in the working of most firms, situations requiring the use of more than one language in an accountant context are on the increase. The benefits of bilingualism in those situations call for a rethinking of some of the requirements for accounting expertise to include the learning of foreign languages.

Tucker made a similar call for bilingualism and its potential effect on international competition:

Internationally if we are to compete effectively, we must communicate more effectively in English as well as in the languages of our clients, our trading partners, and our allies. It is my opinion that we must take steps immediately, rapidly, and increasingly to broaden the base of additive bilingualism in our society because there are cognitive, personal, social, and economic benefits that will occur if we do so. It should be viewed as unacceptable that so few youngsters and so few young adults in the United States develop bilingual language proficiency or have an opportunity to do so, as is now the case. It is not acceptable that fewer than 1% of our youngsters or young adults study or master foreign languages which are spoken by 99% of the world's population. It is not acceptable that the development of a language competent American society should be accorded such a low priority. One of the ways to do this is to examine critically our social needs and objectives and to use the tools of language education planning to implement a language education program that will benefit all American youngsters.[82]

NOTES

1. L. Bloomfield, *Language* (New York: Holt, 1933), 55–56.
2. U. Weinreich, *Languages in Contact: Findings and Problems* (The Hague: Mouton, 1970), 1.

3. W. F. Mackey, "The Description of Bilingualism," in *Readings in the Sociology of Language*, ed. J. A. Fishman (The Hague: Mouton, 1970), 555.

4. A. R. Diebold, "Incipient Bilingualism," *Language* 37 (1961): 97–112.

5. H. Baetens Beardsmore, *Bilingualism: Basic Principles* (Cleveland, OH: Multilingual Matters, 1986).

6. Ibid.

7. J. Pohl, "Bilingualismes," *Revue Roumaine de Linguistique* 10 (1965): 343–349.

8. M. A. K. Halliday, A. McIntosh, and P. Streveus, "The Users and Uses of Language," in *Readings in the Sociology of Language*, ed. J. A. Fishman (The Hague: Mouton, 1970), 139–169.

9. S. H. Houston, *A Survey of Psycholinguistics* (The Hague: Mouton, 1972), 203–225.

10. T. Skutnabb-Kangas, *Bilingualism or Not: The Education of Minorities* (Cleveland, OH: Multilingual Matters, 1981).

11. C. F. Hockett, *A Course in Modern Linguistics* (New York: Macmillan, 1959).

12. J. A. Fishman, "Who Speaks What Language to Whom and When?" *La Linguistic* 2 (1965): 67–68.

13. W. E. Lambert, "Culture and Languages as Factors in Learning and Education," in *Cultural Factors in Learning and Education*, ed. F. E. Aboud and R. D. Meade (Bellingham: Washington State College, 1974).

14. B. McLaughlin, *Second Language Acquisition in Childhood*, vol. 1, *Preschool Children* (Hillsdale, NJ: Lawrence Erlbaum, 1984).

15. C. A. Ferguson, "Diglossia," *Word* 15 (1959): 325–340.

16. J. A. Fishman, "Bilingualism with and Without Diglossia; Diglossia with and Without Bilingualism," *Journal of Social Issues* 2 (1967): 30.

17. Ibid., 29–38.

18. G. Francescato, "Bilingualism and Diglossia in Their Mutual Relationship," in *The Fergusonian Impact*, ed. J. A. Fishman, M. Clyne, A. Tabouret-Keller, H. Krishnamunti, and M. Abdulaziz (Berlin: Mouton de Gruyter, 1986), 396.

19. S. S. Laurie, *Lectures on Language and Linguistic Method in School* (Cambridge: Cambridge University Press, 1980), 15.

20. C. K. Baker, *Key Issues in Bilingualism and Bilingual Education* (Cleveland, OH: Multilingual Matters, 1988).

21. W. R. Jones, *Bilingualism and Intelligence* (Cardiff: University of Wales, 1959).

22. E. Peal, and W. E. Lambert, "The Relationship of Bilingualism to Intelligence," *Psychological Monographs* 76, no. 27 (1962): 1–23.

23. R. M. Diaz, "Thought and Two Languages: The Impact of Bilingualism on Cognitive Development," in *Review of Research in Education*, ed. E. W. Gordon (Washington, DC: American Educational Research Association, 1983), 23–54.

24. Peal and Lambert, "The Relationship of Bilingualism to Intelligence."

25. L. Balkan, *Les effets du bilingualism français-Anglais sur les aptitudes intellectuelles* (Brussels: Aimav, 1970).

26. S. Ben-Zeev, "The Influence of Bilingualism on Cognitive Strategy and Cognitive Development," *Child Development* 48 (1977): 1009–1018.

27. Ibid., 1017.

28. W. E. Tunmer, and M. L. Herriman, "The Development of Metalinguistic

Awareness: A Conceptual Overview," in *Metalinguistic Awareness in Children*, ed. W. E. Tunmer, C. Pratt, and M. L. Herriman (Berlin: Springer-Verlag, 1984), 12.

29. E. Bialystok, "Influences of Bilingual on Metalinguistic Development," *Second Language Research* 3, no. 2 (1987): 154–166.

30. S. J. Galambos, and K. Hakuta, "Subject-Specific and Task-Specific Characteristics of Metalinguistic Awareness in Bilingual Children," *Applied Psycholinguistics*, 5 (1988): 145.

31. B. Bain, "Bilingualism and Cognition: Towards a General Theory," in *Bilingualism, Biculturalism and Education*, ed. S. T. Carey (Edmonton: University of Alberta, 1974).

32. W. W. Liedtke, and L. D. Nelson, "Concept Formation and Bilingualism," *Alberta Journal of Educational Research* 14 (1968): 225–232.

33. C. Baker. *Foundations of Bilingual Education and Bilingualism* (Cleveland, OH: Multilingual Matters, 1993), 119.

34. J. Cummins, "Cognitive Factors Associated with the Attainment of Intermediate Levels of Bilingual Skills," *Modern Language Journal* 61 (1977): 10.

35. S. E. Duncan, and E. A. DeAvila, "Bilingualism and Cognition: Some Recent Findings," *NABE Journal* 4 (1979): 17.

36. Ibid.

37. R. J. Sternberg, *Beyond IQ: A Triarchic Theory of Human Intelligence* Cambridge: Cambridge University Press, 1985).

38. R. J. Sternberg, *The Triarchic Mind: A New Theory of Human Intelligence* (New York: Viking, 1988).

39. A. G. Reynolds, "The Cognitive Consequences of Bilingualism," in *Bilingualism, Multiculturalism, and Second Language Learning*, ed. A. G. Reynolds (Hillsdale, NJ: Lawrence Erlbaum, 1991), 45–182.

40. F. Grosjean, *Life with Two Languages: An Introduction to Bilingualism* (Cambridge: MA: Harvard University Press, 1982).

41. C. Myers-Scotton, "The Negotiation of Identities in Conversation: A Theory of Markedness and Code Choice," *International Journal of the Sociology of Language* 44 (1983): 115–136.

42. I. Sachdev, and R. Bourhis, "Bilinguality and Multilinguality," in *Handbook of Language and Social Psychology*, ed. H. Giles and W. P. Robinson (New York: John Wiley, 1990), 293–306.

43. H. Giles, and P. F. Powesland, *Speech Style and Social Evaluation* (London: Academic Press, 1975).

44. Myers-Scotton, "The Negotiation of Identities in Conversation: A Theory of Markedness and Code Choice," 115.

45. Ibid., 115–130.

46. H. Giles, A. Mulac, J. J. Bradac, and P. Johnson, "Speech Accommodation Theory: The First Decade and Beyond," in *Communication Yearbook*, no. 1, ed. M. L. McLaughlin (Beverly Hills, CA: Sage, 1987), 36–37.

47. H. Giles, R. Y. Bourhis, and D. Taylor, "Towards a Theory of Language in Ethnic Group Relations," in *Language, Ethnicity and Intergroup Relations*, ed. H. Giles (London: Academic Press, 1977), 307–348.

48. R. Y. Bourhis, and I. Sachdev, "Vitality Perceptions and Language Attitudes: Some Canadian Data," *Journal of Language and Social Psychology* 3 (1984): 97–126.

49. I. Sachdev, R. Y. Bourhis, S. W. Phang, and J. D'Eye, "Language Attitudes and Vitality Perceptions: Intergenerational Effects Amongst Chinese Canadian Communities," *Journal of Language and Social Psychology* 6 (1987): 287–307.

50. J. Vaid, and D. G. Hall, "Neuropsychological Perspectives on Bilingualism: Right, Left, and Center," in *Bilingualism, Multiculturalism and Second Language Learning*, ed. A. G. Reynolds (Hillsdale, NJ: Lawrence Erlbaum, 1991), 86.

51. Ibid., 87–90.

52. L. Galloway, "Études cliniques et experimentales sur la repartition hemisphere du traitement cerebral du language chez les bilingues: Modeles theoriques," *Language* 72 (1983): 79–113.

53. Ibid.

54. L. Obler, "Right Hemisphere Participation in Second Language Acquisition," in *Individual Differences and Universals in Language Learning Aptitudes*, ed. K. Diller (Rowley, MA: Newbury House, 1981).

55. E. Schniederman, "Leaning to the Right: Thoughts on Lateralization and Second Language Acquisition," in *Language Processing in Bilinguals: Psycholinguistic and Neuropsychological Perspectives*, ed. J. Vaid (Hillsdale, NJ: Lawrence Erlbaum Associates, 1986).

56. B. McLaughlin, T. Rossman, and B. McLeod, "Second Language Learning: An Information-Processing Perspective," *Language Learning* 33 (1984): 135–158.

57. G. Galloway, and S. Krashen, "Cerebral Organization in Bilingualism and Second Language," in *Research in Second Language Acquisition*, ed. R. Scarcella and S. Krashen (Rowley, MA: Newbury House, 1980).

58. F. Carroll, "Neurolinguistic Processing of a Second Language: Experimental Evidence," in *Research in Second Language Acquisition*, ed. R. Scarcella and S. Krashen (Rowley, MA: Newbury House, 1980).

59. F. Genesee, J. F. Hamers, W. E. Lambert, L. Mononen, M. Seitz, and R. Starck, "Language Processing in Bilinguals," *Brain and Language* 5 (1978): 1–12.

60. Vaid and Hall, "Neuropsychological Perspectives on Bilingualism: Right, Left, and Center," 105–112.

61. Ibid., 104.

62. P. Kolers, "Interlingual Word Association," *Journal of Verbal Learning and Verbal Behavior* 2 (1963): 291–300.

63. A. Paivio, *Mental Representation: A Dual Coding Approach* (Oxford: Oxford University Press, 1986).

64. A. Paivio, and A. Desrochers, "A Dual-Coding Approach to Bilingual Memory," *Canadian Journal of Psychology* 34 (1980): 388–399.

65. Ibid., 388.

66. A. Riahi-Belkaoui, *Accounting Theory*, 3d ed. (London, England: Academic Press, 1992).

67. W. E. Lambert, and G. R. Tucker, "The Benefits of Bilingualism," *Psychology Today* (September 1973): 16–35.

68. J. Monti-Belkaoui, and A. Belkaoui," Bilingualism and the Perception of Professional Concepts," *Journal of Psycholinguistic Research* 12, no. 2 (1983): 111–127. The entire study is reprinted in the Appendix to Chapter 4.

69. W. S. Waller, and W. L. Felix, "The Auditor and Learning from Experience: Some Conjectures," *Accounting, Organizations and Society* (June 1984): 383–406.

70. Ibid., 390.

71. M. Gibbins, "Proposition About the Psychology of Professional Judgement in Public Accounting," *Journal of Accounting Research* (Spring 1984): 103–125.

72. M. Gibbins, "Knowledge Structures and Experienced Auditor Judgement," in *Auditor Productivity in the Year 2000: 1987 Proceedings of the Arthur Young Professor's Roundtable*, ed. A. Bailey (Reston, VA: Arthur Young, 1988), 57.

73. A. Belkaoui, *Judgement in International Accounting: A Theory of Cognition, Cultures, Language and Contacts* (Westport, CT: Greenwood Press, 1990), 8.

74. S. E. Bonner, and N. Pennington, "Cognitive Processes and Knowledge as Determinants of Auditor Experience," *Journal of Accounting Literature* 10 (1991): 1–50.

75. F. Hayes-Roth, D. A. Waterman, and D. B. Lenat, eds., *Building Expert Systems* (Reading, MA: Addison-Wesley, 1983).

76. N. Kogan, "Creativity and Cognitive Styles: A Life-Span Perspective," in *Life-Span Development Psychology: Personality and Socialization*, ed. P. B. Baltes and K. W. Schaie (New York: Academic Press, 1973).

77. R. W. Mason, and I. Nitroff, "A Program for Research in Management Information Systems," *Management Science* 19 (1993): 475–487.

78. H. A. Witkin, D. R. Goodenough, and P. K. Oltman, "Psychological Differentiation: Current Status," *Journal of Personality and Social Psychology* 7 (1979): 1127–1145.

79. J. G. San Miguel, "Human Information Processing and Its Relevance to Accounting: A Laboratory Study," *Accounting, Organizations and Society* 1 (1976): 357–373.

80. J. L. Ho, and W. Rogers, "A Review of Accounting Research on Cognitive Characteristics," *Journal of Accounting Literature* 12 (1993): 101–130.

81. K. Albrecht, with S. Albrecht, *The Creative Corporation* (Homewood, IL: Dow Jones–Irwin, 1987), 91.

82. G. R. Tucker, "Developing a Language-Competent American Society: The Role of Language Planning," in *Bilingualism, Multiculturalism and Second Language Learning*, ed. A. G. Reynolds (Hillsdale, NJ: Lawrence Erlbaum, 1991), 77–78.

REFERENCES

Appel, R., and P. Muysken. *Language Contact and Bilingualism*. London: Edward Arnold, 1987.

Baetens Beardsmore, H. *Bilingualism: Basic Principles*. Cleveland, OH: Multilingual Matters, 1986.

Baker, C. K. *Key Issues in Bilingualism and Bilingual Education*. Cleveland, OH: Multilingual Matters, 1988.

Ben-Zeev, S. "The Effect of Bilingualism in Children of Spanish-English Low Economic Neighborhoods on Cognitive Development and Cognitive Strategy." *Working Papers on Bilingualism* 14 (1977): 83–122.

Ben-Zeev, S. "The Influence of Bilingualism on Cognitive Strategy and Cognitive Development." *Child Development* 48 (1977): 1009–1018.

Bialystok, E. "Influences of Bilingual on Metalinguistic Development." *Second Language Research* 3, no. 2 (1987): 154–166.

Bialystok, E. "Levels of Bilingualism and Levels of Linguistic Awareness." *Developmental Psychology* 24, no. 4 (1988): 560–567.

Bialystok, E., ed. *Language Processing in Bilingual Children*. Cambridge: Cambridge University Press, 1991.

Cummins, J. "Cognitive Factors Associated with the Attainment of Intermediate Levels of Bilingual Skills." *Modern Language Journal* 61 (1977): 3–12.

Cummins, J., and M. Gulutsan. "Some Effects of Bilingualism on Cognitive Functioning." In *Bilingualism, Biculturalism and Education*, edited by S. Carey. Edmonton: University of Alberta Press, 1974.

Darcy, N. T. "A Review of the Literature on the Effects of Bilingualism Upon the Measurement of Intelligence." *Journal of Genetic Psychology* 82 (1953): 21–57.

Diaz, R. M. "Bilingual Cognitive Development: Addressing Three Gaps in Current Research." *Child Development* 56 (1985): 1376–1388.

Diaz, R. M., and C. Klinger. "Towards an Explanatory Model of the Interaction Between Bilingualism and Cognitive Development." In *Language Processing in Bilingual Children*, edited by E. Bialystok. Cambridge: Cambridge University Press, 1991.

Eastman, C. M. "Codeswitching as an Urban Language, Contact Phenomenon." *Journal of Multilingual and Multicultural Development* 13 nos. 1 and 2 (1992): 1–17.

Fishman, J. A. "Bilingualism and Biculturalism as Individual and as Societal Phenomena." *Journal of Multilingual and Multicultural Development* 1 (1980): 3–15.

Genesee, F., G. R. Tucker, and W. E. Lambert. "Communication Skills in Bilingual Children." *Child Development* 46 (1975): 1010–1014.

Giles, H., R. Y. Bourhis, and D. Taylor. "Towards a Theory of Language in Ethnic Group Relations." In *Language, Ethnicity and Intergroup Relations*, edited by H. Giles. London: Academic Press, 1977.

Grosjean, F. *Life with Two Languages: An Introduction to Bilingualism*. Cambridge, MA: Harvard University Press, 1982.

Hamers, J. F., and M. Blanc. "Towards a Social-Psychological Model of Bilingual Development." *Journal of Language and Social Psychology* 1, no. 1 (1982): 29–49.

Hoffman, C. *An Introduction to Bilingualism*. London: Longman, 1991.

Ianco-Worrall, A. D. "Bilingualism and Cognitive Development." *Child Development* 43 (1972): 1390–1400.

Jones, W. R. *Bilingualism and Intelligence*. Cardiff: University of Wales, 1959.

Kardash, C. A., et al. "Bilingual Referents in Cognitive Processing." *Contemporary Educational Psychology* 13 (1988): 45–57.

Kessler, C., and M. E. Quinn. "Cognitive Development in Bilingual Environments." In *Issues in International Bilingual Education. The Role of the Vernacular*, edited by B. Hartford, A. Valdman, and C. R. Foster. New York: Plenum Press, 1982.

Lambert, W. E. "Culture and Languages as Factors in Learning and Education." In *Cultural Factors in Learning and Education*, edited by F. E. Aboud and R. D. Meade. Bellingham: Washington State College, 1974.

Lambert, W. E. "The Social Psychology of Language," In *Language: Social Psychological Perspectives*, edited by H. Giles, W. P. Robinson, and P. M. Smith. Oxford: Pergamon, 1980.

Lambert, W. E., and R. Taylor. *Coping with Cultural and Racial Diversity in Urban America*. New York: Praeger, 1990.

Lambert, W. E., and R. Tucker. *Bilingual Education of Children. The St. Lambert Experiment*. Rowley, MA: Newbury House, 1972.

Macnab, G. L. "Cognition and Bilingualism: A Reanalysis of Studies." *Linguistics* 17 (1979): 231–255.

Martin-Jones, M., and S. Romaine. "Semilingualism: A Half Baked Theory of Communicative Competence." *Applied Linguistics* 7, no. 1 (1986): 26–38.

Ohler, L. "Knowledge and Neurolinguistics: The Case of Bilingualism." *Language Learning* 33, no. 5 (1983): 159–191.

Paivio, A. *Mental Representations: A Dual Coding Approach*. Oxford: Oxford University Press, 1986.

Paivio, A. "Mental Representations in Bilinguals." In *Bilingualism, Multiculturalism, and Second Language Learning*, edited by A. G. Reynolds. Hillsdale, NJ: Lawrence Erlbaum Associates, 1991.

Paivio, A., and A. Desrochers. "A Dual-Coding Approach to Bilingual Memory." *Canadian Journal of Psychology* 34 (1980): 390–401.

Peal, E., and W. E. Lambert. "The Relationship of Bilingualism to Intelligence." *Psychological Monographs* 76, no. 27 (1962): 1–23.

Pintner, R., and S. Arsenian. "The Relation of Bilingualism to Verbal Intelligence and School Adjustment." *Journal of Educational Research* 31 (1937): 255–263.

Ransdell, S. E., and I. Fischler. "Memory in a Monolingual Mode: When Are Bilinguals at a Disadvantage?" *Journal of Memory and Language* 26 (1987): 392–405.

Ransdell, S. E., and I. Fischler. "Effects of Concreteness and Task Context on Recall of Prose Among Bilingual and Monolingual Speakers." *Journal of Memory and Language* 28 (1989): 278–291.

Reynolds, A. G. "The Cognitive Consequences of Bilingualism." In *Bilingualism, Multiculturalism, and Second Language Learning*, edited by A. G. Reynolds. Hillsdale, NJ: Lawrence Erlbaum Associates, 1991.

Saer, D. J. "An Inquiry into the Effect of Bilingualism upon the Intelligence of Young Children." *Journal of Experimental Pedagogy* 6 (1922): 232–240, 266–274.

Saer, D. J. "The Effects of Bilingualism on Intelligence." *British Journal of Psychology* 14 (1923): 25–38.

Spolsky, B. "Review of 'Key Issues in Bilingualism and Bilingual Education.' " *Applied Linguistics* 10, no. 4 (1989): 449–451.

Taylor, D. M. "The Social Psychology of Racial and Cultural Diversity." In *Bilingualism, Multiculturalism, and Second Language Learning*, edited by A. G. Reynolds. Hillsdale, NJ: Lawrence Erlbaum Associates, 1991.

Tunmer, W. E., and M. L. Herriman. "The Development of Metalinguistic Awareness: A Conceptual Overview." In *Metalinguistic Awareness in Children*, edited by W. E. Tunmer, C. Pratt, and M. L. Herriman. Berlin: Springer-Verlag, 1984.

Tunmer, W. E., and M. E. Myhill. "Metalinguistic Awareness and Bilingualism." In *Metalinguistic Awareness in Children*, edited by W. E. Tunmer, C. Pratt, and M. L. Herriman. Berlin: Springer-Verlag, 1984.

Tunmer, W. E., C. Pratt, and M. L. Herriman, eds. *Metalinguistic Awareness in Children: Theory, Research and Implications.* Berlin: Springer-Verlag, 1984.

Vaid, J., and D. G. Hall. "Neuropsychological Perspectives on Bilingualism: Right, Left, and Center." In *Bilingualism, Multiculturalism, and Second Language Learning,* edited by A. G. Reynolds. Hillsdale, NJ: Lawrence Erlbaum Associates, 1991.

Vygotsky, L. S. *Thought and Language.* Cambridge, MA: MIT Press, 1962.

Weinreich, U. *Languages in Contact: Findings and Problems.* The Hague: Mouton, 1968.

Williams, J. D., and G. C. Snipper. *Literacy and Bilingualism.* New York: Longman, 1990.

Willig, A. C. "A Meta-analysis of Selected Studies on the Effectiveness of Bilingual Education." *Review of Educational Research* 55, no. 3 (1985): 269–317.

Appendix: Bilingualism and the Perception of Professional Concepts

Janice Monti-Belkaoui[1] and Ahmed Belkaoui[2]

Accepted August 23, 1982

A selected set of professional concepts was subjected to analysis through two separate multidimensional scaling techniques, the INDSCAL and TORSCA models, to evaluate the intergroup perceptual differences of four experimental groups, made up of unilingual French, unilingual English and bilingual students. The linguistic relativism thesis provided the research hypotheses on the relationship between language access and usage and concept perception. The multidimensional scaling techniques were applied to the matrix of subjects' similarity judgments on pairs of concepts, thus enabling the identification of three dimensions. The dimensions were labelled as conjunctive, relational and disjunctive, and were assumed to be related to the criteria employed by the subjects in their similarity rankings. An analysis of variance of the individual saliences on each dimension provided evidence of linguistic relativism for both the relational and disjunctive dimensions. These findings support the contention that unilingual speakers of separate languages differ from each other and from bilingual speakers in their perception of professional concepts.

INTRODUCTION

Because language mediates our world view, it plays a central role in the development of cognition and perception. Individuals, as they learn a language, acquire not only a store of lexical and grammatical characteristics but also a linguistic mode of cognition and perception:

[1]Department of Sociology, Rosary College, 7900 W. Division, River Forest, Illinois 60305.
[2]Department of Accounting, University of Illinois at Chicago, Box 4348, Chicago, Illinois 60680.

Source: J. Monti-Belkaoui, and A. Belkaoui, "Bilingualism and the Perception of Professional Concepts," *Journal of Psycholinguistic Research* 12, no. 2 (1983): 111–127. Used by permission of the *Journal of Psycholinguisitc Research*.

Language is not a substitute for direct experience; it is itself a mode of
experiencing and an activity of apprehending and transforming direct experience
as well as symbolically mediated experience (Schmidt, 1973; p. 119).

Speakers of different languages therefore acquire and maintain
separate world views. An extension of this line of reasoning suggests that
bilingual individuals possess a different world view from unilinguals
(Lambert & Tucker, 1973). It is not surprising then to note that professional organizations and corporations who operate internationally are
paying increasing attention to language and linguistic differences. One
outcome of this awareness is the growing demand for the international
standardization of professional concepts and techniques. This paper
investigates the hypothesis that unilingual speakers of two different
languages and bilingual speakers of the same languages hold different
perceptions of professional concepts. The study is also an attempt to
validate one of the levels of the "Sapir–Whorf hypothesis" of linguistic
relativism.

SYSTEMATIZATION OF THE "SAPIR–WHORF HYPOTHESIS"

Anthropologists have always emphasized the role of language in their
studies of culture. Sapir's investigations of the linguistic symbolism of a
given culture view language both as instrument and as communication of
thought (Sapir in Mandelbaum, 1956). A given language predisposes its
users to a distinct belief. The idea that language is an active determinant
of thought forms the basis of the principle of linguistic relativism.
According to the Whorfian version of the principle, ways of speaking are
reflections of the metaphysics of a culture (Whorf in Caroll, 1956). These
metaphysics constitute the unstated premises which shape the perception
and thought of those who participate in that culture and predispose them
to a given method of perception (Belkaoui, 1978).

The work of Fishman (1960) is an attempt to systematize this set of
assumptions, known as the "Sapir-Whorf hypothesis." Fishman's four-
fold analytical scheme (Table I) distinguishes between two levels of
language, lexical and grammatical, and two types of behavior, linguistic
and nonlinguistic:

(i) The lexical level refers to all words which compose a language.
Languages differ in the number of terms they possess to describe
phenomena.

(ii) The grammatical level refers to the manner in which the structural
units of a language are organized.

Table I. Fishman's Schematic Systematization of the Sapir–Whorf Hypothesis[a]

	Data of (cognitive) behavior	
Date of language characteristics	Language data ("cultural themes")	Nolinguistic data
Lexical or "semantic" characteristics	Level 1	Level 2
Grammatical characteristics	Level 3	Level 4

[a]see Fishman (1960).

(iii) Linguistic behavior refers to choices among words.

(iv) Nonlinguistic behavior refers to choices among objects. This last distinction will be clarified in the following explanation of the cells in Table I.

(a) Cell 1 posits a relationship between the lexical properties of a language and the speaker's linguistic behavior. Linguistic behavior, the choice of words for describing a particular phenomenon, differs from one language to another.

(b) Cell 2 posits a relationship between the lexical properties of a language and the nonlinguistic behavior of the users of that language. This refers to the idea that speakers of a language that makes certain lexical distinctions will be able to perform tasks better and more rapidly than speakers of languages that do not make such distinctions (Lenneberg, 1973; Brown & Lenneberg, 1954; Lantz, 1953).

(c) Cell 3 posits a relationship between grammatical characteristics and linguistic behavior. This refers to the idea that speakers of a language that uses specific grammatical rules acquire a distinctive world view from speakers of other languages that do not employ such rules (Hoijer, 1951; Ervin-Tripp, 1969).

(d) Cell 4 posits a relationship between grammatical characteristics and non-linguistic behavior. This refers to the idea that speakers of a language that has certain grammatical characteristics will perform non-linguistic tasks differently from speakers of languages that do not have these characteristics (Carol & Casagrande, 1958; Belkaoui, 1980).

This paper reports a study of the perception of professional concepts by unilingual and bilingual speakers as measured by a task of linguistic behavior. The research is designed to answer the following question: Do access and use of two distinct language systems result in differences in the perception of professional concepts? Accordingly, the specific research hypotheses derive from Cell 1 and deal with the relationship between lexical properties of a language and the linguistic behavior of its speakers.

RESEARCH HYPOTHESIS

The research design is based on a perceptual task assigned to three groups of university students, two of which were composed of unilingual and one of bilingual speakers. The groups were selected and matched for their exposure to and understanding of a set of professional techniques and concepts. The major research question is to determine whether language access and usage have any appreciable effect on perception.

The first of the hypotheses represents a direct test of the "Sapir–Whorf" proposition as outlined by Cell 1. It tests whether linguistic behavior, in the form of the choice of words for a particular phenomenon, will differ from one language to another. Specifically, in this case, the hypothesis tests for differences in the perception of professional concepts by unilingual subjects from two different language groups. This is stated in null form as follows:

H_1: The perception of professional concepts by unilingual speakers from two different language groups, as measured by the individual weights assigned to the dimensions of the common perceptual space, will not differ.

The second hypothesis is an extension of the basic relationship expressed by Cell 1. This formulation investigates differences in perception of professional concepts between bilingual and unilingual speakers. It questions whether the two language systems available to bilingual speakers provide cognitive enrichment or linguistic and perceptual confusion. In null form:

H_2: The perception of professional concepts by bilingual and unilingual speakers, as measured by the individual weights assigned to the dimensions of the common perceptual space, will not differ.

The third hypothesis also deals with bilinguals. It tests whether switching from one language to another leads to better perception. Although not strictly derived from Cell 1, this hypothesis is supported by the literature on bilingualism. Language switching has been found to be related to higher levels of creativity (Peal & Lambert, 1962; Landry, 1974), cognitive flexibility (Balkan, 1970), concept formation (Liedke & Nelson, 1968), verbal intelligence (Lambert & Tucker, 1973; Kittell, 1963), and psycholinguistic abilities (Casserly & Edwards, 1973). The null form of this hypothesis is:

H_3: The perception of professional concepts by bilinguals using each of two languages, as measured by the individual weights assigned to the dimensions of the common perceptual space, will not differ from one language to the other.

METHODOLOGY

Subjects

Experimental subjects were recruited from two sections of an accounting theory course given at the University of Ottawa, Ontario, Canada, in the spring semester of 1981. All subjects were fourth-year accounting majors who had fulfilled the same course and degree requirements in preparation for the bachelor degree as well as for the professional degree of C.A., the Chartered Accountant certification. One section of the course was taught in English and the other in French by the same instructor, a bilingual speaker and one of the paper's coauthors. English- and French-language editions of the same textbook, written by the instructor, were used in each respective language section (Belkaoui, 1981 a,b). Testing and evaluation performed at the beginning of the semester revealed that students in both sections were equally unfamiliar with certain advanced accounting concepts and techniques. (The professional training of the students prior to the accounting theory course had been restricted to lower-level courses in conventional bookkeeping). The research design insured that each student was introduced to the same set of concepts, in his or her own language, in the same time period by the same instructor and textbook. Other things being equal, the only difference in the acquisition of the professional concepts was the language of instruction and learning. Because of this, any differences in perception of the concepts may be attributed in great part to the impact of the language used.

Before the conduct of the experiment, some of the students enrolled in the English section were found to be bilingual speakers. Specifically, these students were bilingual Francophones who had elected to take the course in English (primarily because of considerations related to future job-market opportunities in the predominantly English province of Ontario). Because of the presence of these bilingual students, four experimental groups were designated:

(i) Twenty-seven Francophone students enrolled in the French section who performed the experimental task in *French* formed the unilingual French group (UF).

(ii) Twenty-two Anglophone students enrolled in the English section who performed the experimental task in *English* formed the unilingual English group (UE).

(iii) Seventeen bilingual students enrolled in the English section who performed the experimental task in *English* formed the bilingual English group (BE).

(iv) A week later, the same seventeen bilingual students in the English section performed the experimental task in *French*, thus forming the bilingual French group (BF).

Research Design

Subjects in all four experimental groups were given the same questionnaire in an English- or French-language version. The questionnaire required subjects to assign similarity judgments to paired sets of twelve concepts. In multidimensional scaling techniques, such similarity judgments are interpreted as "psychological distances," representing a "mental map" through which respondents view pairs of concepts that are "near" each other as similar and pairs of concepts that are "far apart" as dissimilar. If numerical measures are provided for the similarity judgments, multidimensional scaling techniques may be used to construct a "physical" multidimensional map whose interpoint distances closely relate to the input data.

Two separate multidimensional scaling techniques, the TORSCA and INDSCAL models, were applied to individual similarity judgments to estimate the dimensions of the common perceptual space and each respondent's saliences. Regression was then used to measure the relationship between saliences and selected background variables which included the subjects' age, the number of accounting courses taken, and the grade received in the accounting theory course.

One of the multidimensional scaling techniques used in the study is the TORSCA nonmetric scaling routine (Young, 1968). Given $\frac{n(n-1)}{2}$ similarity/dissimilarity measures, the TORSCA program first yields a set of orthogonal coordinates for the final configuration and then estimates the dimensionality of the data. The other algorithm used in this study is the INDSCAL Model (Caroll & Chang, 1970). In contrast to the TORSCA solution, the stimulus configuration obtained from the INDSCAL algorithm is uniquely oriented. The INDSCAL model assumes that all individuals share a common perceptual space, but assigns differential weights or saliences to the different dimensions of the group stimulus space. These individual saliences provide an ideal operational measure for the evaluation of possible inter- and intra-group perceptual differences.

Professional Concepts and Experimental Decisions

The twelve concepts used in the experiment were chosen to reflect two categories of professional concepts of relevance to accounting theory construction. The terms "going concern," "entity," "stable monetary unit," and "periodicity," represent underlying assumptions of accounting theory while the terms "cost," "revenue," "matching," "objectivity," "consistency," "full disclosure," "materiality," and "conservatism" represent generally accepted accounting principles within the profession (Belkaoui, 1980). At the first class meeting of each language session, the students were required to assign familiarity ratings to the twelve concepts as well as to other unrelated issues and hypotheses in the field of accounting. The seven-point familiarity rating scale ranged from "not familiar" to "extremely familiar." The results revealed that the students had an overwhelming unfamiliarity with the twelve concepts at the beginning of the semester. Two weeks before the end of the semester, the UF experimental group was asked to complete a French language version of the questionnaire containing the experimental task while the UE and BE groups were asked to complete the English version of the questionnaire. One week later, the bilingual subjects, as the BF group, were again asked to complete the questionnaire, this time in a French-language version. The content of both versions of the questionnaire was identical. Subjects were asked to: (a) provide linguistic[3] and background information, (b) assign to each of the paired concepts an integer rating, on a seven-point scale ranging from "very dissimilar" to "very similar," and (c) list the criteria they used for assigning similarity ratings.

ANALYSIS AND RESULTS
Preliminary Findings

The input to TORSCA was a single rank-order similarity matrix computed by averaging the cell ranks obtained from all subjects. The

---

[3]Linguistic information was required to insure against the presence of any undetected bilingual speakers in the two unilingual groups.

resulting average stress indices were .325, .625, and .062 for dimensions 2, 3, and 4, respectively. Based on these results, "goodness of fit" was provided by three dimensions (stress < .05). The input to INDSCAL was a 12 × 12 matrix of similarity judgments for all subjects. "Variance accounted for," a measure of "goodness of fit" in the INDSCAL model was 57%, 65%, and 63%. Goodness of fit improved for three dimensions but tapered off for the fourth. Dimension 4 explained no more variance than could be accounted for in random data. On the basis of both the "stress" and "variance accounted for" measures, the three dimensional solution has been employed. The graphical portrayal of this solution appears in Fig. 1.

Identifying the Dimensions

In the last part of the experimental task, subjects were asked to list, in order of their importance, the criteria used in assigning similarity judgments. Mirroring the results of another experiment where the same treatment was used, (see Belkaoui, 1980) the similarity judgments appear to be assigned on the basis of the presence or absence of perceptual qualities common to each pair of concepts. This process resulted in the three-fold classification of concepts as either conjunctive, relational, or disjunctive (see McDavid & Harari, 1974; pp. 78–79; Hunt & Hovland, 1960; Belkaoui, 1980). Conjunctive concepts are defined as those which have in common one or more perceptual characteristics while disjunctive concepts differ in one or more characteristics. Relational concepts refer to pairs of terms which are linked by a fixed relationship. This classification scheme provides labels for the three dimensions obtained in the INDSCAL solution (see Table II and Fig. 1).

The stimulus configuration depicted in Fig. 1 places the concepts "objectivity," "materiality," and "conservatism" with nearly equal magnitude on the same side of dimension 1. The pairs "period" and "conservatism," "consistency" and "disclosure," "entity" and "stable monetary unit," and "consistency" and "going concern" are also of fairly equal magnitude and placed on opposite sides of dimension 2. "Entity," "going concern," "stable monetary unit," "period," and "materiality" are found on the positive side of dimension 3 while the remaining concepts are on its negative side.

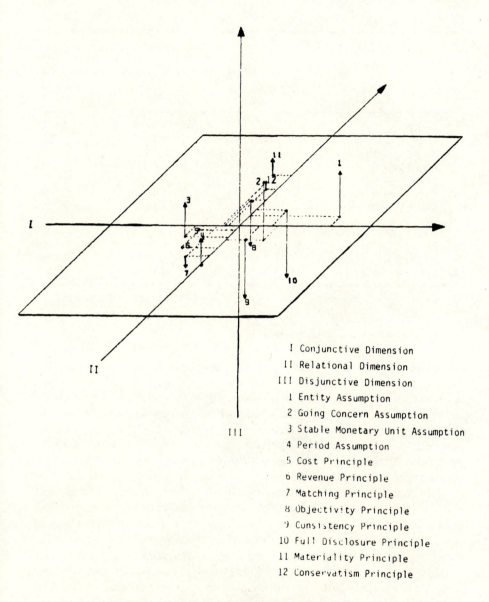

I Conjunctive Dimension
II Relational Dimension
III Disjunctive Dimension

I Conjunctive Dimension
II Relational Dimension
III Disjunctive Dimension
1 Entity Assumption
2 Going Concern Assumption
3 Stable Monetary Unit Assumption
4 Period Assumption
5 Cost Principle
6 Revenue Principle
7 Matching Principle
8 Objectivity Principle
9 Consistency Principle
10 Full Disclosure Principle
11 Materiality Principle
12 Conservatism Principle

Fig. 1. Stimulus configuration.

Table II. Saliences for Professional Concepts on a Three Dimension Solution

	Saliences		
Professional concepts	Conjunctive dimension (1)	Disjunctive dimension (2)	Relational dimension (3)
1. Entity	0.68993	0.10869	0.34030
2. Going concern	0.30491	−0.15673	0.45372
3. Stable monetary unit	−0.34511	−0.11662	0.73046
4. Period concept	0.01261	−0.43953	0.18687
5. Cost principle	−0.29556	−0.08966	−0.01793
6. Revenue principle	−0.27769	−0.23575	−0.00786
7. Matching principle	−0.17216	−0.35309	−0.08010
8. Objectivity	−0.10981	0.27462	−0.33560
9. Consistency	0.15559	−0.15810	−0.44650
10. Full disclosure	0.84349	0.17036	−0.50882
11. Materiality	−0.18402	0.53271	0.13003
12. Conservatism	−0.08213	0.40310	0.04884

Intergroup Differences in Perception

The INDSCAL model produces a spatial representation of the similarity data obtained from subjects as well as a set of dimensional saliences. These saliences are unique to each individual and may be interpreted as indicators of the way in which the individual "distorts" the group stimulus space by "stretching" (represented by the large weights) or "shrinking" (the small weights) the distances between points along the weighted dimensions. The investigation of intergroup differences in perception was accomplished by a one-way analysis of variance of four experimental groups. This determined the extent to which the groups' saliences differed on each of the three dimensions. The results of the analysis of variance are presented in Table III. The general hypothesis of no intergroup differences was accepted for the conjunctive dimension but rejected for the disjunctive and relational dimensions. Each of the four experimental groups assigned different weights to the disjunctive concepts, those which differ on the basis of one or more characteristics, and to the relational concepts, which are linked by fixed relationships. Consensus among all the groups appears to exist only for the conjunctive dimension, for those concepts which share characteristics.

Table III. Results of the Analysis of Variances

| | Dimensions | | | | | | | | | | | |
| | Conjunctive | | | | Disjunctive | | | | Relational | | | |
	Sum of squares	Degrees of freedom	Mean squares	F	Sum of squares	Degrees of freedom	Mean squares	F	Sum of squares	Degrees of freedom	Mean squares	F
Between groups	0.0387	3	0.0129	0.7696	0.1114	3	0.0371	2.2651[a]	0.4936	3	0.1645	9.1501[b]
Within groups	1.3837	79	0.0168		1.2952	79	0.0164		1.4205	79	0.0180	

[a]Significant at $\alpha = 0.0873$.
[b]Significant at $\alpha = 0.0000$.

Table IV. *T*-Test Matrix for Group Means (79 Degrees of Freedom)

	Dimensions											
	Conjunctive				Disjunctive				Relational			
Groups	UE	UF	FB	BE	UE	UF	BF	BE	UE	UF	BF	BE
UE	0.0				0.0				0.0			
UF	0.5384	0.0			-2.1570^a	0.0			3.7646^c	0.0		
BF	−0.2413	−0.7512	0.0		−0.9093	1.0526	0.0		2.4172^d	−0.9711	0.0	
BE	1.8264	0.7796	1.3818	0.0	0.2060	2.2159^b	1.0501	0.0	−1.0265	-4.5629^e	-3.2422^f	0.0

[a]Significant at $\alpha = 0.0341$.
[b]Significant at $\alpha = 0.0896$.
[c]Significant at $\alpha = 0.0003$.
[d]Significant at $\alpha = 0.0187$.
[e]Significant at $\alpha = 0.0000$.
[f]Significant at $\alpha = 0.0017$.

The differences along the disjunctive and relational dimensions were further explored in a *t*-test matrix for group means (Table IV). These findings provide a direct test of the three research hypotheses:

(a) The significant differences in perception between the unilingual French group (UF) and the unilingual English group (UE) along both the disjunctive and relational dimensions provide evidence of differential perception of professional concepts by unilingual speakers from two separate language systems and, thus, makes possible the rejection of H^1. These findings also constitute a direct corroboration of the thesis of linguistic relativism by giving support to its main contention that language behavior, in this case, the perception of word choices for describing a particular phenomenon, i.e., professional concepts, differs from one language to another.

(b) The significant differences between the bilingual English group (BE) and the unilingual French group (UF), along the disjunctive and relational dimensions, and between the bilingual French group (BF) and the unilingual English group (UE), along the relational dimension, provide support for differential perception of concepts between bilingual and unilingual speakers and for the rejection of H_2. These findings suggest that bilingual speakers who have access to two separate language systems perceive concepts differently than unilinguals. Of particular relevance to the linguistic relativism thesis are the findings that the bilingual speakers (who were all exposed to the professional concepts in the English language section of the course) displayed, in the BE experimental treatment, differences along two dimensions from the unilingual French group (who were trained separately in the French section of the course). However, in the BF experimental treatment, these same bilingual speakers differed only along one dimension from their English section classmates, the unilingual English group.

(c) The significant differences in perception between the bilingual English (BE) and bilingual French groups (BF) provide evidence that the habit of switching from one language to another may result in differential perception of concepts which are linked by a fixed relationship. The perceptual differences are not significant, however, for the conjunctive and disjunctive dimensions. These findings provide some support for the contention that language switching may enhance understanding, thus enabling a partial acceptance of the null H_3.

Intragroup Differences in Perception

The saliences for each of the three dimensions were regressed with the background variables, i.e., age, number of accounting courses taken, and the grade received in the accounting theory course, in order to determine if the differences would hold after allowing for variation in the maturity and preparation of the subjects (see Table V). These variables were shown to have no effect on the saliences. The reported differences in the perception of concepts appears to be directly related to language and independent of the effects of these background variables.

DISCUSSION

This study provides some tentative support for the contention that the perception of professional concepts is shaped and mediated by the access to and acquisition of a language. Beyond the theoretical issues raised by the operationalization of the Sapir–Whorf hypothesis, these results also have some practical implications. One obvious implication is in the area of international economic relations and bilingual education.

The increasing volume of international trade during recent years and the decline in the competitive position previously enjoyed by U.S. firms in the international market is seen in part as a function of the linguistic barrier faced by typically unilingual American corporate executives and professionals in dealing with overseas customers and colleagues. Language differences result not only in general communication problems across national boundaries but also in specific perceptual differences in understanding the same concepts used within disciplines, industries, and professions. As a contribution to the literature on the relationship between bilingualism and enhanced perception, our findings may have relevance to those who are concerned with training personnel for careers in inter-ethnic or international contexts. The evidence suggests that fluency in two languages aids in the uniform acquisition and comprehension of professional concepts. The need for (and efficacy of) the bilingual professional is an area that requires further attention from social sciences, economic planners, and the standard-setters of professional organizations.

Table V. Regression Results

Sources of variation	Dimensions											
	Conjunctive				Disjunctive				Relational			
	Sum of squares	DF	Mean square	F	Sum of squares	DF	Mean square	F	Sum of squares	DF	Mean square	F
Regression	0.013	3	0.004	0.248	0.039	3	0.013	0.746	0.026	3	0.009	0.363
Residual	1.350	79	0.017		1.368	79	0.017		1.888	79	0.024	

REFERENCES

Balkan, L. *Les effects du bilinguisme Francais-Anglais sur les aptitudes intellectuelles.* Bruxelles: Aimav, 1970.

Belkaoui, A. Linguistic relativity in accounting. *Accounting, Organizations and Society,* 1978, *3*(2), 97–104.

Belkaoui, A. The impact of socioeconomic accounting statements on the investment decision: An empirical study. *Accounting, Organizations and Society, 5*(3), 263–283.

Belkaoui, A. *Accounting theory.* San Diego: Harcourt, Brace and Jovanovich, 1981(a).

Belkaoui, A. *Theorie comptable.* Quebec City: Presses de l'Universite du Quebec, 1981(b).

Brown, R. W., & Lenneberg, E. H. A study in language and cognition. *Journal of Abnormal and Social Psychology,* 1954, 454–462.

Carol, J. B. & Casagrande, J. B. The functions of language classification in behavior. In E. E. Maccoby, T. M. Newcomb, & E. L. Hartley (Eds.), *Readings in social psychology* (3rd. ed.). New York: Holt, Rinehart and Winston, 1958.

Caroll, J. D., & Chang, J. J. Analysis of individual differences in multidimensional scaling via *N*-way generalization of "Eckart–Young" Decomposition. *Psychometrika,* 1970, *35,* 238–319.

Casserly, M. C., & Edwards, A. P. *Detrimental effects of grade one bilingualism programs: An exploratory study.* Paper Presented to the Annual Conference of the Canadian Psychological Association, 1973.

Erwin-Tripp, S. Sociolinguistics. In L. Berkowitz (Ed.), *Advances in experimental social psychology.* New York: Academic Press, 1969, pp. 91–165.

Fishman, J. A. A systematization of the Whorfian Hypothesis. *Behavioral Science,* 1960, 323–335.

Hoijer, H. Cultural implications of the Navaho linguistic categories. *Language,* 1951, 111–120.

Hunt, D. E., & Hovland, C. I. Order of consideration of different types of concepts. *Journal of Experimental Psychology,* 1960, 220–225.

Kittell, J. E. Intelligence test performance of children from bilingual environments. *Elementary School Journal,* 1963, *64.*

Lambert, W. E. & Tucker, G. R. The benefits of bilingualism. *Psychology Today,* September 1973.

Landry, R. G. A comparison of second language learners and monolinguals on diverging thinking tasks at the elementary school level. *Modern Language Jorunal,* 1974, 58.

Lantz, D. L. Language and cognition revisited. *Journal of Abnormal and Social Psychology,* 1953, 454–462.

Lenneberg, E. H. Cognitions in ethnolinguistics. *Language,* 1973, 463–471.

Liedke, W. W. & Nelson, L. D. Concept formation and bilingualism. *Alberta Journal of Educational Research,* 1968, *4.*

McDavid, J. W. & Harari, H. *Psychology and social bhavior.* New York: Harper and Row, 1974.

Peal, E. & Lambert, W. The relationship of bilingualism to intelligence. *Psychological Monographs,* 1962, 76.

Sapir, E. *Culture, language and personality: Selected essays.* D. G. Mandelbaum (Ed.). Berkeley: University of California Press, 1956.

Schmidt, W. H. O. *Child development: The human, cultural and educational context.* New York: Harper and Row, 1973.

Whorf, B. L. *Language, thought and reality: Selected writings*. J. B. Caroll (ed.), Cambridge, Massachusetts: MIT Press, 1956.

Young, F. W. TORSCA-9: An IBM 360/75 FORTRAN IV program for nonmetric multidimensional scaling. *Journal of Marketing Research*, 1968, 319–320.

INDEX

About the Author

AHMED RIAHI-BELKAOUI is Professor of Accounting in the College of Business Administration, University of Illinois at Chicago. A prolific author of journal articles and scholarly and professional books and textbooks, he serves on the editorial boards for many prestigious journals in his field and is known for his unusual, often groundbreaking research and analysis. This is his twenty-sixth Quorum book.